FRONTIER OF
GERMAN EMPIRE 1914

FRONTIER OF AUSTRO-
HUNGARIAN EMPIRE 1914

FRONTIER OF
RUSSIAN EMPIRE 1914

NEW STATES

AREAS TEMPORARILY
AUTONOMOUS OR
INDEPENDENT

AREAS UNDER
ARMED OCCUPATION

AREAS UNDER
LEAGUE OF NATIONS
HIGH COMMISSIONERS

USSR

DENT
21

UKRAINE
INDEPENDENT
1917-20

USSR

Caspian
Sea

GEORGIA
INDEPENDENT
1918-21

AZERBAIJAN
INDEPENDENT
1918-20

Black Sea

ARMENIA
INDEPENDENT
1918-21

TURKEY

IS. TO ITALY

# War, Peace, and
# All That Jazz

# A  HISTORY  OF  US

The picture on the cover is a watercolor by Dwight Shepler, called *Fighter Scramble—Guadalcanal*. The battle of Guadalcanal was the turning point in the Allies' Pacific campaign against Japan during World War II. The scene shows the fight for Henderson Field, the battle's main objective. When the Japanese attacked from the air, American Marine and Navy pilots would return to the airfield's Fighter Strip One for fuel and ammunition. They often took off three abreast in great clouds of dust. (For more about this battle and the war in the Pacific, turn to chapter 35.) Dwight Shepler was born in 1905 in Massachusetts and studied at Williams College and the Boston Museum School. In 1942 he joined the U.S. Naval Reserve. He was one of the first artists assigned to the Navy's Combat Art Section. Guadalcanal was only one of many important battles Shepler witnessed. After Guadalcanal, he was transferred to Europe, where he painted the Normandy invasion. He then returned to the Pacific to document the battles for the Philippines and Okinawa. In 1971 he published *An Artist's Horizons*, which tells the story of his life and career—you might find it in your local public library.

Oxford University Press

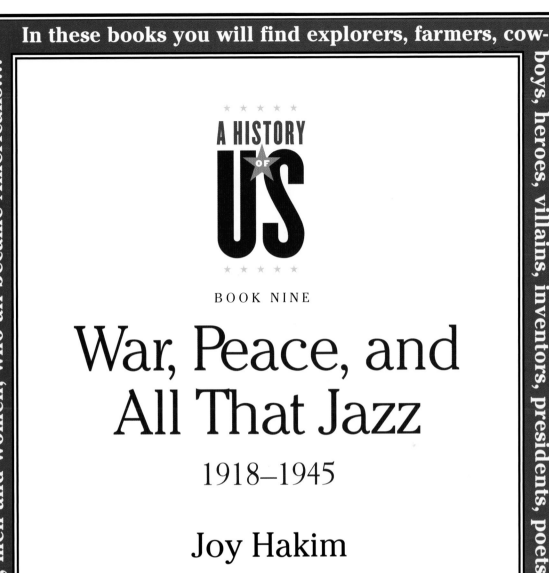

★ ★ ★ ★ ★

# A HISTORY OF US

★ ★ ★ ★ ★ ★

BOOK NINE

# War, Peace, and All That Jazz

## 1918–1945

## Joy Hakim

Oxford University Press
New York

## Oxford University Press

Oxford   New York

Auckland   Bangkok   Buenos Aires
Cape Town   Chennai   Dar es Salaam   Delhi   Hong Kong   Istanbul
Karachi   Kolkata   Kuala Lumpur   Madrid   Melbourne   Mexico City   Mumbai
Nairobi   São Paulo   Shanghai   Taipei   Tokyo   Toronto

### Revised Third Edition

Published by Oxford University Press, Inc.,
198 Madison Avenue, New York, New York  10016
Oxford is a registered trademark of Oxford University Press

**Library of Congress Cataloging-in-Publication Data is available**

ISBN-13: 978-0-19-530738-2
ISBN-13: 978-0-19-532723-6 (Paperback)

5 7 9 8 6
Printed in China

THIS BOOK IS FOR THE TWO BEST TEACHERS I'VE EVER KNOWN:
IDA GINSBURG FRISCH AND JOHN MICHAEL FRISCH

*IDA GINSBURG FRISCH, who played on the first girls' basketball team in Glens Falls, New York, was a flapper who bobbed her long hair and wore a coat with a mink collar.*

*She was hardly beyond her teens when she won an automobile for selling more subscriptions to the GLENS FALLS POST-DISPATCH than anyone else in town. (Having a car was unusual when she was a girl.) She didn't know how to drive, but a license and instructions came with the car, so she convinced her sister, Libbie, to get in with her, and the two of them took off for Saratoga. Fifty years later, Libbie still remembered that drive. "I didn't think I'd live through it," she said.*

*When Ida died, in her eighties, she was the youngest person I knew. She never stopped surprising me with her wit and vitality and curiosity. "What will happen if we try this?" "Or that?" "And let's see for ourselves." I couldn't keep up with her. She was my mother.*

*JOHN MICHAEL FRISCH—"Jack" to those who knew him—was shy and courtly and had strawberry-blond hair. He came to this country at age three, from Zhitomir in Ukraine, the son of poor Jewish immigrants. Soon there were two sisters. Before Jack finished school, his father had died and Jack had to support the family.*

*Photographs from the Roaring Twenties show him as a dandy who went to Broadway openings and wore spats on his shoes. I knew him later, when he sat in a big chair, read newspapers and books, thought about things, and knew the answer to any question my schoolbooks asked.*

*He always said exactly what he meant, and everyone understood that he was a man who could never be unkind or untruthful.*

*He taught me to love ideas and words and to listen to the music in language. Besides that, he could do magic tricks and stand on his head. He was my father.*

# Contents

*Babe Ruth in an eBULLient mood.*

*Two presidents: Herbert Hoover (left) and Franklin Delano Roosevelt, as pictured on the cover of the* New Yorker *magazine on March 4, 1933.*

We Americans today—all of us—we are characters in the living book of democracy. But we are also its author. It falls upon us now to say whether the chapters that are to come will tell a story of retreat or a story of continued advance.

—**Franklin Delano Roosevelt, 1940**

One thing about the past,
It is likely to last.
Some of it is horrid and some sublime,
And there is more of it all the time.

—**Ogden Nash**

What happens to a
  dream deferred?

Does it dry up
  like a raisin in the sun?

Or fester like a sore—
And then run?
Does it stink like rotten
  meat?
Or crust and sugar over—
  like a syrupy sweet?

Maybe it just sags
  like a heavy load.

Or does it explode?

—**Langston Hughes**

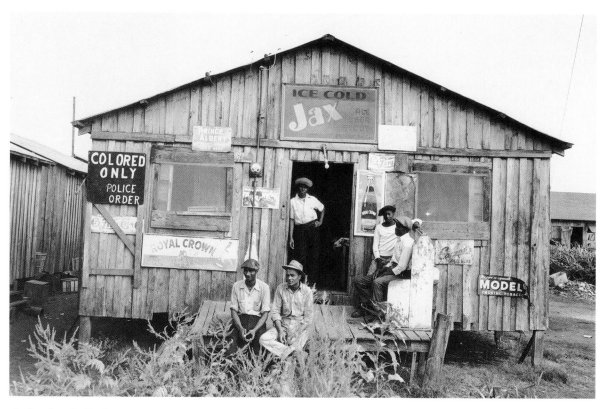

*A shack at Belle Glade, Florida, April 1945.*

# PREFACE
# War and the Start of a New Century

## Some Firsts from the Century's Early Years

**1903:** First World Series and first Hershey Bar.

**1904:** The National Child Labor Committee was formed—first of its kind—to get children out of coal mines and factories.

**1906:** The name "hot dog" was first used, after a cartoon showed a dachshund inside a frankfurter bun.

**1911:** Writer Harriet Quimby became a licensed pilot, the first American woman to do so.

**1912:** The world's first self-service grocery store opened in California.

Uncle Sam sent the Marines to Honduras, Nicaragua, and Cuba, beginning a continuing (and often unwanted) military presence.

**1913:** Henry Ford's first assembly line and the beginning of mass production. It was also the year that the Erector Set was invented (by A.C. Gilbert) and student player Knute Rockne introduced the forward pass at a small college named Notre Dame.

**1914:** Mother's Day was created by President Wilson. (Father's Day had been established in 1910.)

**On August 28, 1917, General Pershing lands in France. President Wilson appointed him Commander of the American Expeditionary Force.**

Gavrilo Princip, a lean angry teenager, was a member of a terrorist organization: the Black Hand. His country, Bosnia-Herzegovina, had broken from Turkish (Ottoman) rule, only to be swallowed by the giant Austro-Hungarian Empire. Princip was determined to set Bosnia free to become part of a greater Serbia. Some radical Serbians had paid to train the Black Hand.

On sunny June 28, 1914, Archduke Franz Ferdinand—heir to the Austro-Hungarian throne—and his wife, Sophie, arrived in Bosnia's capital, Sarajevo. It was a Serbian national holiday, and not the best choice of days for a conquering leader to arrive, but he had come anyway and ceremonial and military events were planned. The royal party climbed into four open cars. What no one there knew was that the Archduke was sympathetic to the aspirations of the Serbs. He had angered his uncle, the Emperor, by suggesting that the Slavs (Bosnians and Serbs) be given separate powers and autonomy within the Empire.

Six Black Hand members, including Gavrillo Princip—all trained to assassinate—stood along the route the motorcade was taking. The first of them threw a bomb. It blew off a wheel and wounded two soldiers. The police quickly arrested the bomb thrower and the procession sped off in the three remaining cars to its destination, the City Hall.

At a public gathering in Munich on August 1, 1914, an exuberant crowd cheered Germany's decision to get on with it. Among those photographed in the mob was a smiling mustached 25-year-old Austrian water-color artist. His name was Adolf Hitler.

Princip, disappointed, headed for a café on Franz Josef Street. Meanwhile the Archduke carried on with his state duties. At the City Hall he remarked (without humor), "So you welcome your guests here with bombs?"

After the ceremonies he asked to be driven to the hospital to see the two injured officers. It was an un-scheduled visit and the driver, Franz Urban, made a wrong turn, which took him into narrow Franz Josef Street. There wasn't room to turn the car around, so Urban stopped before putting the car in reverse. Gavrillo Princip, who was standing on the sidewalk outside the cafe , couldn't believe it. There was the archduke just a few feet away. He stepped forward and fired two shots. Both Franz Ferdinand and Sophie bled to death in the car. Exactly a month later, on July 28th, Austria-Hungary de-clared war on Serbia. Russia and France were allies of Serbia. Within weeks, all of Europe was at war.

George Washington had warned Americans to stay out of foreign entanglements; President Wilson agreed. Besides, there were German-Americans and British-Americans and divided opinions on this European war. The United States stayed neutral.

On May 1, 1915, the German Embassy in Washington placed an advertisement in the leading New York newspapers. The ad said, "Travelers intending to embark on the Atlantic voyage are remind-ed that a state of war exists between Germany and Great Britain. . . vessels flying the British flag. . .are liable to destruction." This warn-ing was published next to an advertisement for a British passenger liner, the *Lusitania*, "Fastest and Largest Steamer now in Atlantic Service."

That same morning the luxurious *Lusitania* set sail for England, filled with tourists, business people, and others who wanted to get to England. (You couldn't go by plane then.) Many of the voyagers were nervous about the trip—but passenger ships had traditionally been safe from military attack. Six days later, within sight of the Irish coast, most were preparing for a festive last evening dinner. A German submarine, the U-20, was about to cancel the meal. A single torpedo was fired without warning. Eighteen minutes later the *Lusitania* was beneath the waves. Of 2,000 passengers, 1,198 drowned. The captain, who had ignored official warnings and instructions, was washed from the deck and saved.

Meanwhile, Mexico was having a revolution (some called it a civil war). Russia would soon have one, too. The desire for independence—from imperialist empires and emperors—underlay the times. It went along with freedom movements and a rising belief in democracy and self-rule and people power, themes that would dominate the 20th century.

For 30 years, Mexico had been under the fist of an iron dictator, General Porfirio Diaz. Outside of Mexico, his rule was often seen as beneficent and orderly, but under the surface it was brutally cruel and corrupt. A small group of immensely wealthy landowners dominated peasants who lived in a state very close to slavery. It's not surprising that rebels—some idealistic, some opportunistic— would attempt to change things. The story of what happened is one of the fascinating tales of the time. If you want to know more, you can start by finding out about Pancho Villa, Emiliano Zapata, and Victoriano Huerta. Those three will lead you to an astonishing cast of characters.

When Mexican bands began raiding small towns and ranches in the United States, President Wilson sent General John Pershing south of the border. The United States was not very popular in Mexico, so stories of the American action were often distorted. For a while it looked as if there might be war with Mexico. And that was exactly what Germany hoped. After more than two years, the war in Europe was eating soldiers and national economies and getting nowhere. The United States was under increasing pressure to enter the fray. U-boat warfare was making many Americans very angry with Germany and its allies. If the United States got involved, it would be on the side of Britain and France. But President Wilson still seemed determined to stay neutral. In 1916 he campaigned for president on a platform of peace.

Then, on January 16, 1917, the German foreign minister, Arthur von Zimmermann, sent a telegram to Mexico City. Before it was

The assassination of Archduke Ferdinand and his wife, Sophia, as seen in *Le Paris Journal* on July 12, 1914.

**Gavrillo Princip being arrested.**

The Panama Canal opened to ships in August 1914. (That was the same month that Germany invaded Belgium and got World War I going.) Nearly 35,000 workers were needed to build the canal, which was, at the time, the greatest construction project the world had ever seen. Ships going from the Atlantic to the Pacific could now skip the long, dangerous voyage around the tip of South America.

read there it was intercepted by British Intelligence and decoded by their astonishing cryptographers (code readers). The telegram suggested an alliance between Germany and Mexico against the United States. When they won the war, as Germany was sure they would, Mexico would recover "the lost territory of Texas, New Mexico and Arizona." (The telegram actually said Kansas when it meant Texas. To Zimmermann they may seem the same, but if you're from either state, well, I don't have to go further.)

That same evening, Admiral von Capelle, speaking to the Reichstag (German ruling body), said, "From a military point of view, America is a nothing." Being a foreign minister, or an admiral, doesn't necessarily mean that you are smart. The Zimmerman telegram has gone down in history as one of the biggest diplomatic goofs of all time. When its contents were made known to the American public, it helped bring the United States into what had begun as a European war. Admiral Capelle's opinion of Americans as fighters? We would make him eat those words. General Pershing, who gained fame in Mexico, would lead America's Expeditionary Force. An angry teenager, a captain who didn't worry enough about his passengers' safety, and a pompous foreign minister—would they define the first half of the 20th century? No, those misfits were going to end up as minor characters in history books. The decades to come—despite two devastating wars and a depression—would be full of achievement and innovation. This was a time when science and technology would blossom with astonishing discoveries and inventions. Musicians, artists, and writers were going to break old rules—looking at the world through creative new lenses—and sharing their visions. Women and minorities would be laying seeds for triumphs to come. America, in the early years of the century, was a bit like most adolescents in a growing spurt—eager to try new things, and full of vigor and hope.

# 1 War's End

Calamity Jane was one of the huge heavy-artillery guns that fired a final fusillade at 10:59 A.M. on November 11, 1918.

In Europe, in 1918, on the 11th hour of the 11th day of the 11th month, it suddenly became quiet. The cannons were still. For the first time since 1914, men could hear each other without shouting. The Great War—soon to be known as World War I—was over.

It had been a horrible war. Nine million men died. It was not fought soldier against soldier, like medieval battles of knights in armor. The new weapons of killing—machine guns, tanks, long-range artillery, grenades, and poison gas—led to mass slaughter. "War," wrote one soldier, "is nothing but murder."

But now the guns were silent; the dying was finished.

In Washington, D.C., even though it was six o'clock in the morning, America's 28th president, Woodrow Wilson, was up and at his desk. Because he was considerate, and feared his clackety typewriter would wake his wife and staff, he sat and wrote these words with a pen on White House stationery:

> *Everything for which America has fought has been accomplished. It will now be our fortunate duty to assist by example, by sober, friendly counsel, and by material aid, in the establishment of just democracy throughout the world.*

They were the words of a high-minded leader. The slim, frail, bookish man had proved to be a great war president. In amazingly fast order he had

**No one** could buy his way out of service in World War I (unlike the Civil War). And for the first time women served officially in the armed forces.

Stretcher bearers carry the wounded from the ruined French town of Vaux, which was captured by the U.S. Army's 2nd Division.

*Left:* officers of the 129th Field Artillery. Second row, third from right, is a captain named Harry S. Truman. (More about him at the end of this book.) *Right:* Company M, 6th Regiment, greets the Armistice.

turned a peaceful nation into a strong fighting force. The country's factories had gone from making corsets, bicycles, and brooms to production of guns, ships, and uniforms. In just over a year—beginning in April 1917—more than a million American men had been drafted into the army, trained, and sent overseas. And just in time. In Europe the fighting had been going on for three years; both sides were near collapse.

It had been a heartbreaker of a war—awful, dreary, bloody—begun in Europe for selfish reasons. It ended up making nations and people cruel, and bitter, and angry, and it led to another terrible war.

The Central Powers (Germany, Austria-Hungary, and the Turkish Ottoman Empire) were on one side, against the Allies (Britain, France, Russia, Japan, and Italy), with a few other nations involved, too.

The Germans had taken a gamble. Before the United States entered the war, Germany sank neutral American ships carrying food and supplies. American lives were lost. The Germans knew that might bring the United States into

## Gee, How They Sang!

*Lieutenant Harry G. Rennagel of the 101st Infantry wrote his family:*

Nothing quite so electrical in effect as the sudden stop that came at 11 A.M. has ever occurred to me. It was 10:60 precisely and—the roar stopped like a motor car hitting a wall. The resulting quiet was uncanny in comparison. From somewhere far below ground, Germans began to appear. They clambered to parapets and began to shout wildly. They threw their rifles, hats, bandoliers, bayonets, and trench knives toward us. They began to sing. Came one bewhiskered Hun with a concertina and he began goose stepping along the parapet followed in close file by fifty others—all goose stepping.... We kept the boys under restraint as long as we could. Finally the strain was too great. A big Yank named Carter ran out into No Man's Land and planted the Stars and Stripes on a signal pole in the lip of a shell hole. Keasby, a bugler, got out in front and began playing "The Star-Spangled Banner" on a German trumpet he'd found in Thiaucourt. And they sang—Gee, how they sang!

the war. They weren't worried. They thought it would take several years for the United States to get ready to fight. By that time they expected the war in Europe to be over. Most German leaders believed that the American system of government was very slow.

The scholarly, honorable man who was president stunned them. He was stronger than they thought possible. He asked Congress for special war powers; he was able to act quickly.

Woodrow Wilson's greatest strength was his integrity. People trusted him because they knew he was trustworthy. He inspired others. He believed in the American dream—in Jefferson's words about how all people have a right to "life, liberty and the pursuit of happiness." Wilson wanted to see that dream spread around the world. He convinced the people of the United States to go to war without thought of gain for themselves. He made it clear to everyone that America's only goal was "to make the world safe for democracy." He made America's participation in the war seem noble and unselfish.

It was still dark, but on November 11, 1918, the news of war's end was too good to wait for daybreak. Whistles tooted, church bells rang, and sirens blared. Before long the streets across the nation were filled with people cheering, shouting, hugging, and kissing. America had gone to war and the world was going to be a better place because of it, or so it seemed on that Armistice Day.

The morning is chilly. Mother and I wear sweaters as I follow her around the big old house. Suddenly bells begin to ring, the bells of Yamhill [Oregon]'s three churches, and the fire bell. Mother seizes my hand and begins to run, out of the house, down the steps, across the muddy barnyard toward the barn where my father is working. My short legs cannot keep up. I trip, stumble, and fall, tearing holes in the knees of my long brown cotton stockings, skinning my knees.

"You must never, never forget this day as long as you live," Mother tells me as Father comes running out of the barn to meet us.

Years later, I asked Mother what was so important about that day when all the bells in Yamhill rang, the day I was never to forget. She looked at me in astonishment and said, "Why, that was the end of the First World War." I was two years old at the time.

—BEVERLY CLEARY,
*A GIRL FROM YAMHILL*

Armistice Day, New York City. "The...crowds," said one observer, "rarely raised a cheer....It was enough to walk...with 10,000 strangers, and to realize in that moment of good news not one of them was really a stranger."

# 2 Fourteen Points

President Wilson in London with King George V. Wilson stayed in Buckingham Palace, which was freezing (due to wartime coal shortages). The king gave him a small electric heater—it didn't help much.

I can predict with absolute certainty that within another generation there will be another world war if the nations of the world do not concert the method by which to prevent it.

—WOODROW WILSON, ON A 1919 SPEAKING TOUR

Wilson's Fourteen Points were supposed to bring about a world government run by popular votes and open discussion. Wilson talked of "peace without victory," with no punishment for the losers. He didn't get his way.

The innocent, optimistic, sure-of-itself 19th century didn't actually end in America until the First World War began. The real start of the 20th century came in 1917. No question about it, the war changed things. It changed people. They began to question old ideas that had never been questioned before. Hardly anyone seemed sure of anything.

Except Woodrow Wilson. He was like an old-time Puritan, convinced of God's grace and very sure of himself. Wilson would do everything possible to lead his nation and the world on a path of righteousness. His father had been a minister; he had the preacher's genes. He spoke eloquently and told the world how to behave. Unfortunately, some people don't like being told what to do—even if the teller is right.

Before the war ended Woodrow Wilson came up with "Fourteen Points" on which the peace was to be based. Wilson didn't believe in revenge; he believed in the power of kindness. He said he wanted "peace without victory." Now that was a startling statement in a nation that had cheered Ulysses Grant when he called for "unconditional surrender." But Woodrow Wilson had grown up in the defeated South. He knew about the hatreds that can come after a war. He didn't think an enemy needed to be shamed, or made poor. He intended to lead the world toward a generous and lasting peace.

Wilson's Fourteen Points may have been the most forgiving peace plan ever. Under the Fourteen Points, people all over the world were to determine their own fate—by vote. It was called "self-determination." Self-determination was to end the old imperialist system that let winning nations grasp foreign colonies. The Fourteen Points also called for:

- *free trade (that means no tariffs)*
- *an end to secret pacts between nations*
- *freedom of the seas*
- *arms reduction*
- *the forming of a world organization—a League of Nations*

Wilson expected this league to guarantee freedom to all the world's peoples and keep the peace between nations.

Leaflets describing the Fourteen Points were dropped over Germany from those new vehicles that had been used, for the first time, as instruments of war: wood-framed airplanes. The German people—who were tired of the war and close to rebellion—read the leaflets, hoped for peace, and soon forced their ruler, the Kaiser (KY-zer), to flee the country.

With the war over, Wilson set off for Europe, the first American president ever to do so while in office. He wanted America to lead the world to a just peace, and he wanted to be the peacemaker. The European people were wild with admiration for Woodrow Wilson. They greeted him with flowers and cheers. They called him the savior of the world.

Too bad he went, say some historians. Others say it would have been worse if he'd stayed at home. Everyone agrees: Wilson didn't get what he wanted. Perhaps because of that, the Great War, which was called the "war to end wars," didn't end anything. It turned out to be World War I. Another world war—which was much worse—followed 21 years later.

What went wrong? Why didn't Wilson get his just peace?

Was it because he was too sure of himself?

Wilson's Fourteen Points provided for self-determination of the peoples of Europe. But in fact many of the new national boundaries were decided by the Allied politicians in secret meetings where they drew lines and argued over huge maps.

**17**

At Versailles: *(above, left to right)* the Big Four—Lloyd George of Britain, Orlando of Italy, Clemenceau of France, and Wilson; *(below)* inside the Hall of Mirrors during the signing of the peace terms, June 28, 1919. "England and France," wrote Wilson, "have not the same views with regard to the peace by any means."

Or because he didn't worry enough about jealous politicians, at home and in Europe? Was it the tragedy of his health? (Before he left the presidency, he exhausted himself, lost contact with reality, and became unable to fight for his beliefs.) Maybe it was all of those things—and more, too. After four years of war, many Americans seemed to have stopped caring. Most just wanted to get on with their lives; some didn't want to be bothered by ideals; others were disappointed that we hadn't smashed the enemy. Besides, President Wilson's sermons were getting tiresome.

France's crafty old premier (prime minister), Georges Clemenceau (cleh-mon-SO)—who was called "the Tiger"—said, "God gave us his Ten Commandments and we broke them. Wilson gave us his Fourteen Points—we shall see."

What Clemenceau saw was that France did, indeed, want revenge. Germany had invaded France twice within his memory (in 1870 and 1914). Two generations of young Frenchmen were dead. The French countryside was devastated. The French wanted protection and repayment for what they had suffered. They, and England and Italy, wanted—and got—a hard peace. They were angry with Germany.

The peace treaty was signed at a gorgeous French royal palace called Versailles (vair-SY). Some of Wilson's most important points got thrown out of the window at Versailles. Germany was blamed for the whole war and given a huge bill for war costs. The Germans (who had surrendered, in part, because of their faith in the Fourteen Points) felt betrayed. But the 14th point, which meant most to Wilson—the League of Nations—was saved. He believed that the League would right the wrongs of the Old World order.

And it might have done so, if the nation that was now the most important power in the world had joined the League. (What nation could that be?)

American treaties with foreign powers must be agreed to by two-thirds of the members of the Senate—a simple majority won't do. At first, most Americans believed in the League of Nations. But there were strong senators who hated Wilson. Some were Republicans who were anxious to win the next election; they thought that a triumph for Wilson would hurt their party's chances.

When Wilson went to Europe he brought many advisers with him; they were either professors or Democrats. None were prominent Republicans. That wasn't wise or generous on Wilson's part. Some Republican senators began to fight the idea of the League. Many Americans, Democrats as well as Republicans, worried about America getting involved in Europe's problems.

Woodrow Wilson knew that the problems of any one part of the globe were now the problems of all peoples. America could not hide from world responsibility. So the president decided to do what he did best: explain things to the American people. That had worked for him before. But, in those days before radio and TV, it meant getting on a train and giving speeches. Wilson crossed the country; he gave three or four speeches a day talking about the importance of the League of Nations.

*Above:* signing the peace treaty. Wilson wanted "open covenants of peace, openly arrived at." He did not get them.

Wilson underestimated Republican opposition to the League of Nations—and ordinary Americans' lack of interest in it. With Congress against him, he took his treaty to the people. But he failed to drum up enough enthusiasm.

Senator Henry Cabot Lodge of Massachusetts led Republican opposition to the League.

It was too much for his health. Wilson had been working hard. In Paris he had been ill and had acted strangely. In Pueblo, Colorado, he was so sick he could not finish his speech. Then he had a stroke. He was never the same again.

Those who opposed the League in the Senate were now able to defeat it. The United States did not join the League of Nations. You can imagine how Woodrow Wilson felt. He believed that without a strong league to enforce peace, there might be another war—and that it would be much worse than the Great War. "What the Germans used were toys compared to what would be used in the next war," he said.

But we didn't listen. The United States embarked on a period of "isolation." We tried to stay away from the rest of the world and its concerns. We would learn that could no longer be done. Like it or not, the United States was now a world leader.

*Justice Oliver Wendell Holmes, Jr.*

## No Clear and Present Danger

**A**mericans had roots in many different countries. Because of hereditary ties to other nations, the issue of possible disloyalty began to concern the U.S. government. As a result, in 1917 Congress passed an Espionage Act. In 1918 it passed a Sedition Act. (*Espionage* is spying; *sedition* means "inciting others to rebel.") Those acts were meant to ban speech that might harm the war effort.

The First Amendment guarantees free speech. Were these acts unconstitutional? Or do things change in wartime? Clearly, war demands national unity.

When anarchists threw 5,000 anti-war leaflets from a New York hat factory, and were arrested and convicted, the case was appealed all the way to the Supreme Court.

The court upheld the convictions, but two justices—Louis D. Brandeis and Oliver Wendell Holmes, Jr.—disagreed. Holmes said that speech may be punished only if it presents "a clear and present danger" of producing evils that the Constitution tries to prevent. "Now nobody can suppose that the surreptitious publishing of a silly leaflet...would present any immediate danger." His opinion was that "the defendants were deprived of their rights under the Constitution of the United States." Today, the concept of *clear and present danger* is used as a test of whether speech should be censored. Holmes became known as the "Great Dissenter."

*The Supreme Court invites Brandeis to join her ranks while fat cats look on in horror.*

# 3 Another Kind of War

**INFLUENZA**
FREQUENTLY COMPLICATED WITH
**PNEUMONIA**
IS PREVALENT AT THIS TIME THROUGHOUT AMERICA.
THIS THEATRE IS CO-OPERATING WITH THE DEPARTMENT OF HEALTH.
**YOU MUST DO THE SAME**
IF YOU HAVE A COLD AND ARE COUGHING AND
SNEEZING. DO NOT ENTER THIS THEATRE
**GO HOME AND GO TO BED UNTIL YOU ARE WELL**
Coughing, Sneezing or Spitting Will Not Be
Permitted In The Theatre. In case you
must cough or Sneeze, do so in your own hand-
kerchief, and if the Coughing or Sneezing
Persists Leave The Theatre At Once.

This Theatre has agreed to co-operate with
the Department Of Health in disseminating
the truth about Influenza, and thus serve
a great educational purpose.
**HELP US TO KEEP CHICAGO THE
HEALTHIEST CITY IN THE WORLD**
JOHN DILL ROBERTSON
COMMISSIONER OF HEALTH

**The usual October death rate from influenza and pneumonia was 4,000. In 1918 it was about 194,000.**

*I had a little bird,*
*And his name was Enza;*
*I opened the window,*
*And in flew Enza.*

*In flew Enza*—say it fast and it becomes "influenza." It was a catchy little rhyme, and boys and girls skipped rope to it. It was also an epidemic; no, it was worse than that. It was a *pandemic*, which means a disease that spreads across many nations. This one went around the globe. And it was deadly.

Diseases don't fly in the window, but the influenza of 1918 almost seemed to. It lasted about nine months, and, worldwide, killed 20 million people. That was more than the total of deaths during the four years of the Great War. Mysteriously, it struck at about the same time in India, and Russia, and China—no major nation escaped. In the United States there were more than half a million victims. On one terrible day in Philadelphia, almost 1,000 people died. Neither doctors, nor hospitals, nor cemeteries could handle the

**Returning soldiers, and anybody who didn't wear a mask, could be fined $100 and jailed.** *Obey the laws, and wear the gauze, protect your jaws from septic paws,* went one ditty. But the masks were useless.

The word ***influenza*** first appeared in 1743 after an epidemic in Italy. It is an Italian word, related to *influence,* and it means an "intangible visitation" (a visit by something you can't touch). ***Pandemic*** comes from the Greek words *pan* ("all") and *demos* ("people").

A public-health doctor in Washington, D.C., found that the only way he could be sure of having enough room in his emergency hospital was to keep undertakers always waiting outside the door so that the dead could be taken away immediately.

awful burdens put upon them. In those days before the discovery of modern medicines, there was little doctors could do.

In New York and Chicago, laws were passed making it illegal to sneeze or cough in public without using a handkerchief. Police dutifully hauled sneezers and coughers to court, where they were given stiff fines. The police had time to worry about influenza because the robbers and murderers were sick, too. In October 1918, Chicago's crime rate dropped by almost half.

**Today,** scientists believe that the 1918 influenza epidemic may have stopped killing people because of the way the influenza virus behaves. Dr. Michèle Barry, an infectious-diseases specialist at Yale University Medical School, says: "Every year, the influenza virus changes the coat of protein that surrounds it. Some protein coats seem to make the virus weaker or stronger. We think that during the course of the 1918 epidemic, the virus changed its protein coat and became weaker." She adds that it's also possible that after the disease killed off the most vulnerable victims (especially old people), the people who were left were tougher and less likely to die.

The epidemic spread most rapidly in cities—where people are crowded together—but many in the countryside died, too. A prominent senator lost a son and daughter. Soldiers, fighting heroically against enemies they could see, fell to invisible germs. In America the flu took 10 times as many lives as the war. The last week of October in 1918, 2,700 American soldiers died fighting in Europe; that same week, 21,000 Americans died at home of the flu.

It was called Spanish influenza—because people

New York City's phone company begged people to make only urgent calls—many switchboard operators were hit by flu, too.

One of the wounded soldiers who came home to find things changing was a young man named Ernest Hemingway *(left),* who was soon writing novels and stories (of war and life between the wars).

thought it had started in Spain. It hadn't. It may have begun in the United States, from a disease of hogs (it is sometimes called "swine flu," after the hogs). Some say it was the worst pandemic in history. It wasn't that it killed the most people; it was that it killed so rapidly. Someone figured, mathematically, that if it had continued spreading for another year, at the rate it was going, the world's population would have been wiped out.

By Armistice Day, November 11, the peak had passed. The disease soon departed as mysteriously as it had arrived. It left the country exhausted. Wasn't a war trouble enough? Everyone had worked hard supporting the war effort. Americans had done astonishing things in factories and on the farms. They'd fed Europe with an amazing harvest of grain; they'd armed the Allies. Citizens had given up luxuries and even some necessities to help others. That flu epidemic was the final straw. Someone needed to find something to cheer people up.

Soon a new word was being used. It was *normalcy.* That's what people wanted. They wanted to go back to the good old days before the war. But time won't march backward.

Those boys and girls who were skipping rope in 1918 had no idea what was ahead of them. They wouldn't have believed it if you had told them. Normalcy? No way. They were going to live in a world of radio, TV, computers, jets, and rockets. In 1918 that was the stuff of science fiction. Their

## If you were sick

in 1920, you didn't go to the doctor's office. The doctor came to your house. He brought a black satchel with him. It was stuffed with medical supplies: pills, salves, bandages, and maybe a stethoscope and a thermometer. Those two pieces of equipment were about as high-tech as medicine got. The world of the modern hospital, and sophisticated equipment, was still decades away.

## From Art to Science

**A**braham Flexner, an educator who was asked (by the Carnegie Foundation) to study medical schools in America, inspected each of the country's 155 medical schools, and in 1910, described them in a study that became very influential. Mostly, he thought American medical schools weren't very good and that they turned out poorly trained physicians. Flexner was especially critical of women's medical colleges (there were 16 of them) and black medical schools (there were 10). Doctors then earned little money and relied chiefly on experience and observation in treating patients. Flexner said that medicine needed to be a science. His report helped make it just that. It also drove most women and minorities from the practice.

world was slow-paced, and mostly powered by horses and mules.

Their older brothers—the soldiers who came home from Europe in 1919—had exciting things to tell them. They'd been to Paris and had seen fancy nightclubs, stunning buildings, and splendid boulevards. Some bragged about their heroism in battle, which was understandable; you had to be tough—or lucky—to be a survivor. A few came home without arms or legs. Some didn't want to talk about the war at all. They, too, were looking for normalcy.

The returning soldiers were surprised to find that America had changed in the year they'd been gone. They noticed two things right away. One had to do with beer and liquor. During the war it was considered unpatriotic to drink alcohol. Beer is made from grain, and grain was needed to feed soldiers. Now that the war was over, many people wanted to put an end to all liquor drinking. It would make the world a much better place, they said.

The other change gave some of the soldiers a chuckle. Imagine, women were demanding equal rights: they wanted to be full citizens. Why, soon they'd probably want to wear pants, too!

## The Wild Beasts

It was a cold winter day in 1913 when the doors opened at an old, drafty armory on 25th Street and Lexington Avenue in New York City, and people got to see some new paintings and sculpture (including many from Europe). American art was never the same again. Some of the paintings in the Armory Show were done by Henri Matisse, Paul Cézanne, Pablo Picasso, Paul Gauguin, and Vincent van Gogh. Today we know them all as great artists, but in 1913 their work was unlike anything most people here had seen before. Matisse was part of a French group called Les Fauves, or "the wild beasts." Many viewers thought it a good title for all the artists.

One painting, by Marcel Duchamp, was called *Nude Descending a Staircase*. Classical paintings often showed naked figures reclining on couches. This painting showed what seemed to be a bunch of sticks— or maybe a figure; it was hard to tell—but something very active *was* happening on the canvas. It was worth a second, and even a third look. Many of the paintings included unrecognizable objects. Before, art had always more or less imitated reality. These paintings were completely different. In Chicago some art students burned effigies (stuffed figures) of Henri Matisse. But many Americans were profoundly changed by the new modernism. The artist Stuart Davis said that the Armory Show was "the greatest single experience...in all my work." He was not alone.

*Marcel Duchamp's* Nude Descending a Staircase; *to some it was an outrage.*

# 4 The Prohibition Amendment

You couldn't get drier than a camel—it became the symbol of Prohibition party supporters.

The Constitution does not give Congress the right to tell people what they may eat or drink. If someone wants to drink poison, only a state can make laws to try to keep him from doing so.

Many people say that alcohol can be a kind of poison. No one disagrees that drinking too much is harmful.

Drunkenness was a special problem in early America. Most drinking was done in sa-

*Women's Christian Temperance Union Parade,* painted by Ben Shahn around 1934. The ladies of the WCTU campaigned "for God, for home, for native land." But lawmakers found that it was hard to make a crime out of drinking, which many had never seen as a crime before.

loons, where women were not admitted. Some men took their paychecks, went to a saloon, drank up, and then went home drunk, with no money left for their families. Reformers decided to attack the problem. Some of them believed in *temperance,* which means "moderation." Others believed in *prohibition,* which means "outlawing all drinking."

Some women's groups fought for prohibition. Several religious groups—especially Methodists and Baptists—joined the battle. Many states became *dry.* In a dry state it was against state law to buy or sell liquor. Some people wanted to go further. They wanted the whole nation to be dry. A constitutional amendment was needed.

It was the Progressive Era: people thought that laws could help make people perfect—or close to it. It took about 20 years to get the

Prohibition agents got to work disposing of booze. But there were only 1,500 agents, not really enough to enforce the law—especially when they were up against the ruthless gangsters who sold the liquor.

In this painting, *Bootleggers* (1934), Ben Shahn shows three ways to hide alcohol: tie a bottle to your leg; tie it behind your back; or empty it into a hollow walking stick. In the background two men make whiskey in a homemade still.

18th Amendment passed, but finally it was done. The Prohibition amendment became law in 1920. The amendment made it illegal to sell liquor anywhere in the United States. Most people thought it a very good idea. All but two states passed the Prohibition amendment.

It didn't work. Many people who wanted to drink kept drinking—although per capita (see page 28) alcohol consumption did fall during Prohibition years.

# The Constitution of the United States, Article V

*The Congress, whenever two thirds of both Houses shall deem it necessary, shall propose Amendments to this Constitution, or, on the Application of the Legislatures of two thirds of the several States, shall call a Convention for proposing Amendments, which, in either Case, shall be valid to all Intents and Purposes, as Part of this Constitution, when ratified by the Legislatures of three fourths of the several States, or by Conventions in three fourths thereof.*

What does all that mean? Read it slowly and it isn't as difficult as it may seem. What it means is that the men who wrote the Constitution—James Madison, Gouverneur Morris, Ben Franklin, John Adams, and the others—understood that a constitution needs to be adaptable. The Founding Fathers wanted people in the future—you and me—to be able to change the Constitution. But they didn't want to make it too easy to change. If they did that the Constitution wouldn't have much lasting value: it would get changed all the time.

So they came up with the idea of amendments as a way to change the Constitution. It has been more than 200 years since the Constitution was written; hundreds of amendments have been proposed, but only 26 have been passed.

For an amendment to succeed, two-thirds of the Congress must pass it—that means two-thirds of both the Senate and the House of Representatives. Then three-fourths of the states must also approve the amendment. (The Constitution may also be amended if a constitutional convention is called by three-fourths of the states—that has never been done.)

Remember, we have a federal form of government. Power is shared among the national government in Washington, D.C., and the state governments. The Constitution lists all the things the president, Congress, and the courts can control. Any powers not listed in the Constitution belong to the states.

**Per capita** (pur-CAP-it-uh) is Latin, and means "by heads" or per person. In other words, the total amount of liquor consumed in the U.S., divided by the number of people in the U.S., showed there was less alcohol drunk during Prohibition than before. But many new kinds of people began drinking; that was the problem.

**After** the Prohibition amendment was passed, Congress needed to provide for its enforcement. That was done with a law called the Volstead Act. Prohibition didn't make it illegal to drink, or even to buy liquor; it just made it illegal to sell it.

But some people, especially some women and young people, who had not drunk before, decided to try it. Prohibition wasn't supposed to do this, but in some crowds it made drinking fashionable. (Maybe it had to do with disillusionment after the war. Writers were calling this a "lost generation." People weren't really lost, but they were confused about right and wrong.)

Since selling liquor was now a crime, gangsters took over that activity. People who sold liquor were called "bootleggers." (Some of them stuck flasks inside high boots.) Ships running whiskey from foreign suppliers to coastal ports were called "rumrunners." Illegal bars, where drinks were sold, were called "speakeasies." (If people spoke loudly, and the police heard them, the bar would be raided. So they spoke "easy.")

No one expected it, but Prohibition made crime a big business in the United States. Americans learned that some kinds of prohibition must be done by persuasion and education. Laws and force don't always work.

Another amendment was needed to get rid of the Prohibition amendment. The 21st Amendment was passed in December 1933. It ended what was a well-meaning experiment. The experiment had failed.

But how do you get people to stop doing something that isn't good for them? Do the lessons of Prohibition apply to drugs? Some people say we should make it legal to buy drugs; then criminals could not earn big money selling drugs. Others say that would encourage people to use drugs. What do you think?

In 1933, the country had more than 200,000 illegal speakeasies. This painting, like those on pages 25, 27, and 35, was made by artist Ben Shahn, who put many of the social and political issues of his time on canvas.

# 5 Mom, Did You Vote?

The suffragists had become experts at getting publicity for the cause.

We're heading back in time—just a bit. It is 1917, and some women are marching in front of the White House. They carry a big banner that says 20 MILLION AMERICAN WOMEN ARE NOT SELF-GOVERNED. In Europe, American soldiers are fighting for democracy; these women feel they should fight for it at home.

Day after day, for months, the women march in front of the president's house. They are peaceful and respectful, but persistent. Some people don't like it; they say the suffragists shouldn't annoy the president during wartime. The police tell the women to leave. "Has the law been changed?" asks Alice Paul, leader of the group. "No," says the police officer, "but you must stop."

"We have consulted our lawyers," says Alice Paul. "We have a legal right to picket."

The next day two women, Lucy Burns and Katherine Morey, are arrested. Other arrests soon follow.

On the Fourth of July a congressman speaks to a large crowd gathered behind the White House. "Governments derive their just powers from the consent of the governed," he says. Police keep the crowd orderly and protect the congressman's right to free speech.

Alice Paul went to England and learned tough tactics—chaining oneself to railings, disrupting public meetings—from British suffragists.

**In 1915,** Alice Paul organized a women's suffrage motorcade that went from San Francisco to Washington, D.C., with a petition 18,000 feet long. It carried half a million names.

This is what we are doing with our banners before the White House, petitioning the most powerful representative of the government, the President of the United States, for a redress of grievances; we are asking him to use his great power to secure the passage of the national suffrage amendment.

—ANNE MARTIN

**Dr. W. W. Parker** of Richmond, Virginia, wrote an essay that he read to the Medical Society of Virginia. Women, he said, were "superior morally, inferior mentally, to man—not qualified for medicine or law." Then he continued, "God having finished this splendid world, placed at its grand arched gateway imperial man, stately and stalwart, with will and wisdom stamped upon his lofty brow."

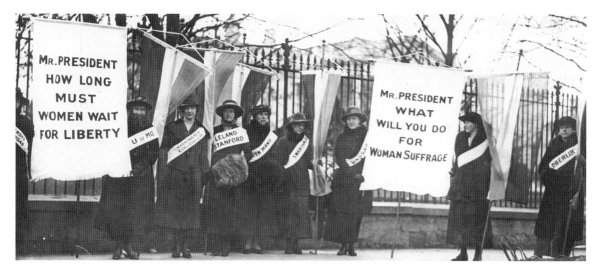

At one demonstration outside the White House, men from the crowd tore the suffragists' banners down and pelted the women with eggs, tomatoes, and apples. Twenty-two banners and 14 party flags were destroyed.

**Many Americans**—men and women—don't bother to be active citizens. Many don't vote. The whole point of a democracy is that it gives everyone power. Those who don't vote give up their power.

In front of the White House a group of 13 women silently holds a banner with those very same words from the Declaration of Independence. Some are young women, some white-haired grandmothers; all are arrested. The women are taken to court and fined. They refuse to pay their fines—to do so would mean to admit they are guilty. They do not believe themselves guilty of any crime. The police take them to jail. More women are arrested. Anne Martin speaks out in court:

> As long as the government and the representatives of the government prefer to send women to jail on petty and technical charges we will go to jail. Persecution has always advanced the cause of justice. The right of American women to work for democracy must be maintained.

More women go to jail. They are separated from each other. Prison conditions are awful. For 17 days Ada Davenport Kendall is given nothing to eat but bread and water. Some women are held in solitary confinement. Some, who go on hunger strikes, are held down and fed against their will. Anne Martin, Lucy Burns, and Elizabeth McShane are force fed. Burns is bruised on her lips and face; McShane throws up. Now the women have become interested in prison reform, as well as in women's suffrage. One woman writes that it is "necessary to make a stand for the ordinary rights of human beings for all the inmates."

## Utter Nonsense

When Susan B. Anthony was a girl she asked the schoolmaster one day if she could learn long division with the boys. "Nonsense! Utter nonsense!" he told her. "A girl needs to know how to read her Bible and count her egg money, nothing more." But Susan Anthony was determined. So, slyly, she sat on a bench behind the boys and listened and worked problems and learned long division. Anthony never did what others did, unless she thought it right.

Suffragists parade through New York City in 1913.

In the White House, Woodrow Wilson has other concerns. He is fighting a war—that war for democracy. Wilson says he isn't against women's suffrage—in fact he is for it—but, like many men, he thinks that most other issues are more important.

The women keep marching. All kinds of women. Rich and poor. Could it be that they understand democracy in a way the president doesn't?

Mrs. John Rogers, Jr., is arrested. She is a descendant of Roger Sherman (a signer of the Declaration of Independence). Like her plain-speaking ancestor, Mrs. Rogers says what she thinks. She tells the judge:

> We are not guilty of any offense...we know full well that we stand
> here because the president of the United States refuses to give liberty

**The right of citizens of the United States to vote shall not be denied or abridged by the United States or by any state on account of sex.**

—19TH AMENDMENT
TO THE CONSTITUTION

**31**

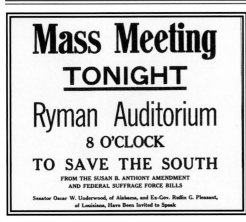

# Mass Meeting
## TONIGHT
### Ryman Auditorium
#### 8 O'CLOCK
## TO SAVE THE SOUTH
FROM THE SUSAN B. ANTHONY AMENDMENT
AND FEDERAL SUFFRAGE FORCE BILLS

Senator Oscar W. Underwood, of Alabama, and Ex-Gov. Ruffin G. Pleasant, of Louisiana, Have Been Invited to Speak

Many people—women as well as men—fought desperately to block the 19th Amendment. At right, an antisuffrage propaganda poster implies that "emancipated" women abandoned their suffering families to pursue the vote.

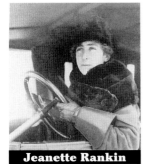

**Jeanette Rankin**

Montana's Jeanette Rankin was the first woman elected to Congress. She served two terms in the House (1917–1919; 1941–1943). Rebecca Latimer Felton, age 87, was the first woman in the Senate. She didn't do much. After a Georgia senator died, she was appointed to fill the vacancy for two days in November 1922.

**Rebecca Latimer Felton**

*to American women. We believe, your honor, that the wrong persons are before the bar in this court....We believe the president is the guilty one and that we are innocent.*

Now, isn't that what America is all about? The right of every citizen to speak out—even against the president.

Mrs. Rogers's cause is just, but her comments aren't quite fair. It is Congress that is holding things up, not Woodrow Wilson. But the president hasn't helped. Finally, he does. He urges Congress to pass the 19th Amendment. It is known as the Susan B. Anthony amendment. This battle for women's suffrage is not something new. Susan Anthony and her friend Elizabeth Cady Stanton began the fight in the mid-19th century. They spent their lives fighting for women's rights. So did Carrie Chapman Catt, the head of the National American Woman Suffrage Association.

Many men and women have worked hard for this cause. Most are people you have never even heard

## Female Takeover

*The perpetrators of Yoncalla's conspiracy of women after their takeover of the town council, with Mayor Mary Burt in the middle.*

In 1920, the women of Yoncalla, Oregon, got together and made plans to take over the town government. They didn't tell anyone, not even their brothers or husbands. Men outnumbered women two to one in this community of fewer than 350 persons, but the women all voted. According to *Literary Digest,* they were "stirred by the alleged inefficiency of the municipal officials, and swept every masculine office-holder out of his job." When they went to the polls they elected an all-women's slate of town officials. Mrs. Mary Burt became the new mayor. The out-of-a-job former mayor, a Mr. Laswell, was said to be "much surprised."

Said Mr. Jones in Nineteen-Ten:
"Women, subject yourselves to men."
Nineteen-Eleven heard him quote:
"They rule the world without the vote."
By Nineteen-Twelve, he would submit
"When all the women wanted it."
By Nineteen-Thirteen, looking glum,
He said that it was bound to come.
This year I heard him say with pride:
"No reasons on the other side!"
By Nineteen-Fifteen, he'll insist
He's always been a suffragist.
And what is really stranger, too,
He'll think that what he says is true.

—ALICE DUERR MILLER, "EVOLUTION,"
IN *ARE WOMEN PEOPLE? A BOOK OF RHYMES FOR SUFFRAGE TIMES*, 1915

Carrie Chapman Catt campaigned all over Tennessee to get the amendment ratified. "The summer heat was endless, and many legislators lived in remote villages," she said. "Yet the women trailed these legislators, by train, by motor, by wagons, on foot...no woman faltered."

about. (See if you can find a history of the women's suffrage movement in your community.) In Tennessee, Harry Burn was 24 and the youngest representative in the legislature when he got a letter from his mother. "Don't forget to be a good boy," wrote his mother, "and help Mrs. Catt put the 'Rat' in ratification."

The Tennessee legislators were trying to decide whether to approve the 19th Amendment or not. Half were for women's suffrage, half were not. Burn held the deciding vote. He followed his mother's advice. It was 1919, and Tennessee was the last state needed to ratify. The following year, 1920, America's women finally went to the polls.

# 6 Red Scare

"Whose country is it anyway?" Uncle Sam takes care of "reds."

Communists were called **reds** after the red flag of the International, which was the worldwide communist organization.

Some people in America were scared by Russia's ideas. They were afraid of *communism*. Others were attracted to those ideas. Under communism, most property and goods belong to the state. People are expected to share. That sounds noble; it just never seems to work unless forced upon people. Communist nations have not been free nations.

After the world war, some people were scared that communists wanted to take over in the United States. There were a few communists in this country—but they were not successful. Most American people were not attracted to communism.

## Russia Revolts

Russia fought with the Allies in World War I until the Russian people decided they'd had enough of the war. It was more important, as far as they were concerned, to solve their own problems. They wanted to get rid of their ruler—the tsar (ZAR). They wanted to end the big gap between rich and poor in Russia. They wanted what Americans had wanted in 1776. They wanted freedom. So they had a freedom revolution.

At first, it looked as if they might get freedom. The people who overthrew the tsar (in 1917) were trying to create a demo-cratic government. Then a revolutionary named Vladimir Lenin, who was living in Europe in exile, came back to Russia. That man changed the fate of Russia and the world. He became dictator of Russia. He didn't believe in democracy.

Things had been bad in Russia when the tsar was ruler. They got much worse under Lenin and the ruler who followed, Joseph Stalin. Lenin and Stalin brought totalitarianism to Russia. They brought repression, murder, state control, and misery. They brought an economic system called communism.

Lenin took Russia out of the war. That let Germany move troops from eastern Europe to France. It made the Great War tougher for the Allies.

What does all this have to do with U.S. history? A lot. You see, the world had become smaller. Not smaller in size, but in accessibility. At the beginning of the 19th century, it took at least two years for a ship to go from Salem, Massachusetts, to China and back. Now, with the telephone, communication was almost instantaneous. Modern technology meant that the ideas of one nation could spread quickly to others.

*Left:* In September 1920, a bomb exploded on Wall Street, killing 38 people and fueling fears that communists threatened the nation's existence. *Above:* A. Mitchell Palmer, President Wilson's attorney general.

In that same postwar time, there were also some *anarchists* in America. Anarchists don't believe in government at all. You don't have to be very smart to realize that anarchy doesn't work. But, when the anarchists looked around and saw poverty, war, and evil, they thought that this was the fault of governments. Some may have really believed that the answer was to do away with all governments. A few tried to do that by setting off bombs intended to kill government leaders. That, of course, was criminal behavior. Newspapers made big headlines of the bombs. Many Americans were frightened. But what A. Mitchell Palmer, President Wilson's attorney general, did was irresponsible and criminal. (He got away with it—but not in the history books.)

Palmer went on a witch hunt. The witches he went after were communists and anarchists. He took the law in his hands, and, in two days of raids in major cities (in 1920), agents invaded homes, clubs, union halls, pool halls, and coffee shops, rounding up nearly 5,000 people, who were held in jail, not allowed to call anyone, and treated terribly. Those without citizenship papers were sent out of the country—to Russia. Most weren't guilty of anything.

## Sacco and Vanzetti

**N**icola Sacco and Bartolomeo Vanzetti were accused of murdering a paymaster and his guard at a shoe factory in South Braintree, Massachusetts. Did they do it? Even today, no one is sure. But they were convicted and executed. Sacco and Vanzetti were anarchists, and many said it was radical beliefs that were on trial. The trial was a *cause célèbre* (which, in French, means "a famous happening").

*Ben Shahn made 23 paintings of the Sacco and Vanzetti case in 1931–1932, including this portrait from their trial.*

**In 1789,** Congress passed an Alien law. It kept certain people from emigrating to the United States. A sedition law made it a crime to speak against the government. People were jailed for their ideas. The people who supported those laws said they wanted to keep "dangerous foreigners" out of the country. At the time, the foreigners they feared were French.

Behind the red scare was a fear of foreigners. These men being taken to prison are all immigrant aliens.

Communists are sometimes called "reds." Mitchell Palmer took advantage of America's fear of communism. He helped create a "red scare." He hoped it would make him president. During the red scare, Americans were not free to speak out about communism. They weren't free to criticize the government. Some people's lives were ruined.

Witch-hunting turns up every once in a while in American history. (It happened in Salem, Massachusetts, in colonial days; it happened after World War II with a senator named Joe McCarthy.) The good thing is, it never seems to last long. Persecution for ideas is not the American way.

Everywhere reds were under the bed—or, as in this cartoon, slithering under cover of the Stars and Stripes.

The 1st Amendment (part of our Bill of Rights) says: *Congress shall make no law...abridging the freedom of speech.* Does that mean that communists and anarchists are free to speak out here—as long as they do not engage in criminal activity or plot to overthrow the government?

Thomas Jefferson wrote: *Truth is great and will prevail if left to herself,* and *errors cease to be dangerous when it is permitted freely to contradict them.* He believed that when everyone's ideas are heard, people will make wise choices. Do you agree with him?

The Ku Klux Klan grew hugely in the 1920s. The Klan no longer limited its hatred and bigotry to blacks; it was anti-foreign, anti-communist, anti-Catholic, anti-Jewish.

# 7 Soft-Hearted Harding

Harding in 1882, age 16, when he graduated from college and taught school for a year.

The two presidents sat together in the elegant Pierce-Arrow touring car. The car had running boards on its sides, the presidential seal on its door, and no roof.

Both men wore tall black silk hats and fashionable coats with black velvet collars. Woodrow Wilson's face was ash white. He had always been slim; now he seemed shrunken, like a dry reed. It had taken all his energy to walk from the White House door to the automobile. Just two years earlier, Wilson had been the world's hero. Now he was ill and ignored. His country seemed to have no use for him or his ideas, and he knew it.

Sitting next to him was the president-elect. The candidate the people had chosen—enthusiastically—as 29th president: Warren Gamaliel (guh-MAY-lee-ul) Harding. If a movie director were casting a president's part, he might pick Harding. The man *looked* presidential. His hair was silver, his eyebrows black, his skin tanned bronze, his voice golden. He was handsome, well groomed, and distinguished looking. He was also a good-natured, pleasant man.

The Pierce-Arrow pulled up to the Capitol, where Woodrow Wilson signed his last official papers as president. The new vice president, Calvin Coolidge, was sworn into office in the Senate chambers. Then Warren Harding took his place at the center of the grandstand built for his inauguration in front of the Capitol. He put his hand on the Bible and swore to execute the office of president to the best of his ability. He had chosen a line from the Old Testament book of Micah, and he read it in a clear voice amplified by loudspeakers:

A **running board** was a long entry step that ran along the side of an automobile.

**Florence Harding** managed a lot of firsts along with being First Lady. She was the first president's wife to fly in an airplane and the first to hold press conferences for women reporters. She worked, successfully, to found the first rehabilitation penitentiary for women (that's a jail where prisoners are helped to change their criminal behavior rather than just punished for it). And she spoke out for women's equality in sports, schools, employment, and politics.

The scandal in the Harding administration centered on some naval oil reserves, including one at Teapot Dome, near Casper, Wyoming. (Geologists call a swollen upward curve in the earth's surface a "dome.") Congress was concerned that the military services have enough oil in case of emergencies, so it had set aside certain oil-rich areas for government use. Harding had appointed men who gave secret rights to those government oil lands to individuals and private companies that got rich on oil meant for public use.

Thanks to Thomas Nast (see *A History of US,* book 8) cartoonists often represent the Republican, or "Grand Old" Party (GOP), as an elephant (and the Democratic party as a donkey). The Teapot Dome scandal got the Republican party elephant into some very hot water.

*What doth the Lord require of thee, but to do justly, and to love mercy, and to walk humbly with thy God.*

The Marine band played "America."

After the stormy war years, this low-key, modest inaugural seemed just right. "We must strive for normalcy," said Warren Harding, and the public applauded.

Two years and five months later, Harding was dead, and the nation wept as it had not done since the death of Abraham Lincoln. In his lifetime, Warren Harding was one of the most popular presidents ever.

He is said to have died of heart failure, but perhaps it was of a broken heart. For he knew, before he died, that his friends, whom he trusted with important government jobs, had betrayed him and

The mustachioed men are Interior Secretary Albert Fall *(left)* and Edward Doheny. Doheny bribed Fall to lease the Teapot Dome oil fields.

the nation. They had stolen and plundered. They had given away priceless oil reserves, laughed at the conservationists, and taken bribes from business and criminal interests. They had become very rich.

And what did the American people think when they heard the news? At first they were angry at the senators and journalists who told them. Later, they became angry when they thought about Harding. Before long, historians were calling him the worst of all presidents.

Montana Senator Thomas Walsh investigated Teapot Dome. He was harassed by the FBI, which tapped his phones, opened his mail, and made anonymous threats on his life.

He wasn't the worst. He created the Bureau of the Budget, reduced the national debt, cut taxes, and appointed black men to public office. It's a myth that he didn't work hard (although he did play a lot of poker and golf). But he may not have been tough enough, or smart enough, to handle the presidency. A president has to make hard decisions.

If you are president you need to appoint good people to the cabinet and to thousands of administrative jobs. You need to be a leader of the armed forces. You need to make a huge budget to run the country. You need to come up with ideas for domestic policies that will make the country prosperous and happy. You need to make foreign policies to guide the nation in its relations with other nations. You need to get along with Congress. You need to get along with the states and their governors. You need to be a role model for millions of citizens with differing ideas and desires. Being president is an enormous, complicated job.

Warren Harding, as I said, was a pleasant man, always gracious and considerate. Maybe it was because he was so good-hearted that he wanted to help his old friends. Maybe that's why he put some

> ## Loudspeakers
> were used at Harding's inauguration for the first time in the event's history.

> ## "Lord, Lord, man!"
> said one of Harding's aides to reporter William Allen White of the *Emporia Gazette.* "You can't know what the president is going through. You see he doesn't understand it; he just doesn't know a thousand things he ought to know. And he realizes his ignorance, and he is afraid. He has no idea where to turn."

## Political Advice: Don't Say Yes—or No

Harding was the first president to address the nation over the radio.

**W**arren Harding, 29th president, was the owner and editor of a newspaper in Marion, Ohio, when he entered politics. He became a senator. In 1920, the Republican National Convention couldn't decide on a candidate—the delegates were deadlocked—so on the 10th ballot the party turned to well-liked, easygoing Senator Harding, and nominated him. During his campaign, Harding wouldn't say if he was for the League of Nations or against it. His opponent, Democrat James M. Cox (also of Ohio), said he was for the League. Cox lost the election.

of those friends in important jobs. Most weren't qualified for those jobs. Some were crooks who stole a whole lot of money from the nation.

Harding didn't realize it. But he should have. That was his job. A more able president might have saved the country a lot of grief.

## Chicken-Bone Specials

**B**etween 1910 and 1920, more than 1 million black people headed north. Working conditions in the South were awful; schools were worse; and most blacks couldn't vote. The North held the hope of better jobs, better schooling, and a chance to get ahead. For a while, the Pennsylvania Railroad offered free passage to blacks who could recruit others to come north. The trains came to be called "chicken-bone specials"; blacks weren't allowed to eat in the dining cars, so they had to bring their own food—usually fried chicken. New York's black population (centered in Harlem) increased by 66 percent in that 10-year period. Chicago's black population (centered in the South Side) increased by 50 percent. That black migration—from field to factory, from rural to urban—continued through most of the century. Jacob Lawrence painted the migration in a series of paintings that are small in size but powerful in impact.

*Jacob Lawrence's* The Migration of the Negro, Panel No. 1 *(1940–41). "There is absolutely nothing before them on the farm," said a government report on Southern labor, "no prospect...but to continue until they die." Instead, they fled.*

# 8 Silent Cal and the Roaring Twenties

Coolidge was happy to play the tunes big business wanted to hear—and it was music to the fat cats' ears.

Thrifty, Vermont-born Calvin Coolidge became president when Harding died. He had been an active governor of Massachusetts and, like most Vermonters, he didn't waste words, but he did get a lot done. So most people thought he would be an energetic and decisive chief executive. And he started that way. In his first message to Congress he called for federal laws to punish "the hideous act of lynching," and for more attention to education, minimum wages for women workers, and other progressive measures.

But then something terrible happened. Coolidge's son, 16-year-old Calvin Jr., died of blood poisoning, which developed from a toe blister he had gotten playing tennis. Coolidge was overwhelmed with grief. He couldn't concentrate. He developed an assortment of illnesses, including severe depression. His work suffered.

Still, the times were prosperous, he was popular, and almost no one, besides his wife and close friends, knew what was happening to him. Today, he is mostly remembered as a president who didn't say or do much—but he held more than seven press conferences a month, which was more than Theodore Roosevelt or Woodrow Wilson did before him or Franklin Roosevelt did after him. As for not doing much, that was part of his philosophy. He was against ac-

**1925:** Wyoming elects the first woman governor in U.S. history, Nellie Taylor Ross. *The New Yorker* is introduced as a magazine for "caviar sophisticates… not for the old lady in Dubuque." The first issue costs 15 cents. At Nome, Alaska, dog-team relays bring serum to combat a serious diphtheria epidemic. Born in 1925: Robert F. Kennedy, Rod Steiger, and Malcolm X.

**1926:** The first motion picture with synchronized sound, *Don Juan,* stars heartthrob John Barrymore. The sound comes from a phonograph record. (Until now, theaters have usually hired a piano player to play along with the films.)

**1927:** The United States Supreme Court in *Nixon* v. *Herndon* rules unanimously that a Texas law forbidding blacks to vote in primary elections violates the 14th Amendment and is unconstitutional. The first talking picture, *The Jazz Singer,* starring Al Jolson, opens.

The '20s were the age of fad contests. People tried to set records for doing something the most, the fastest, or the longest. Dance marathons went to extremes. Resting only 15 minutes an hour, couples danced for days, even weeks. The last couple left won a little bit of money.

Hardly anyone remembers Philo Farnsworth, but they should. Farnsworth is the man who invented TV. The idea for the TV picture tube came to him when he was 14 and a farm boy in Idaho tilling a potato field, back and forth. He realized an electron beam could scan images the same way. He was right. In 1927 he transmitted his first electronic image. He talked it out with his high school chemistry teacher, Justin Tolman, who encouraged him to go further.

Women wearing bathing suits were measured to see if they were showing too much leg. Here, Chicago police make an arrest for "indecent exposure" in 1922.

tive government. "Perhaps one of the most important accomplishments of my administration has been minding my own business," he said. The argument between active government and stand-aside government continues today. Most Americans at the time thought Coolidge a splendid president.

He had a wry wit—typical of Vermonters. When a woman told him she had bet someone that she could get him to say more than three words to her, he responded, "You lose."

It was the 1920s. Some called the decade the "Roaring Twenties," some called it the "Jazz Age," and some the "Dance Age." Whichever you chose, it seemed like a time of fun and change.

More people had more money than ever before. And, mostly, they were intent on having a good time. Hardly anyone seemed to worry that some people were left out of the prosperity boom.

In 1919, before the '20s began their roar, women's ankles sometimes could be glimpsed beneath long skirts. Those ankles, however, were modestly hidden beneath high-topped shoes. Then skirts started going up, and up, and up.

That made it a tough time to be the parent of a girl. It wasn't easy to be a girl then either. Most young women were cutting their hair—short. They called it "bobbing." Some parents wouldn't allow it. Short hair seemed indecent to the older generation, but up to the minute to those who did it. The girls who weren't allowed to cut their hair felt old-fashioned.

Some daring women were wearing bathing suits that left their legs uncovered. Police arrested women on the beaches for doing that. And makeup! "Nice" women started wearing lipstick, rouge, and powder. The older generation worried. "What is the world coming to?"

Those girls who bobbed their hair and wore short skirts and lipstick were called "flappers." They did other things, too. They drove automobiles, got jobs, went to the movies, read romantic novels, played Ping-Pong, and danced. My, did they dance! It was the big thing in the '20s. And the big dance was the Charleston. (In New York City, Gimbel's department store advertised special Charleston dresses that swung loose on the body. The price was $1.58.) When you danced the Charleston you swung your arms, kicked up your heels, knocked your knees together, and moved frantically.

*Frantic* is a good word to describe the '20s. The idealism of the Wilson years seemed to have come to nothing. After the war, everything was supposed to be better. But anyone could see that it wasn't. And there was the Prohibition idea. Americans wanted to have a good nation—where all people behaved themselves and didn't get drunk—but that wasn't working either. If you read the newspapers you could see that criminals were becoming rich and powerful selling liquor. So maybe the best thing to do was to forget about ideals and have a good time—frantically—which was what a

**In 1927,** sculptor Gutzon Borglum, using a steam shovel and dynamite as chisel and mallet, begins carving four gigantic heads (60 feet high) on Mount Rushmore in South Dakota. (Whose heads are they?)

**President** Coolidge had a dog named Prudence Prim.

By the time Henry Ford brought out his Model A, in 1927, there were 21 million cars in America—and the traffic jam was beginning to be a familiar phenomenon.

lot of Americans did in the '20s.

It was a materialistic age. People concentrated on making money and buying things for themselves. Successful businesspeople became national heroes. There were more rich people than ever before in American history. No one seemed to notice, however, that there were also growing numbers of unemployed people—people who were desperately poor. And many farmers were in terrible trouble.

But for most Americans, the times seemed good. The stock market—like women's hems—went up and up and up. Land values boomed. People were able to buy things they never could buy before. In 1920 the car was a novelty. Ten years later, almost every family had a car. Many Americans who didn't have indoor toilets in their homes had motorcars in their yards. The automobile was becoming a necessity.

Before the war, life had been slow-paced; now change was coming with cyclone speed. Ordinary people owned radios and listened to comedy shows and the nightly news. In Florida, in 1924, a schoolboy named Red Barber heard radio for the first time at a friend's house. Barber was so excited he stayed up most of the night listening to news from around the nation. It was a new experience. "A man...in Pittsburgh said it was snowing there...someone sang in New York...a banjo plunked in Chicago...it was sleeting in New Orleans." (Red Barber later became a radio sports broadcaster.)

## Monkeys on Trial

Jesus said, "Ye shall know the truth, and the truth shall make you free." Now here are some other words to think about: Thomas Jefferson, in the *Virginia Statute for Religious Freedom,* said, "Truth is great and will prevail if left to herself." Consider that idea—it has become a guiding philosophy in America. Our government doesn't tell its citizens what to believe. Jefferson's statute led directly to the First Amendment to the Constitution, which states that, "Congress shall make no law respecting an establishment of religion. . ." This section of the First Amendment, often called the "establishment clause," is the foundation of the American idea of separation of church and state.

But will truth "prevail if left to herself," or do you have to help it? And how do you determine what is true? Is religious truth different from scientific truth? Is it natural for them to be in conflict? The great American 20th century chemist Linus Pauling, the only person to win two unshared Nobel prizes (one for science and one for his peace efforts), said, "Science is the search for truth—it is not a game in which one tries to beat his opponent." Swiss-born Louis Agassiz, who became professor of zoology and geology at Harvard and a strong spokesman for science in 19th century America, said, "The time has come when scientific truth must cease to be the property of the few, when it must be woven into the common life of the world."

Now, with those thoughts in your head, take yourself to the town of Dayton, Tennessee. It is 1925 and Dayton has 1,600 citizens, down from the 3,000 who lived there in the 1890s. Mule-drawn wagons and old Model Ts are rolling down the dusty roads. Hot-dog and soft-drink vendors seem to be on every street corner. More than 100 reporters have arrived in town. So have photographers and motion-picture makers. A telegraph office—with 22 operators—is set up in a grocery store. A bookseller hawks biology texts. Another sells Bibles. Everywhere there are monkeys: monkey postcards, stuffed toy monkeys, and souvenir buttons that say *Your old man is a monkey.* Dayton has never seen so many people. What's going on?

It's a sensational court case; the best-known trial of the decade. Newspaper headlines are calling it the "monkey trial," and readers and radio listeners all over the country (and in other countries, too) can't seem to get enough of it.

A young schoolteacher is on trial because of what he is teaching in his classroom. In Tennessee it is illegal to teach the theory of evolution. Evolution traces life on earth through millions of years of development from one-celled creatures to plants and animals to humans. (Since apes and monkeys are a stage below us on the evolutionary ladder, jokesters have come up with the monkey label for the trial.)

Fundamentalist Christians believe in the exact words of the Bible, and the Bible says that the world was created in six days and that Adam and Eve—humans—were part of the Creation from the very beginning. Many find evolution a disturbing issue: Can you be both a Christian and a believer in evolution? Most Christians (but not fundamentalists) say you can. The theory of evolution is accepted at all of our major universities.

In 1925 Tennessee passes a bill that states that it is *unlawful for any teacher . . . to teach any theory that denies the story of the divine creation of man as taught in the Bible, and to teach instead that man has descended from a lower order of animals.*

That state law is telling schools that they should teach the Bible's version of creation. Critics say a church doctrine is being imposed on public schools and that is unconstitutional.

Many schoolteachers break the law and keep teaching from their science textbooks. The American Civil Liberties Union (founded in 1920 to protect civil rights) says it will pay the legal expenses of anyone who wants to test the law. In Dayton, some citizens sitting in Robinson's drugstore are concerned that their little town seems to be dying. They ask 24-year-old John Scopes (who teaches evolution in his high school biology class) if he would mind being arrested. They all joke that a trial might put Dayton on the map. It turns out to be no joke.

William Jennings Bryan learns of the trial and volunteers to be the prosecutor (in favor of the Tennessee law). Bryan has run for president three times; everyone knows him. He is kind, well liked, and a fundamentalist. Clarence Darrow volunteers to defend Scopes. Darrow is a brilliant lawyer, a friend of the underdog, and an agnostic (someone who is not sure if there is a God or not).

When the trial begins, it is hot, and the old courthouse is so crowded it acts as if it might collapse;

*Clarence Darrow* (left), *famous Chicago lawyer, and William Jennings Bryan* (right), *defender of fundamentalism, share a friendly moment at the Scopes trial in 1925.*

the judge moves everyone outdoors. Darrow is in shirtsleeves and wears lavender suspenders to hold up his pants. Bryan turns his collar inside his shirt, ties a handkerchief around his neck, and cools himself with a palm-leaf fan.

It is an angry trial, full of bad feelings, and it doesn't settle much of anything. Bryan wins the case: the courts agree that Scopes broke Tennessee law. (That law stays on the books until 1967.)

But, in most of the nation, people chuckle about "the monkey trial" and don't take it seriously. Which is too bad. This is an issue—involving the separation of church and state—that will keep coming up. In 1968 and again in 1987, the Supreme Court rules that laws requiring the teaching of creationism (the Bible's story of Creation) are in violation of the First Amendment. For many citizens, those Supreme Court decisions don't decide things either. Back in the 5th century in North Africa, Saint Augustine asked, "Why does truth call forth hatred?" In this debate, both sides claim ownership of truth.

45

## A Writer for the Jazz Age

Francis Scott Fitzgerald, a young Minnesotan (named for an ancestor, Francis Scott Key), had a tough time in school—but he loved to write:

*When I lived in St. Paul and was about 12, I wrote all through every class in school in the back of my geography book and first-year Latin book and in the margins of themes and mathematics problems. Two years later my family decided that the only way to force me to study was to send me to boarding school. That was a mistake. It took my mind off my writing.*

But not for long. In a short life (he died at age 44), Fitzgerald wrote five novels, more than 150 short stories, and many essays. Hardly anyone described America of the 1920s and '30s as well as he did. It was he who labeled the times the "Jazz Age." His characters tried to turn life into a glittering party, and then couldn't understand why they weren't happy. Something was wrong, Fitzgerald said. His generation had "grown up to find all Gods dead, all wars fought, all faiths in man shaken."

**F. Scott and Zelda Fitzgerald**

Young people were flocking to the movies and, in 1927, movies began to talk. Talk about fun!

The following year, in Hollywood, California, a young filmmaker named Walt Disney produced the first animated sound film, *Steamboat Willie,* and introduced a little mouse named Mickey to the American public.

Suddenly, America seemed filled with artistic geniuses: musicians George Gershwin and Aaron Copland; writers Ernest Hemingway, William Faulkner, and F. Scott Fitzgerald; and artists Mary Cassatt, Grant Wood, and Thomas Hart Benton. And those are just a few of the names.

Harlem (a part of New York City with a rapidly growing black population) began vibrating with artistry. It was contagious. Playwrights, poets, musicians, artists, and actors, all living within a few blocks of each other, were sharing ideas. Langston Hughes, Claude McKay, and Countee Cullen began writing poetry. Zora Neale Hurston and Jean Toomer wrote novels. Jacob Lawrence and Romare Bearden painted pictures. And Duke Ellington and a whole lot of other people made music. Artistic excellence was something that the segregationists couldn't suppress. And Harlem, during this time known as the "Harlem Renaissance," exploded with creativity.

While this was going on, sad, grieving Calvin Coolidge sat in the White House and did little. His campaign slogan, "Keep Cool with Coolidge," seemed right for the times. The country was thriving, so when he said, "The chief business of America is business," many agreed, without ever hearing the rest of his speech. "The accumulation of wealth cannot be justified as the chief end of existence....So long as wealth is made the means and not the end, we need not greatly fear it." He added, "I cannot repeat too often that America is a nation of idealists. That [idealism] is the only motive to which they [Americans] ever give any strong and lasting reaction."

Do you think he was right?

Coolidge was uncomfortable in front of the camera—in this down-home photo opportunity he looks as if he's never been on a farm in his life.

# 9 Everyone's Hero

Ruth the rookie found even riding in an elevator exciting. "Why, he's just a babe in the woods," his teammates said.

George Ruth, Jr. *(right)*, age seven, at St. Mary's with his baseball buddy John DeTullio

George Herman Ruth certainly didn't look like a hero. His body was shaped like a barrel with spindly legs sticking out of its bottom. His face wasn't much to look at either. In the middle was a mashed-in nose.

But none of that mattered, because Ruth—who was known as "the Babe"—turned beautiful when he stepped onto a baseball field. He was the most famous ballplayer of all time.

He had an awful childhood. He wasn't an orphan, as some books say, but his parents, who ran a tavern, didn't care for him much. So he spent most of his time on the streets of Baltimore, got in trouble, and, at age eight, was sent to a Catholic boys' home (where he played a lot of baseball). He was tough—he had to be—but not bitter or angry. Actually, he was funny and friendly, and had all the instincts of a natural ham actor. He loved playing baseball, he broke all its records, and he was always himself, which means no one could predict what he would do or say next. The crowds adored him.

Ruth was a lefty—a southpaw—and he started out as a pitcher (in 1914) with the Boston Red Sox. He was sensational. But he could also hit—harder and farther than anyone. So Boston had him pitch some days and sometimes had him play first base. In 1918 he was about the best left-handed pitcher in the game, and that year he also led the American League in home runs.

But Boston needed money, so they traded him to the New York Yankees. The Yankees put him in the outfield. Pitchers play only every three or four days. An outfielder plays every day. The Yankees were

## Black Sox

**B**abe Ruth was a godsend for a national game deep in scandal. In 1919, members of the Chicago White Sox (forever after known as the "Black Sox") took money from gamblers and lost the World Series on purpose. Only a larger-than-life figure like Ruth could distract the millions of baseball fans from the ugly scandal and restore the game's innocence. Ruth, with his prodigious hitting, flamboyant behavior, and childlike enthusiasm, was just what the country needed.

Ruth *(second from right)* as a Red Sox rookie in 1914. His first professional baseball experience was with the Baltimore Orioles, who were down on their luck and in the minors. The owner was short of cash and sold Ruth to Boston after five months. By 1916 the Babe was the best left-handed pitcher in baseball.

**America** fell in love with organized sports during the Roaring Twenties. Sports stars became American heroes. Working hours were changing, and more Americans had more leisure time. They could go to ballparks or listen to games on radio. (Red Barber was now one of their favorite sportscasters.) They could also play sports themselves. When the Great War ended there were very few tennis courts or golf courses in the nation. Some states didn't have any at all. Those sports were mainly played by rich folks. By the end of the '20s, golf courses and tennis courts were popping up everywhere. Americans were hard at play.

counting on Babe Ruth's hitting.

Were they ever right! Before Ruth, baseball had been a low-scoring game. Pitchers were the stars, and batters did a lot of bunting and base-stealing. Ruth made it a hitter's game.

The all-time home-run record—set in 1884—was 27 home runs in one season. In 1920, Ruth hit 54 home runs. People came to the ballpark just to see those homers. Other ballplayers began holding the bat the way he did and swinging with all their might. Scores began going up. High-scoring games are a lot more exciting than pitchers' duels. The fans went wild. Baseball teams agreed to switch to a lively ball that went farther than the ball they had been using. The game got really exciting.

In 1921, Babe Ruth hit 59 home runs and scored a total of 177 runs. Yankee baseball attendance doubled. In 1923, the New York Yankees built big, beautiful Yankee Stadium. They used the money that came from increased attendance. It was called "the house that Ruth built."

Those who couldn't get to Yankee Stadium could still enjoy the game. The first radio station, KDKA in Pittsburgh, began broadcasting in October of 1920. Four years later there were 576 licensed stations and five million radio sets in use. People in Kansas could hear the Yankees play baseball. Radio announcers went to the ball games and described what was happening, play by play. At home, families clustered around their wood-covered radio sets, and, if the static wasn't too bad, listened for the swat of Babe Ruth's bat.

He was trying to beat his own home-run record. But when a reporter asked, "Which one was that, Babe?" the slugger was cool. "I'll hit 'em, you count 'em," he said.

In 1927, the Babe hit 60 home runs. That record stood for

34 years, until 1961, when Roger Maris hit 61. (There were 154 games in the 1927 season and 162 games in 1961.) It took 13 more years for someone to top his career home-run total—714 of them. (Atlanta Brave Hank Aaron did that.)

Babe Ruth loved kids. Someone told him that one of his young fans was dying in the hospital. Ruth went to see the boy, gave him an autographed ball, and promised to hit a home run for him that very afternoon. He did it. The boy recovered and Babe Ruth said, "A home run is the best medicine in the world." At least, that was the story the publicity agents told. It was hard to separate the truth about Ruth from the legend. Eleven-year-old Johnny Sylvester was badly hurt when he fell off a horse—but he wasn't dying.

*Above, left:* the house that Ruth built—Yankee Stadium. *Right:* the most famous swing in the history of baseball. At Ruth's funeral in 1948, an old newsman said, "I stopped talking about the Babe for the simple reason that I realized that those who had never seen him didn't believe me."

## The End of a Streak

The first great baseball game—at least, the first that wowed the press and public—was played in Brooklyn, New York, on June 14, 1870. Some 12,000 fans tried to squeeze into a park built for 5,000 people to see the Cincinnati Red Stockings (the first professional team) play the Brooklyn Atlantics. The Red Stockings had an undefeated 91-game streak; the Atlantics had a lot of grit. They went nose to nose for nine innings until the game ended in a 5–5 tie. How about extra innings? The rules weren't exactly the same as they are today. The game was supposed to be over. But the crowd wouldn't go home—they wanted a winner. So the teams got back on the field,

and the pitchers held on, with the tension shifting back and forth, back and forth, until dusk came and the players could barely see. Top of the 12th and Cincinnati got two runs. Things looked desperate for the Atlantics until Joe Start (known as "Old Reliable") came to bat, hit a line drive (with a man on third), and a Brooklyn fan climbed on the back of a Cincinnati fielder (which did slow his throw a bit, just enough to let the runner score). Then right-handed Brooklyn captain Bob Ferguson surprised everyone by batting left-handed (being thus the first recorded switch hitter) and getting a hit. When Cincinnati's first baseman flubbed a grounder, the Red Stockings' winning streak was over.

## The Other Babe

**W**hen Mildred Didrikson was growing up in Beaumont, Texas, she played baseball with the neighborhood boys. When she began hitting homers the boys couldn't catch, they gave her a nickname. What do you think it was? Why, Babe, of course. When it came to athletics, Babe Didrikson seemed to do it all. She was an all-American basketball player. She was a softball star and pitched in baseball exhibition games against major-league teams. She competed in swimming and diving events and played competitive tennis. She did some boxing. She became a national heroine when she earned three medals in track and field at the 1932 Olympic Games at Los Angeles, California. But she is best known as one of America's outstanding women golfers. Once she won 17 golf tournaments in a row. Babe became Babe Didrikson Zaharias (zuh-HAIR-ee-us) in 1938 when she married wrestler George Zaharias. She has been called the outstanding woman athlete of the first half of the 20th century. No American woman before or since has been a champion in so many sports.

*"Is there anything you don't play?" a reporter asked Babe. "Yes," she said. "Dolls."*

Babe Ruth was a photographer's dream; he loved to clown for the camera (*below,* in a movie publicity still). Said one of his friends: "There was only one Babe Ruth."

Still, the public couldn't get enough stories about Ruth, and he did spend a lot of time visiting children in orphanages and hospitals.

Babe did everything in a big way—including eating and drinking. So, when he got sick, with a fever and stomach cramps, reporters said it was because he ate 12 hot dogs and drank eight bottles of soda pop. That wasn't true. He ate like that regularly. But this time he was really sick. It was called "the bellyache heard round the world."

In 1935 Ruth was fat from eating too much. He was 40 years old. Still, there was no stopping him. He was now playing for the Boston Braves, and, in his last professional game, hit three home runs! His final home run was said to be the longest ever hit in Forbes Field.

# 10 Only the Ball Was White

Josh Gibson *(above)* "can do everything. He hits the ball a mile....Throws like a rifle," said pitching whiz Walter Johnson.

"Don't look back," said Satchel Paige *(left)*. "Something might be gaining on you." James Bell *(right)* was pitching for the St. Louis Stars and struck out some tough players. "That kid's cool," said a teammate. So they called him "Cool." But that didn't seem enough of a name, until someone added "Papa." It was 1922; he was 19.

Some people said that Josh Gibson once hit a ball over the roof at Yankee Stadium—which was farther than the Babe ever did. As for the unbelievable Satchel Paige, his pitching was so accurate they say he could have stayed in the strike zone pitching to Tom Thumb. Did he have a fast ball? Why, Satchel practically invented the fast ball. Someone who batted against him said that you never saw his pitched balls—just heard the thump in the catcher's mitt and knew they'd gone by. And Cool Papa Bell? Well, Paige himself swore that Bell ran so fast he could turn off the light switch and make it to bed before the light went out.

That lights-out story got repeated as a tall tale and a joke, although it happened to be true. Bell explained that he bet Paige he could do it one night when he learned a light switch was faulty. He won the bet. But usually he didn't need trickery. Cool Papa Bell was fast as Mercury (maybe faster), and Paige and everyone else knew it.

Paige and Bell and Gibson were stars of the Negro Leagues. These were Jim Crow times, when, in much of the United States, schools and ball teams and other things for blacks and whites were separate and unequal. Baseball didn't start that way. The brothers Fleet and

Two Cuban teams, the Cuban Stars and the New York Cubans, added a cosmopolitan touch to the Negro Leagues. Martin Dihigo, who played with the Cubans and with the Vera Cruz (Mexico) Eagles, ended up in baseball halls of fame in Cuba, Mexico, *and* the United States. In a league where everyone seemed versatile, he still managed to be outstanding. As one player said, "I seen them all for the past fifty years and I still think Dihigo was in a class by himself. He'd pitch one day, play center field the next, and the next day he'd be at first base. Sometimes he even played two or three positions in a single game."

*Playing for the Cuban Giants, 1905*

**51**

Moses (Fleet) Walker played 42 games for the Toledo Blue Stockings in 1884. That was the major-league record for a black player until 1947. A black man, he said, could never become "a full man ...of this Republic."

Welday Walker had played in the old American Association. But when the association died in 1892, Cap Anson (who was a big hitter and a big bigot) made sure that the new leagues fielded whites-only teams. So men of color formed their own leagues.

The Negro Leagues were filled with talented players who played hard and seemed to have a whole lot of fun, too. Not that it was an easy life. Money was usually short, the equipment shabby, the travel brutal, and, in segregated times, blacks almost always had trouble finding hotel rooms or restaurants to eat in. Sometimes they played 200 or 300 games in a six-month season. (Figure the math on that one.) Since they had no ballparks of their own, they had to rent, and the managers wanted to get their money's worth—so, when lights got put in ballfields, they'd often play a doubleheader, and then a night game, too.

What they did best, besides the regular league games, was barnstorm around the country bringing entertainment and fancy ballplaying to blacks (and some whites) in a whole lot of American towns. They were to baseball what

Cap Anson (back row, second from right) and the Chicago White Stockings in 1888, the year Anson started purging baseball of black players. He seemed to think it was okay to have a black mascot (in front of Anson).

Satchel Paige and his All Stars on a barnstorming tour against white pitcher Bob Feller's All Stars (Paige is in the doorway on the left). "This was a gravy train," said one of the team members. "My share was $7,500 for 17 days' work....Each team had a private plane. Segregated luxury."

the Harlem Globetrotters later became to basketball: wizards. Sometimes they played in formal attire, sometimes in clown costumes, sometimes in uniforms. They did comic routines, they juggled, they did ball tricks. Sometimes they came with a band and a midway. It was carnival, it was fun, and it was skilled ball, too. You had to love baseball to keep up the pace. Josh Gibson and Ted Page remembered playing a twilight game in Pittsburgh, driving to St. Louis for a day game, and then on to scorching Kansas City for a doubleheader. That evening the two of them made it to a hotel porch, where they sat, dog-tired, until they heard some kids playing sandlot ball. Naturally, they couldn't resist that, so they joined the game.

Except for the traveling, most of the ballplayers had a good time, although a few hated having to clown around. They just wanted to play ball. But,

## Were the Men Scared?

It was 1931, and the Yankees were playing an exhibition game against the Chattanooga (Tennessee) Look-outs. Chattanooga's owner, Joe Engle (who once traded a ballplayer for a Thanksgiving turkey), had just signed a 17-year-old pitcher, Jackie Mitchell. When the great Babe came to the plate, the new pitcher was called to the mound—and SURPRISE: Mitchell was a *she*.

Her first pitch was low and a ball. The Sultan of Swat swung at the next—and missed. Ditto the next. Babe Ruth didn't like missing anyone's pitch—and a woman's! Babe demanded to see the ball. There was nothing wrong with it. Mitchell wound up, let go, and the Babe watched the pitch fly by. "Stee-rike!" The Bambino threw his bat, stalked off, and the crowd roared. The next batter was big hitter Lou Gehrig. Jackie threw three times. Gehrig swung three times. And that was that.

Some said that Ruth and Gehrig were just being polite to a woman, but no one who was there believed it. Years later, Jackie Mitchell said, "I had a drop pitch and when I was throwing it right, you couldn't touch it." Baseball's commissioner, Judge Kenesaw Mountain Landis, didn't care. He was a misogynist (miss-SODGE-ih-nist—someone who dislikes women). Landis said Mitchell's contract was void, and baseball lost out.

In 1941, Josh Gibson *(top, fourth from left)*, played for Vera Cruz in the Mexican League, hitting 33 home runs. *Center:* Oscar Charleston, the phenomenal Indiana outfielder, nicknamed the Hoosier Comet. *Right:* Smokey Joe Williams. Satchel Paige said he was "the greatest pitcher I've ever seen."

## World Beater

**S**ometimes Jesse Owens joined the barnstorming Toledo Crawfords. Then the team had a big track star to help draw the crowds. Owens won four gold medals at the 1936 Olympics in Berlin, Germany (no one had ever won four at once before). That displeased the German leader, Adolf Hitler, who believed in Aryan (white northern European) supremacy and thought Negroes were inferior. Owens would race anyone who wanted to run against him (fans got a 10-yard lead). The only person he ever refused to race was Cool Papa Bell, who said he wanted to race around the bases. Owens even raced a horse—and won!

*Owens flies past 26 feet, 5 inches for a gold medal in the long jump and an Olympic record in Berlin, 1936.*

being black, or dark-skinned Cuban, or Mexican, they couldn't join the major leagues. It was crazy. One excuse was that blacks and whites wouldn't play together. But that wasn't so. White all-star teams often barnstormed with the blacks, playing exhibition games. (Black teams won more than they lost.) Everyone knew that players like Oscar Charleston, Smokey Joe Williams, and Buck Leonard were major talents.

"I have played against a Negro all-star team that was so good we didn't think we had even a chance," admitted white Dizzy Dean, who pitched for the St. Louis Cardinals and the Chicago Cubs. "There is no room in baseball for discrimination," said Lou Gehrig (one of the best first basemen ever). White catcher Gabby Hartnett (whose three sisters barnstormed in a women's league) said, "If managers were given permission there'd be a mad rush to sign up Negroes." Which is what finally happened (see book 10 of *A History of US* for that story). "Democracy is killing Negro baseball," lamented one black sportswriter. But it was a death most people welcomed.

## Joe Louis—Making Mom Feel Proud

*The Brown Bomber KO's Max Schmeling in one round in 1938.*

**I**f [Joe Louis] is not the best boxer that ever lived, he is as near to it as we are ever likely to know. He was born in 1914 on a sharecropper's cotton patch in Alabama and was as country-poor as it is possible to be. In theory the farm was —it had been rented as—a cotton and vegetable farm. But the vegetables did not feed the family, not by the time Joe, the seventh child, came along. His father broke, as sharecroppers do, from the daily strain of not making enough in crops either to feed his children or to put shoes on them. They had no money to send him to a hospital. So he was carried off to a state institution, where he died. A widower came to help out and soon married Joe's mother. And his five children moved in with the eight Louises. Joe got a little more food and went to a one-room school. Then the family moved to Detroit, where the stepfather worked in an automobile factory. Joe went to trade school and worked in the evening doing the rounds with an ice wagon. Then came the Depression, and the family went on relief. This, said Joe, made his mother feel very bad. Years later Joe wrote out a careful check, for two hundred and sixty-nine dollars, which was the amount of relief checks they had had from the government. That, said Joe, made Mrs. Brooks, as she now was, feel better.

—ALISTAIR COOKE, *JOE LOUIS*

54

# 11 American Music

Trumpeter Louis Armstrong in 1931. He started as a street kid and learned to play cornet at the Waifs' Home.

Do you ever stop and listen to the sounds around you? Have you noticed that indoor sounds are different from outdoor sounds?

Concentrate for a minute. It doesn't matter if it seems noisy or quiet; concentrate hard. You will hear sounds you were unaware of before. What you are hearing is the music of your world. Imagine what the music is like—that natural-sound music—if you are sitting on a California beach near the Pacific Ocean. Then pretend you are skiing in Colorado's Rocky Mountains and listen to the sounds around you. And then open your ears and take an imaginary walk down Broadway in New York City. Think of the differences between city sounds and country sounds, between sea sounds and mountain sounds. Some places, of course, have more sounds than other places.

New Orleans is one of those places with a lot of music in the air. If you look at a map, you'll find New Orleans down in Louisiana at the mouth of the Mississippi River. You can understand that New Orleans has water sounds: sounds from shrimp boats and tankers in the Gulf of Mexico,

**There were once** about 30 different tribes of Native Americans in the Louisiana region, including the Attakapa, Caddo, Chitimacha, and Tunica.

New Orleans kids made music with whatever they could find. This street band includes homemade drum set, trombone, harmonica, and dancers.

The great riverboats that plied up and down the Mississippi were a home for jazz bands—Louis Armstrong played on them—and often the place where people outside New Orleans heard jazz for the first time.

## At the Back of the Bus

*Sarah and Bessie Delany grew up in segregated North Carolina, and describe what life under Jim Crow was like in their book* Having Our Say: The Delany Sisters' First 100 Years *(written with Amy Hill Hearth).*

We encountered Jim Crow laws for the first time on a summer Sunday afternoon. We were about five and seven years old at the time. Mama and Papa used to take us to Pullen Park in Raleigh [N.C.] for picnics, and that particular day, the trolley driver told us to go to the back. We children objected loudly, because we always liked to sit in front where the breeze would blow your hair. But Mama and Papa just gently told us to hush and took us to the back without making a fuss. When we got to Pullen Park, we found changes there, too. The spring where you got water now had a big wooden sign across the middle. On one side, the word "white" was painted, and on the other, the word "colored." Why, what in the world was all this about? We may have been little children, but, honey, we got the message loud and clear. But when nobody was looking, Bessie took the dipper from the white side and drank from it.

sounds of water lapping the shores of the city's Lake Pontchartrain, and dock and riverboat sounds from the great Mississippi.

Because New Orleans has a warm climate, people are out of doors most of the time. So there are people-on-the-street sounds. Today in New Orleans, you can also hear cars, trucks, motorcycles, and airplanes.

Back in 1900, the music of the streets was different. Oh, there were many of the same people sounds—but there were also chickens and pigs in the city, and they scratched and squealed. There was the clippety-clop of horses' hoofs, and the rolling sounds of wooden-wheeled wagons, the hoots of trains, and the sad notes of riverboat foghorns.

Some of the people sounds were different then, too. There were no big supermarkets, so people bought ice, milk, bread, fresh fruit, vegetables, meat, and other things from the backs of the clippety-cloppety wagons. The wagon drivers had to tell people what they were selling. Usually they sang their message. It was the same idea as a TV-commercial jingle, but it might go like this: *I got tomatoes big and fine, I got watermelons red to the rind.* Or like this: *My mule is white, the coal is black; I sell my coal two bits a sack.* Imagine a whole lot of street peddlers all singing their wares at the same time.

Now, on top of all this, New Orleans had, and has, an unusual mixture of peoples. The city was settled by the French in 1718. (In 1803, President Thomas Jefferson bought New Orleans as part of the Louisiana Purchase.) The French language stuck. Some of the sounds and words of that language can be heard in New Orleans even today.

Many of the French and Spanish men who came to New Orleans in the 18th century married African-American women. Their biracial children, called Creoles, often spoke French or Spanish as well as English.

Out of the sounds of New Orleans, and the mixed heritage of its people, a new music arose. It was American music—unlike anything heard in the world before. It combined the rhythm and drum beat of Africa with the instruments and heritage of Europe. It added a dash from the spirituals of the black Protestant churches, and much from the talents of some black musical geniuses who could be heard in street bands and nightclubs. It was called "jazz." It was unique (you-NEEK)—which means totally unlike anything before it. Have you ever mixed red paint with yellow? The color you get is not red, or yellow. It is orange. It is unique. Jazz is like that. It is not African music, or European music. It is uniquely American.

In 1900 nobody much outside of New Orleans had ever heard of it. But in the 1920s jazz began to spread: first to Chicago, then across the country, and then around the whole world.

The best way to learn about jazz is to listen to it. You could start with one of the greatest jazz performers: Louis Armstrong.

Louis was one of those boys who sold coal in New Orleans for two bits a sack. He was very poor. Then someone gave him a trumpet. It

By the mid-1920s, dance halls and speakeasies, like this club scene painted in 1929 by Archibald Motley, Jr., were booming in New York and Chicago. Jazz musicians went north, and soon Chicago had replaced New Orleans as the home of jazz and swing.

**The first jazz** is said to have been played by funeral bands that wailed music full of soul and sadness as they followed horsedrawn hearses down the streets of New Orleans. It was blues music.

## Talking Without Drums

*Willie Ruff plays the French horn. He knows a lot about jazz. He has taught about it at Yale University. Here is what Mr. Ruff says of the origins of jazz:*

In Africa the drum is the most important musical instrument...people use their drums to talk. Please imagine that the drum method of speech is so exquisite that Africans can, without recourse to words, recite proverbs, record history, and send long messages. The drum is to West African society what the book is to literate society.

"In the seventeenth century," Ruff continues, "when West Africans were captured and brought to America as slaves, they brought their drums with them. But the slave owners were afraid of the drum because it was so potent; it could be used to incite the slaves to revolt. So they outlawed the drum. This very shrewd law had a tremendous effect on the development of black people's music. Our ancestors had to develop a variety of drum substitutes. One of them, for example, was tap dancing....By the time jazz started to develop, all African instruments in America had disappeared. So jazz borrowed the instruments of Western music."

*Jazz is not African music, but it is mainly the creation of American blacks. But, from the beginning, white musicians also played jazz, and some made important contributions to the music. While the roots of jazz can be found in Africa, the fruit is a hybrid. (Willie Ruff is wrong to say all African instruments died out in America. The banjo is based on an African instrument.)*

*Above:* Bessie Smith, one of the pioneer female jazz singers, in 1936. *Right:* Many of the early jazz leaders—such as Joe "King" Oliver (back row, on cornet, with his Creole Jazz Band)—were trumpeters, probably because the trumpet could be played while marching, and because its sweet, high sound carried over the street noise. Kneeling, front, is Louis Armstrong.

must have been a good angel. Louis Armstrong was born to play the trumpet. People began calling him "satchelmouth," because his cheeks seemed to hold a suitcase full of air. "Satchmo" was soon playing on riverboats that went up and down the Mississippi. Then he went to Chicago and began making history.

Satchmo had a big grin, but when he played the trumpet he closed his eyes and blew clear, heavenly tones. Listen to some of his recordings, and see what you think.

As soon as you start listening you will learn something: no two jazz performances are exactly alike. Composers who compose European-style music write down notes and expect musicians to play those notes just as they are written. That isn't so in true jazz. You see, an important part of jazz is *improvisation*. Improvising means doing your own thing. Jazz musicians talk to each other with their instruments. It is something like African drum talk. One musician leads with a theme. Then someone answers that theme. He plays the theme his own way. Then maybe the first musician improvises with another variation on the theme. Soon the whole band is playing with it. Does that sound wild? It isn't easy to do it well.

People in the 1920s were crazy about jazz. The 1920s were called the "Jazz Age." When the Jazz Age '20s ended—with a big thud called the "Depression"—jazz continued to grow in popularity. Today, many people call it America's most original art form.

## The Duke Roars with the Twenties

He wore dandy suits, ruffled shirts, top hats, and slicked-back hair. His high-school friends called him "The Duke," because he dressed like royalty. "He was wearing velvet slippers!" remembers one adoring fan. "No man I knew would have dared wear velvet slippers!" The Duke was a man of supreme grace—taking to heart his father's credo that "pretty can only get prettier, but beauty compounds itself."

But beneath the elegance and flash was music. Wild music. Some people called it *jazz,* but not Duke Ellington—that was too small a category. By the late '20s, his music was taking off. It was a time when everyone was desperately trying to be young again. The Great War was over; it had exhausted the world and killed much of its youth. Now that world was ready to party.

Painters came to New York to paint in bold new styles that forsook form altogether. Novelist F. Scott Fitzgerald sketched portraits of the fast life—decadent dreams where characters had such pressing observations as "I like big parties…at small parties there isn't any privacy." Duke Ellington, himself a painter turned composer, created music in colors with songs like "Mood

**Duke Ellington**

Indigo," "Magenta Haze," and "Blue Cellophane."

The sound of the '20s was jazz, originated by blacks but embraced by whites. Innovative jazzmen appeared all over the country. Louis Armstrong showcased his individual talent—many credit him with inventing the jazz solo. Duke's music borrowed from his African heritage, from European atonal theory, and from Western classical tradition—but the music he created was completely his own. It was deeply thoughtful music, sometimes achingly sad, and it reflected the romanticism and gentleness of its creator.

Duke had experienced a comfortable, middle-class childhood in Washington, D.C.—in his own words, he was "pampered and spoiled rotten." He was a man of infinite mystery; as his sister said, "There was just veil after veil after veil." We know that he never liked to argue, that, when confronted with racism, he "took the energy it takes to pout and wrote some blues." His music remains hard to classify; some people still wonder exactly what jazz is. "If you gotta ask," said Louis Armstrong, "you'll never know."

—DANNY HAKIM
(COURTESY OF *TLC MONTHLY*)

# Rhapsodies in Red, White, and Blue

*Americans have always made music—in the fields, in wagons heading west, on whaling boats, and in church. But it wasn't until the beginning of the 20th century that composers took that singing and fiddling and stomping and turned it into music that could hold its own in concert halls around the world. Here are three who led the way.*

## CHARLES IVES (1874–1954)

**W**hen Charles Ives was born—in Connecticut, toward the end of the 19th century—everyone who composed or played or listened to symphonies understood that serious music had rules and forms that had been established by the great European composers.

By the time Ives died—in the middle of the 20th century—many of those rules had been blown away. It was Charles Ives, as much as any other American, who set the dynamite charges.

He heard music everywhere: in revival hymns, in off-key singing, in children's shouts, in fire-engine whistles, in factory bells, and in the cacophony of city street noise. He took all those kinds of sounds, which were often discordant, and composed with them.

**B**efore Ives, American composers tried to make their music sound like Beethoven or Mozart. Ives used some ideas from the European masters, but, since he talked like an American, he thought he should compose like an American. And he did. He quoted bits of barn-dance tunes, hymns, speeches, and songs in his music long before others

**Charles Ives**

began doing that. Most composers start with a simple theme and make it more complex. Ives often did just the opposite. He anticipated much of the "new" music of the 20th century.

**B**eing way ahead of your time isn't easy. Ives needed to earn a living, so he became an insurance man and, eventually, president of the largest insurance company in the world. Few people have been creators in both the world of business and the world of the arts. Charles Ives was exceptional.

The best way to understand a composer is to listen to his music. You might start with "Putnam's Camp," which is part of a composition called *Three Places in New England*. It is narrative music that tells the story of a Fourth of July celebration during the Revolutionary War.

## RICHARD CHARLES RODGERS (1902-1979)

**R**ichard Rodgers's music is played more than that of any other composer—and that includes Beethoven and Bach. He began composing when he was nine, had a show in a Broadway theater when he was 18, and kept going for the next six decades.

You can call him prolific and popular and be right on target.

Rodgers was a New York Jewish boy whose father was a doctor and whose mother sang to him. He heard beautiful melodies in his head and played them on a piano. But he wanted his music to be sung, so it needed words. He teamed up with a friend, Lorenz Hart, who also turned out to be a genius. Rodgers wrote music; Hart supplied lyrics. They began averaging two new Broadway musicals each season and, because they were full of ideas and imagination, they were soon doing exciting things with dance and costumes and staging as well as music. When Hart died, at age 48, Rodgers needed a new lyricist. He turned to another old friend, Oscar Hammerstein II, who had been writing operettas. Together they helped develop a new form: the musical play. Their first was *Oklahoma*, it was followed by *Carousel, South Pacific, The King and I, The Sound of Music*, and others. They tackled serious subjects, like racism and hatred, and by putting their ideas in songs and stories they reached a lot of people. They won Tony Awards, Academy Awards, Pulitzer Prizes, Grammy Awards, Emmys, and even got their faces on a postage stamp. See if you can find some of Richard Rodgers's songs; they'll get you singing.

## AARON COPLAND (1900–1990)

Aaron Copland was born right as the century began, to a Jewish family living in Brooklyn, New York, on a street that he described as "drab." It was an unlikely environment for an aspiring musician. "Music was the last thing anyone would have connected with it," he said. Copland went to public school and his older sister taught him to play piano. He soon knew that he wanted to be a composer, and he sent for a through-the-mail course in musical harmony.

**Aaron Copland**

Then he set out to learn from the best teachers he could find in New York. But when he heard a piece by Charles Ives, a teacher told him not to be "contaminated" by it. After that, at age 20, he went off to Paris and found a great music teacher, Nadia Boulanger, who polished his talents as she did those of some other American musicians. In Paris Copland met important European composers and musicians: Prokofiev, Milhaud, Koussevitzky. He realized that their music reflected their origins. He decided that his music should reflect America.

When Copland returned to America, in 1924, he was ready to take America's indigenous (in-DIDGE-in-uss—it means "native") music—especially jazz and folk songs—and make it symphonic. Eight years later he was recognized as an important composer, so when he played music by Charles Ives at a summer festival, people listened. He helped introduce Ives's music to a generation of young musicians. (Some were gladly "contaminated.")

Aaron Copland wrote symphonies and chamber music and film scores. His ballets *Billy the Kid* (1938) and *Rodeo* (1942) are all-American compositions and favorites of mine. Listen to one; I think you will like it.

Copland brought a youthful exuberance to all his endeavors; it gladdened his colleagues and inspired his music. He was a gentle man, and gracious, and he became a great teacher as well as a musician. To learn more, read Aaron Copland, *What to Listen for in Music* (McGraw-Hill, 1988).

## GEORGE GERSHWIN (1898–1937)

George Gershwin heard a live jazz performance when he was six, and that hooked him for life. He was a poor boy, but he managed to get some piano lessons and, at 14, got his first song published. It was a good thing he started early and worked quickly, because he died at age 39. In that short lifetime, he became one of the most important of America's composers. He took jazz and popular music and blended them with elements of classical music to create works that are original and wonderful. (Gershwin never stopped studying. One of his teachers was a Russian composer known for his mathematical approach to music.)

It was in Broadway's musical theater that Gershwin came to fame. But he also wrote film scores and compositions for orchestra and piano. *Rhapsody in Blue, An American in Paris,* and *Lady Be Good* are among his best-known works. His brother Ira wrote lyrics for many of his songs.

If you've never heard Gershwin's opera *Porgy and Bess,* see if you can find a video to watch, or listen to a recording, or, if you're lucky, find a live performance. Gershwin began it after he read a novel by DuBose Heyward called *Porgy.* It was about African-Americans who lived on the coastal islands near Charleston, South Carolina. Gershwin went to the islands, lived there for a summer, heard the rhythms and sounds of the region, and composed a masterpiece.

**George Gershwin**

# Hooray for Hollywood!

Hollywood, which is the name of a suburb of Los Angeles, was the capital of a make-believe world: nothing was quite real, although everything was made to seem real.

In its golden age, which was the 1930s, Hollywood was a movietown filled with studios where makeup artists, costumers, carpenters, writers, directors, and camera crews created scenes and characters that put dreams and laughter and exotic settings onto a big screen. It was pure enchantment, and it possessed the nation. In later years, the cameras would leave the studios and go "on location" to real places. Then computer technology would make astonishing effects possible; but none of it came close to capturing people the way those Hollywood films did.

Maybe it was the Depression that made people love going to the movies. Maybe cute Shirley Temple, dashing Clark Gable, the comical Marx Brothers, and glamorous Greta Garbo made people forget their troubles. Whatever the reason, some 80 million movie tickets sold each week in 1938—that equaled 65 percent of the U.S. population (although some people went more than once a week, which skewed the figures a bit). Compare it to this: in 1990 about 20 million tickets sold every week, representing less than 10 percent of the population. In the 1930s, movies mattered; now they entertain.

*Tyrone Power and Gene Tierney* (foreground) *in a passionate embrace while filming* The Razor's Edge *for Twentieth Century Fox before an intimate audience of at least 50 enthralled grips, continuity girls, lighting designers, cameramen, director, and producers.*

*Miss Shirley Temple and Bill "Bojangles" Robinson tap dance down the stairs to fame.*

**TO HOLLYWOOD IN STYLE**
*In 1931, it took five days on two trains to get to Hollywood [from New York], but what a deluxe five days! Because that traffic was supported by the film industry, the* Twentieth Century *to Chicago and the* Santa Fe Super Chief *[trains] to Los Angeles glittered with polished mahogany, shiny brass, and red brocade; the seats flaunted antimacassars of heavy lace.* —ANITA LOOS, CAST OF THOUSANDS

# 12 Hubba, Hubba Hubble!

**Edwin Hubble's ideas helped increase the understanding of our universe. Here's a beautiful picture of the planet Saturn.**

This chapter is about a man who did just what he wanted with his life, and changed the world in doing it. But, before you read about him, it will help to know the meaning of two words:

- "galaxy" (pronounced GAL axe see) and,
- "nebulae" (pronounced NEB you lie, it is the plural of *nebula* (NEB you luh).

A *galaxy* is a huge collection of stars, planets, and stardust moving around (orbiting) a common center. The average galaxy contains about 100 billion stars—all held together by gravity. Our sun and its planets (including Earth) are part of the Milky Way galaxy.

*Nebula* comes from a Latin root that means "cloud." Today scientists use the word to describe clouds of dust and gas in space that are birthplaces of stars. They are not galaxies. Only three galaxies (besides the Milky Way) can be seen from Earth with the naked eye. (That means without the help of a telescope.) Those three look like fuzzy clouds or blobs (you can't see the individual stars), so scientists called these "nebulae," because they didn't know what they were. But in the 18th century, a famous German thinker named Immanuel Kant thought the nebulae might be "island universes." In other words, he thought they could be separate galaxies, full of stars.

By the 20th century that idea had been mostly rejected. Here is what astronomer Agnes Clerke wrote in 1905:

*The question whether nebulae are external galaxies. . .has been*

"You will behold through the telescope a host of other stars, which escape the unassisted sight, so numerous as to be almost beyond belief." Galileo Galilei, writing in 1610, about his first observations of the night sky with a telescope.

**63**

*answered by the progress of research. No competent thinker. . .can now, it is safe to say, maintain any single nebula to be a star system [like] the Milky Way.*

Clerke went on to say that the whole universe is one galaxy; she called it "a mighty aggregation." In other words, the Milky Way was the whole cosmic ballgame.

Another famous astronomer, Harlow Shapley, had made his reputation measuring the Milky Way. It was all there was, he said.

Edwin Hubble, sitting at what was the world's largest telescope, on top of chilly Mt. Wilson in southern California, was soon to overturn that idea. And that would lead to our modern understanding of the universe.

Hubble was tall (6"2'), handsome, a super athlete, very smart, and maybe a bit conceited. Born in Marshfield, Missouri, he won a scholarship to the University of Chicago. There he not only got outstanding grades, he also got letters in basketball and boxing. He was such a good boxer that a promoter wanted to train him to fight for the world championship. But Hubble had other things in mind. He won a Rhodes Scholarship, which took him to Oxford University where he ran track, played on one of the first baseball teams in England, kept getting good grades, and picked up an English accent and a pipe.

He made a promise to his dying father to study law. Which he did. Then he came home, taught Spanish in high school, and practiced law. But he longed to be an astronomer. "All I want is astronomy," he said. "I would much rather be a second-

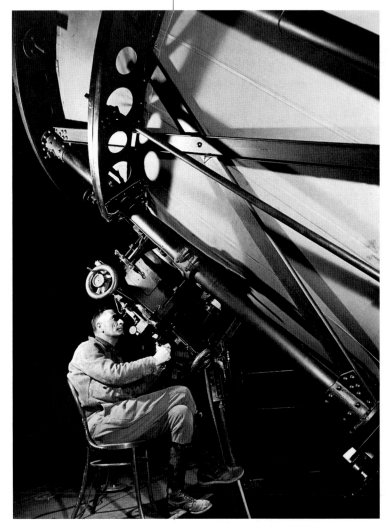

Margaret Bourke-White, a famous photographer, took this picture of Edwin Hubble studying the skies.

rate astronomer than a first-rate lawyer." But there was nothing second rate about Edwin Hubble. He went back to Chicago and got a graduate degree in science. Then World War I erupted and, being cut out for heroic things, he joined the army, fought in France, and came home a major. Finally, in 1919, he was ready to accept an offer he'd received from the Mount Wilson observatory.

For the next few years he painstakingly analyzed photographs and other data from the giant telescope on the peak of Mt. Wilson. Today astronomers study data on computer screens. But Edwin Hubble cranked and turned the huge cyclops until it pointed where he wanted it, put his eye to the eyepiece, and saw stars that had never been seen before. When he pointed the powerful scope at a fuzzy area in the heavens, then called the Andromeda nebula, he saw a swirling collection of stars. He realized he was seeing a separate galaxy with a spiral shape much like our own Milky Way. He soon understood that the universe is much, much bigger than anyone had imagined and that it is strewn with galaxies. But it was when he figured out that the galaxies are all moving—moving away from each other at an astonishing speed—that he changed almost everything we had believed about the heavens.

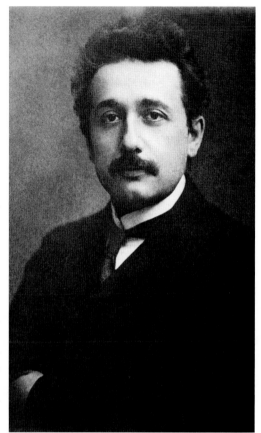

Albert Einstein in 1905, the year he published his Special Theory of Relativity.

Over in Switzerland, Albert Einstein had come up with a Theory of Relativity that showed mathematically that the universe is expanding. But no one could believe it. Not even Einstein. He thought he had made a mistake. Most people believed the universe was exactly as it had been at the creation. Others thought the universe had always existed as it is; they said it had no beginning and no end. Then Edwin Hubble looked through his telescope, understood what he was seeing, and confirmed Einstein's theory. The universe isn't static, it has changed over time, which means it has a story to tell, it has a history.

*Cyclops* (SEYE klops) was a one-eyed giant, a Titan, from Greek mythology.

Science is a dual thing: it takes ideas and proofs. Einstein's theories and Hubble's proofs would set a direction for much of 20th century science. (They would take us on a trip to the Moon.) Einstein was elated when he heard of Hubble's conclusions. In 1931 he traveled to Mt. Wilson and personally thanked the great astronomer.

# Stars In Women's Eyes

The director of the Harvard College Observatory needed help classifying stars. It was an important but tedious job. He couldn't find many men to do it. Then he realized he could hire educated women at one third the salary he paid men with the same abilities. That's how some unusual women became astronomers. They not only did tiresome work willingly, they used their brains (which women were not expected to do) and made outstanding contributions to the field.

Henrietta Swan Leavitt (1868- 1921) noticed that some stars (called Cepheid stars) vary in brightness at a consistent rate. In 1912 she figured out how to use that information to measure distances between stars. That made Edwin Hubble's discoveries possible.

Annie Jump Cannon (1863-1941) was a graduate of a new woman's college with an excellent physics lab: Wellesley College. She went to work at Harvard classifying stars; no one was able to do the job as well as she. Cannon cataloged more than half a million stars. Doing that, she discovered hundreds of variable stars and novae. Her work served as a foundation for 20th century astronomy. Despite her renown, Harvard waited until 1938 to officially appoint her an astronomer at the university; she was then 75 years old.

Sitting here on our small planet in our minor solar system in the Milky Way galaxy we are not moving from here to

Annie Jump Cannon

there through space. Space itself is expanding. Think of a lump of bread dough with raisins. As the dough rises the raisins get farther and farther away from each other. So do the molecules of dough. Space is like that dough and the raisins like the stars. The expanding galaxies are creating space/time.

We perceive the universe through our senses, especially our eyes and ears. And what we see is different from what we hear. Astronomy has eyes and ears. Some telescopes "see" like that at Mt. Wilson and the Hubble Telescope. Others hear. They are big discs called radio telescopes.

Henrietta Leavitt

# 13 Space's Pioneer

**Robert Goddard in his lab in 1935, the year he became the first to shoot a liquid-fuel rocket at supersonic speed.**

It was cold in Auburn, Massachusetts, on March 16, 1926. The three men and the woman who stood in an open field wore warm coats, and, as they talked, their breath turned into misty clouds of frost.

That didn't seem to concern them. They were concentrating on a tall structure. It was built of metal pipes. Actually, there was nothing special about the structure. What was attached to it was special. It was a small rocket.

The woman was Esther Kisk Goddard, and she held a motion-picture camera. She would film what was about to occur. Her husband, Robert Hutchings Goddard, a college professor, was in charge. The two other men were his assistants. They were standing in Goddard's Aunt Effie's field.

The rocket had a two-foot-long motor. Pipes ran from the base of the motor to two attached tanks: one tank held gasoline, the other oxygen. Goddard touched a blowtorch to an opening at the top of the rocket. The rocket let out a roar. Slowly it lifted off the launch pad—that is what the metal-pipe structure was—and rose into the air, speeding upward at 60 miles an hour. Then it crashed into the snowy field. The flight lasted three seconds. The space age had begun.

Robert Goddard and his assistants went back to their laboratory. They were physicists, and New England Yankees, and they understood the value of hard work. They knew they had much yet to do.

They also knew that what they had done that day was as important as what had been done by two brothers from Dayton, Ohio, at Kitty Hawk, North Carolina, in December of 1903. But almost no one

**Esther Goddard's 1929 film of one of Robert's successful liftoffs. Even when the rockets worked, people laughed and called him "Moony" Goddard.**

It took astronomer Percival Lowell 25 years of searching, but in 1930 he found a ninth planet and named it Pluto. It was mathematical investigation of the planet Uranus that made him believe another planet existed in our solar system.

*Right:* The launch pad in Aunt Effie's Auburn, Massachusetts, meadow. Goddard's liquid fuels were the same ones that would be used for Germany's V-2 rockets in World War II (more on them later).

else knew that. In 1926, most people would have laughed at a scientist who took the idea of space travel seriously. It would be a long time before the world understood about rockets and rocket travel. Few people ever knew about Robert Goddard.

Maybe that was because he was shy. No, it wasn't just his shyness. It was more than that. He was a loner, and a dedicated scientist. He didn't have much use for publicity. He wanted to get on with his work. He wanted to realize his dream.

He had dreamed of space and interplanetary travel from the time he was a boy. It all began with two books. One was *The War of the Worlds,* which was written by an Englishman, H. G. Wells. The other was *From the Earth to the Moon,* written by a Frenchman, Jules Verne. They are two of the earliest, and best, of the modern science-fiction novels. Goddard read them, reread them, and then read them again.

They made him believe that space travel was possible. In Jules Verne's book, astronauts catapult into space inside a capsule shot from a gigantic cannon. That didn't sound plausible to Robert Goddard. He decided that rockets were the way space would be conquered.

## Rocket Science

In 1232, at the battle of Kai-Keng, the Chinese had gunpowder-filled tubes attached to long arrows. When the end of the tube was lit, the burning powder made fire, smoke, and a gas that produced a thrust and sent the blazing arrow through the air. Those early rockets were probably not very destructive, but they must have terrified the Mongols who saw them coming.

The Mongols soon produced their own rockets and brought them to Europe; Europeans began experimenting with them. In England, a monk named Roger Bacon improved them. In France, Jean Froissart launched rockets from inside a tube (like a modern bazooka). Joannes de Fontana of Italy designed a rocket-powered torpedo that zoomed across the surface of the water and set ships on fire. The English sometimes shot rockets to scare enemies. Otherwise they did little damage. It was in "the rockets' red glare" that Francis Scott Key composed a famous poem. (During which war?)

Automobile age meets space age. At 17, Goddard had a dream about building a space-flight machine. "I imagined how wonderful it would be to make some device which had even the *possibility* of ascending to Mars," he wrote.

He had three good reasons for that belief. Rockets have more push, or "thrust," than other engines of the same weight. Rockets can be designed to hold within themselves all that is needed to make them operate. Since rockets lose weight as they use up their fuel, their highest speeds can come at the end of a flight.

Rockets were nothing new. The Chinese had designed rockets way back in the 11th century. The Chinese rockets were powered by explosive powders. You lit the powder and, whammo, the rocket lifted off and the fuel was all used up. Chinese rockets were mostly used for fireworks.

Goddard realized that if a rocket was to soar out of Earth's atmosphere and beyond, it would need a fuel that provided steady power, a fuel that wouldn't burn up all at once. A liquid seemed the answer, but liquid fuels demand oxygen in order to burn. There is no oxygen in space. Now, it doesn't sound terribly complicated to figure all that out and build a rocket that carries its own fuel and oxygen tanks. It doesn't seem difficult because we now know it can be done. The first person to come up with an idea isn't sure it can be done. Or how to do it. It took Robert Goddard 10 years of experimenting to build the little rocket that climbed into the sky on that icy-cold March day in 1926.

A few other scientists—in Germany and Russia—were working on the same problem. They worked with theories. Theories are ideas. Goddard was different. He started with theories, but then he tested them. That is the true scientific way.

When he was 38 (six years before the 1926 test flight), Goddard wrote a paper for the Smithsonian Institution in which he theorized that a rocket of 10 tons might be made

Goddard drew these plans for a patent application on a "rocket apparatus" in 1914.

**Sir Isaac Newton** (1643–1727), England's great scientific genius, came up with three laws of motion that explain how rockets work and why they can fly in space's vacuum. If you are interested in rocketry, study those laws.

**69**

By the 1930s, a Goddard rocket *(left)* had gone as high as a mile above earth. At right, Goddard *(center)* with Harry Guggenheim *(left)*, and Charles Lindbergh, who asked Guggenheim's millionaire father, Daniel, to help Goddard; more about Lindbergh on the next page.

powerful enough to reach the moon. He spent much of the rest of his life working to make that possible.

New England isn't a good place to test rockets: too many trees and people. Goddard decided to do his testing in New Mexico, over the desert. Soon his rockets were traveling at 700 miles an hour; some were rising as much as a mile and a half high. He worked out ways to guide and control rockets. He developed the idea of a series of rockets as a means of reaching the moon. He devised parachutes to allow rockets to return to earth smoothly. He patented more than 200 of his ideas.

He didn't live to see his dream fulfilled. Robert Goddard died in 1945, 24 years before Apollo 11 landed on the moon. But his spirit must have been riding with the astronauts on that voyage, probably with Jules Verne and H. G. Wells tucked under its arms.

**There is** an old Chinese story of a low-ranking but inventive Chinese official named Wan Hu who is said to have designed a rocket-powered flying chair. Two large kites were attached to the chair; attached to the kites were 47 fire-arrow rockets. On the day that Wan Hu decided to test his invention, he sat in the chair and his assistants rushed forward with torches and lit the 47 rockets. According to the story, when the smoke cleared, Wan Hu and the chair were gone— never to be seen again. Today, no one knows what actually happened, but rockets are as likely to explode as to fly.

# 14 The Lone Eagle

**Lindbergh quit college in his second year to go to flying school and buy a World War I biplane.**

Robert Goddard might never have gone farther than that field in Auburn, Massachusetts, if a young man hadn't come to visit him. The young man was Charles A. Lindbergh, Jr., and he was famous. Newspapers were saying he was the most famous man on the planet. He may have been.

Lindbergh was wise enough not to be too impressed with himself. He was also wise enough to know the importance of Goddard's work. Lindbergh talked to a philanthropist (fil-AN-thro-pist) named Daniel Guggenheim. (A philanthropist is a person who gives money to good causes.) The Guggenheim Foundation gave Goddard money to build a laboratory in New Mexico.

Why was Lindbergh so famous? Well, back in 1919, a wealthy hotel man offered a prize of $25,000 to anyone who could fly from New York to Paris (or Paris to New York). Several pilots tried for the prize. None made it. Then, in 1927, the competition got fierce. Besides the money, everyone knew there would be much glory for the pilot who first crossed the Atlantic.

In April, Richard E. Byrd took off, crashed, and broke his wrist. (The Byrd family had been well known in America since the days of George Washington and even before.) That same April, two pilots set out from Virginia, crashed, and were killed. In early May, two French aces (top pilots) left Paris, headed out over the Atlantic, and were never heard of again.

In mid-May, three planes were being made ready. Newspapers were full of their stories. The competition had captured the imagination of people on both sides of the Atlantic. Most of the newspaper attention focused on Byrd, who was famous and eager to try again. His plane had three engines and a well-trained crew. The second plane,

## Byrd Man

Richard Evelyn Byrd was the most renowned American explorer of his generation. In May 1926, he and co-pilot Floyd Bennett flew over the North Pole. (Much later, scientists discovered his calculations were off and he had missed the North Pole—but not by much.) Byrd was a superb leader and a naval officer who took polar exploration from dog-sled individualism to the discipline of government-sponsored science.

Naturally, one pole led to the other. In 1928, he headed an Antarctic expedition, set up a scientific base there named Little America, and, in 1929, flew over the South Pole. Byrd's radio reports of his adventures were listened to eagerly at home. He wrote books, made lecture tours, and opened Antarctica to scientific research.

While Lindbergh was an airmail pilot flying out of St. Louis he met the businessman who paid for the plane he would later fly to Paris. *Above:* Lindbergh loads the world's first sack of airmail. *Inset:* Lindbergh with the *Spirit of St. Louis.*

**In 1922,** Bessie Coleman becomes America's first licensed black pilot. Because of prejudice, she has to learn to fly in France.

with two engines, was to be flown by two experienced pilots. The third plane, a small single-engine craft, could hold only one person. It was called the *Spirit of St. Louis,* because a group of St. Louis businessmen had helped pay for it. The pilot, Charles Lindbergh, was little known. He'd been a barnstormer, a pilot who went around doing trick flying: circles and loops and daredevil things, and then taking people on plane rides for $5 a spin. That was the kind of thing most pilots did in those days. People didn't use airplanes for transportation. Trains were used to get places. Airplanes? No one was quite sure where the future of aviation lay. But if planes could fly across the ocean safely, they might have an important future.

Lindbergh was a good pilot. He was the first man to fly the U.S. mail

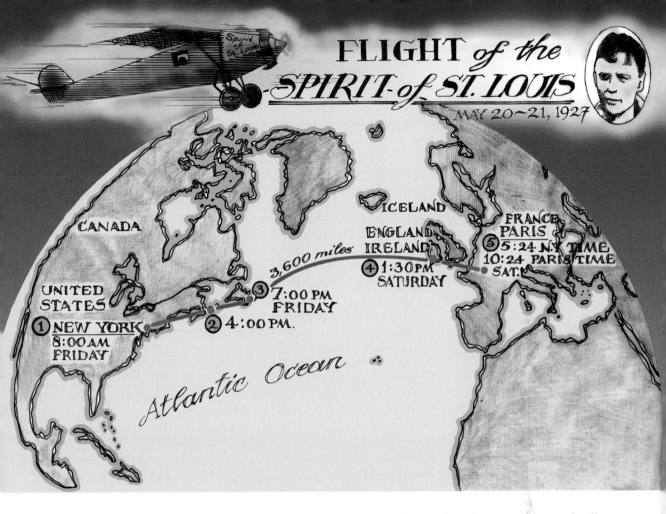

3,600 miles

CANADA

ICELAND

ENGLAND
IRELAND

FRANCE
PARIS
⑤ 5:24 N.Y TIME
10:24 PARIS TIME
SAT.

④ 1:30 PM
SATURDAY

③ 7:00 PM
FRIDAY

UNITED
STATES
① NEW YORK
8:00 AM
FRIDAY

② 4:00 PM.

Atlantic Ocean

from St. Louis to Chicago. And the first to survive four forced parachute jumps. (Forced because his planes developed troubles.) There was a bold, daring side to him, and another side that was careful and methodical. It was a rare combination. In a crisis he would not panic.

Something about him attracted people. Partly it was his looks. He was tall—six-foot-two—skinny, with light, curly hair and a boyish grin. He looked younger than his 25 years. He was quiet, and was always more at ease with machines, or nature, than with people. He'd grown up in Minnesota, where his father was a congressman. He never did well in school—maybe because he went to a different school almost every year. But he was smart enough to do a lot of reading. He wrote well.

It was 8 A.M. on May 20 when he took off. The weather wasn't good, but he was anxious to

I slip Massachusetts into the map pocket, and pull out my Mercator's projection of the North Atlantic. What endless hours I worked over this chart in California, measuring, drawing, rechecking each 100-mile segment of its great-circle route, each theoretical hour of my flight. But only now, as I lay it on my knees, do I realize its full significance. A few lines and figures on a strip of paper, a few ounces of weight, this strip is my key to Europe. With it, I can fly the ocean. With it, that black dot at the other end marked "Paris" will turn into a famous French city with an aerodrome where I can land. But without this chart, all my years of training, all that went into preparing for this flight, no matter how perfectly the engine runs or how long the fuel lasts, all would be as directionless as those columns of smoke in the New England valleys behind me.

—CHARLES LINDBERGH,
*THE SPIRIT OF ST. LOUIS*

**In 1929,** Lieutenant James Doolittle, of the Army Air Corps, makes the first blind airplane landing, using instruments only.

**In 1939,** 12 years after Lucky Lindy's flight (that became Lindbergh's nickname), 22 passengers leave New York on the first commercial transatlantic flight. Their Pan American Airways Clipper has passenger compartments, sleeping berths, a dining room, and a bridal suite. The passengers each pay $375, and, with stops in the Azores and Portugal, it takes them 42 hours and 22 minutes to get to their destination: Marseilles, France.

**Lindbergh** was a genuine hero as long as he stuck to his specialty—flying. When he got involved with politics he was out of his league. More on that to come in this book.

beat the others, and he was used to flying the mail in all kinds of weather.

His little plane carried so much gasoline that some people thought it would never get into the air. But Lindbergh had planned carefully. There wasn't an extra ounce on the plane. He sat in a light wicker chair and carried little besides the fuel, a quart of water, a paper sack full of sandwiches, and a rubber raft. There was no parachute—it would be of no use over the ocean—and there was no radio. He would be on his own once he left the East Coast.

He headed out to sea, and people around the world learned of it on their radios. And then there was nothing to hear. That evening, during a boxing match at Yankee Stadium, the spectators rose and said a prayer for Charles Lindbergh, somewhere over the Atlantic Ocean. Boxing fans are not usually the prayingest people, but that night they were.

Lindbergh, meanwhile, was having a hard time. He had to stay awake or crash. After eight or ten hours of sitting in one place he began to doze. The night before the flight he had been so excited, and had had so much to do, that he had not slept at all. So he was tired before he got into the air. He got more tired, much more tired.

Luckily the plane was frail. It banged about in the wind, and each time he started to nod it went careening down toward the water. That woke him. Then, miraculously, the fatigue ended, he looked down, and there was Ireland. He was exactly where the charts—the charts he had drawn —said he should be. Lindbergh, like Columbus, was a superb navigator.

He didn't know that his plane was spotted over Ireland and the news radioed to America and France. People cheered and wept with relief. He was seen over London, and then over the English Channel. Thirty-three and a half hours after he left the United States, he circled the Eiffel Tower in Paris. It had taken less time than he expected, so he was worried that no one would be at the airport to meet him. Since he didn't speak French, he wondered how he would find his way from the airport into Paris. Then he looked down and saw a mob of people. They were waving and screaming.

The young flyer, who had brought nothing with him but the paper bag (which still had some sandwiches), was carried about on shoulders and hugged and kissed and cheered. He was rescued from the crowd only after his helmet was put on another American and the mob thought he was Lindbergh. Then the real Charles Lindbergh was taken to the American ambassador's house, where a butler ran his bath and put him to bed. Soon he was meeting kings and princes and more crowds of admirers. He wanted to stay in Europe and see the sights, but Calvin Coolidge sent a naval cruiser to Europe just to carry him and the *Spirit of St. Louis* back to America. He was a world hero.

People lost their heads over Charles Lindbergh. All over America there were parades and dinners and celebrations for the man they called the "Lone Eagle." It was wild. Nothing quite like it had ever happened before. Why did people go so crazy over Lindbergh?

What he did was daring and brave. But others did daring things. What he did was important. But if he hadn't flown the ocean, someone else would have soon enough. There was more to it than that. The frantic, roaring world of the '20s needed a hero. Lindbergh turned out to be just what was wanted.

You see, he was decent. He didn't drink and he didn't smoke. He was modest. He had good manners. He was offered a great deal of money to pretend to smoke for an advertisement. He wouldn't do it. He wouldn't do anything he didn't believe in.

A publisher offered to hire a ghost writer to help him write a book about his flight. He said he'd write it himself. And he did. He turned down many money-making opportunities. He had values and standards, and he stuck to them.

In the Roaring Twenties, when many people thought only of having fun, or making money, or showing off, Lindbergh reminded people that courage, determination, and modesty were perhaps more satisfying. The American people had found a pretty good hero.

*Left*: New York City greets Charles Lindbergh in a blizzard of confetti and ticker tape. Later, Lindbergh flew all over the world and pioneered many commercial airline routes. *Right*: Amelia Earhart was working at a settlement house in Boston in 1928 when she got a chance to be the first woman to cross the Atlantic in an airplane. She was just a passenger, but it made her a celebrity. In 1932 she flew the Atlantic herself, as Lindbergh had done. It was a big moment for women and for aviation. Then she decided to fly around the world. She wrote her husband, "I am quite aware of the hazards. I want to do it because I want to do it. Women must try to do things as men have tried." It was her last flight; she disappeared over the Pacific Ocean.

# 15 The Prosperity Balloon

Al Smith *(left)* lost the 1928 presidential election to Herbert Hoover *(right)*. As secretary of commerce, Hoover had tried to restrain big business and the stock market—and failed. That led to big trouble during his presidency.

At its peak, in the mid-'20s, the Ku Klux Klan had 4 million members and political clout in the Midwest as well as the South.

Nineteen twenty-eight was an election year. Two good men were running for president. One was Herbert Hoover, an engineer and businessman, who had a reputation for accomplishing things. As a young college graduate, Hoover had managed a gold mine in the Australian desert and then gone to China as a mining expert. After that he got involved (successfully) with Burmese tin and Russian oil. He became known as a very capable man. When Woodrow Wilson needed someone to help feed Europe's starving people (during and after the First World War), he chose Herbert Hoover. He couldn't have found a better man for that job.

The other presidential candidate was the governor of New York. His name was Al Smith, and he was called the "Happy Warrior." Smith was colorful, full of fun, and honest and efficient, too. The governor introduced progressive reforms into New York State, appointed women and minorities to state jobs, and was fiscally responsible. (That means he did a good job with New York's budget.) The Happy Warrior was Catholic, Irish, and a New York City boy.

One of the reasons for reading history is to learn from past mistakes. That campaign was a mistake. Hoover didn't do bad things, but some of his supporters did.

They ran an anti-Catholic hate campaign. It was anti-city and anti-immigrant, too. The miserable Ku Klux Klan was still a powerful force in parts of America. Those are the people who put sheets over their heads and minds. They, and other hate groups, said that the only real Americans were those whose backgrounds were Protestant, English, and white. They said that Catholics, Jews, Asians, Arabs, Germans, Irish, Italians, blacks, and American Indians—of all people—were not real Americans. And then, on top of that, they said they didn't like city people. They said that if Al Smith got elected, the Catholic pope would be ruling America from Rome. Would you believe that nonsense?

Well, sadly, a whole lot of people did.

Hoover was elected by an enormous majority. Perhaps Americans would have chosen him anyway, but the mean-spiritedness of that election should not have happened.

What kind of president was Herbert Hoover? Poor President Hoover. He wore stiff collars and he had a kind of stiff personality, but he didn't deserve the bad luck he had. He worked hard, yet his presidency was a disaster. But anyone elected in 1928 would have been in trouble.

No one understood that then. In 1928 most Americans were rejoicing. America seemed to have acquired King Midas's golden touch. (Although hardly anyone thought to remember what happened to Midas in the end.)

By 1928 the balloon of prosperity had been pumped so full of hot air that no one had ever seen anything quite like it. Many people were saying that something new had been found: an economic balloon that would just keep expanding. A few others were saying: "Stand back, cover your ears, and watch out."

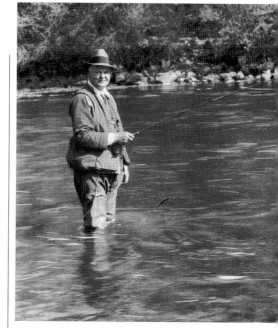

The president goes fishin'. "There is no cause for worry," said Hoover's treasury secretary, Andrew Mellon. "The high tide of prosperity will continue."

In 1922 this advertisement ran in support of an anti-lynching bill. The bill passed in the House but was defeated in the Senate.

## Back to Africa

Marcus Garvey came to the United States from Jamaica in 1916 to launch his Universal Negro Improvement Association. Garvey, the most influential black leader of the 1920s, promoted self-help and race pride and urged blacks to return to their African heritage.

*Marcus Garvey in 1922*

# 16 Getting Rich Quickly

*Oh hush thee, my babe, granny's bought some
  more shares,
Daddy's gone out to play with the bulls and the bears,
Mother's buying on tips and she simply can't lose,
And baby shall have some expensive new shoes.*
—SATURDAY EVENING POST

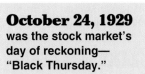

In 1929 the stock market crashed, and some stockholders committed suicide.

In 1927, '28, and '29 it was easy to get rich. All you had to do was put a little money in the stock market. Then you could watch it turn into a whole lot of money. Here is how it worked.

Imagine that you are the owner of a large company: the ABC Automobile Company. You manufacture cars—good cars—and now you want to expand. You want to add new models. You need to build a new plant and buy a lot of equipment. You need money. So you decide to look for investors. You *go public*. You sell *shares* in your company. You sell 10,000 shares at $100 each. The shares are called "stock." Anyone who buys that stock becomes a part owner of the ABC Auto Company.

The new automobile models are a big success. The company earns a great deal of money. The stockholders get a percentage of the profits. The money they get is called a "dividend." The future of your company looks very good; many people want to buy stock in the ABC Company. Here is where a rule of economics, called *the law of supply and demand,* comes in. There are only 10,000 shares available. (That may sound like a lot, but it really isn't.) There is a big demand for ABC stock. People will pay $110 a share for it. Then they will pay $120 a share. Before long, ABC stock is selling for $200.

One stockholder, Mr. Jones, bought 10 shares at $100 each. (How much money did he spend?) Now he will sell them at $200 each. How much money will he have now? What is his profit? (You can do some problem-solving math here!)

Easy to make money that way, isn't it? Well, hold on. In the '20s it was even easier than that. People bought stocks on *margin*. (That means they borrowed most of the money. Today, laws restrict margin buying.) Margin means you don't have to pay $100 for $100 worth of stock. In 1927, you could pay $10, and borrow the other $90 from the stockbroker. (The person who buys and sells stock for you is called a "stockbroker.")

Now, if Mr. Jones puts $100 into ABC stock and buys on margin at 10 percent, he can have 10 shares instead of one. For $1,000, he will get 100 shares. If he sells the shares for $200 each, how much money will he have? He has to pay back the money he borrowed—$90 per share—but he still makes a whole lot of money. See if you can figure out how much. The good idea that many people soon had was to buy a lot of stock for very little money and get rich quickly.

The business of buying and selling stocks is called the "stock market." The place where stocks are bought and sold is called a "stock exchange." The most important stock exchange is in New York City, on Wall Street. Brokers from all over the world call Wall Street with orders to buy and sell.

The stock market usually reflects the business world. If things

**The Securities** and Exchange Commission (SEC), an independent government agency, was formed in 1934 to regulate securities (stocks and bonds) markets and investment businesses in the United States. Joseph P. Kennedy was its first chairman. Kennedy had a 17-year-old son, John Fitzgerald, with a big job in his future.

Conducting business at the New York Stock Exchange. A newspaper columnist wrote in 1928, "If buying and selling stocks is wrong, the government should close the Stock Exchange. If not, [it] should mind its own business."

Plans for New York City's Empire State Building (for many years the world's tallest) began at the height of the stock-market boom. By the time it was built, in 1931, half the office floors had to be closed because there were no businesses to occupy them.

*Acumen* (ACK-yoo-min) is "smarts."

**In 1928** everyone was singing Eddie Cantor's hit, "Makin' Whoopee." A year later, there wasn't much whoopee around. Depression songs included: "I Got Plenty o' Nuthin'," "Shanty in an Old Shanty Town," the ironic "Life Is Just a Bowl of Cherries," and Eddie Cantor's new hit— "Potatoes are cheaper, Tomatoes are cheaper, Now's the time to fall in love."

Before he left office, President Coolidge said the stock market was "absolutely sound." Seven months later, this *New York Times* headline told a different story.

are going well, stocks go up. If business is poor, stocks go down. Brokers have a nickname for an "up" market. They call it a "bull" market. A down market is a "bear" market. The '20s were a prosperous time. Around 1924, the stock market started rising. At first it was a slow, moderate rise. Then the bulls got frisky.

In 1927, the market began to rise like fury. Almost overnight, stocks doubled and sometimes tripled in value. Everyone was talking about it. Newspapers wrote about it. The country's political leaders were all smiling. They felt it was their good leadership that was causing it. The business leaders were happy, too. Of course they thought it was their business acumen that was causing the stock-market boom. Many politicians and business leaders were saying that something new was happening. They said that the boom would just go on and on. That there was not going to be an end to it. And it wasn't just the business and political leaders who were saying all this. Professors from the nation's great universities were saying the same thing.

Now, suppose you are living in 1927. All your friends are getting rich and you aren't. You feel like a dummy, don't you? Why don't you take all your savings and buy as many stocks as you can? Buy them on margin so you can get lots of shares for your money. That's the smart thing to do, say many business experts.

## Some Stock Prices

| Company | SEPTEMBER 3, 1929 | NOVEMBER 13, 1929 |
|---|---|---|
| Radio Corporation of America (RCA) | 505 | 28 |
| Montgomery Ward | 466½ | 49¼ |
| General Motors | 73 | 36 |

*When the stock market crashed, artist James Rosenberg drew this picture of Wall Street with a panicked crowd, people jumping from collapsing buildings, thunderclouds and lightning, and flocks of black birds flying overhead. He called it Oct. 29 Dies Irae—Latin for "Day of Wrath," the name of a hymn sung in the mass for the dead.*

So that is just what you do—in July of 1929. And some of your friends do it, too. The stock boom is phenomenal before July. That summer it is fantastic. Some people are buying stock in anything. It doesn't matter if the company has any real worth or not. No one seems to care. Just give me stock and more stock, I want to get rich. The stock balloon grows bigger and bigger and bigger.

And then guess what happens?

Picture a balloon being pumped up. Now watch that pin. You thought the balloon went up fast? Well, *whoosh*, it will come down much faster.

It happens in October of 1929. It is called the "panic." People go wild trying to sell. But now almost no one wants to buy.

Remember that $100 stock you bought on margin for $10? Well, when the price drops, your broker sells it. Too bad—you lose your $10. No. It's worse than that.

You see, you owe $90 on that stock. Deduct from the $90 the price your broker gets when he sells the stock. You owe the rest. But you bought 100 shares of stock—or was it 1,000, or 10,000? You put all your savings into the stock market. The experts said that was the smart thing to do.

Sorry, you owe the money. You don't have any money? You can sell your house, or your car, or both.

You just lost your job, too? You worked at the ABC Auto Company. Oh, that's too bad. Most people have stopped buying cars. Now the company is losing money. It has to sell that beautiful

**The broker** has to sell when the stock price falls unless you come up with more money to pay for the drop in value—immediately.

*What was the pin that brought down the stock-market balloon in 1929?*

**After** the Wall Street Crash, some people who once had good jobs were now selling apples on street corners.

81

**This man, a victim of the Wall Street Crash, offers his car at a bargain price**

As fall the leaves by
   Autumn blown,
So fell those lovely
   shares I own.
Forlorn, disconsolate
   I sing,
Goodbye, goodbye to
   everything!

To car and plane and
   gleaming yacht
And rather ducal
   country cot
That all seemed surely
   mine by Spring,
Goodbye, goodbye to
   everything!
   —*NEW YORK TIMES,*
   **NOVEMBER 3, 1929**

new plant. Why doesn't it sell stock to try to raise money? Are you kidding? No one is buying stock now.

And you know about the banks, don't you? The banks are all in trouble, too. You see, the banks lent money to the brokers and all those people who were buying stocks. Now they have no money. They are closing their doors.

What is happening in America?

We're having a depression, that's what. It will go on for 10 years. People will be out of work. The country will be in terrible shape.

Years later, economic historians will look at the wild stock-market boom and the awful depression and say that they didn't have to happen. If there had been good leadership and sensible regulations, they could have been prevented. That's where greed gets you, they'll say. That's where out-of-date thinking gets you, they'll say.

But where were those economists when they were needed?

And wasn't it fun while it lasted? (For some of us, anyway.) Those roaring, prosperous '20s are great to remember. Didn't we think we were smart that summer of 1929! Will you ever forget what it was like to be rich?

# 17 Down and Out

*The Depression is an embarrassing thing. It is a shame to the system: the American Way that seemed so successful. All of a sudden, things broke down and didn't work. It's a difficult thing to understand today. To imagine this system, all of a sudden—for reasons having to do with paper, money, abstract things—breaking down.*

—STUDS TERKEL,
*HARD TIMES: AN ORAL HISTORY OF THE GREAT DEPRESSION*

There were no jobs for 12 million. Many more had their hours and pay cut.

By 1932, at least 12 million people were out of work. That was one in four of all those who normally would work. Count your friends: pretend that the parents of every fourth person are unemployed. Start with yourself. Suddenly, your family has no income. What are you going to do?

America had had depressions before. They were supposed to be a kind of self-regulating part of capitalism. All the early depressions had something in common: it was the poorest workers who were hurt. They lost their jobs. They went hungry. The wealthy and the middle class suffered only slightly.

The Great Depression (which is what it came to be called) was different. It hurt more people—rich and poor—than any previous depression. And it went on, and on, and on.

To begin, the census of 1920 had shown that for the first time more than half the nation was urban. (Cities in the 1920s were small by today's measures; still, they were a

U.S. Steel's payroll of full-time workers fell from 225,000 in 1929 to zero on April 1, 1933; even the hands employed part-time in 1933 numbered only half as many as the full-time force of 1929. In Seattle, jobless families whose lights had been cut off spent every evening in darkness, some even without candles to light the blackened room. In December 1932, a New York couple moved to a cave in Central Park, where they lived for the next year.

—WILLIAM E. LEUCHTENBURG

In William Gropper's *Migration* a desperate farm family heads west, carrying their belongings. More than 3 million people left the Great Plains during the 1930s. They were called "Okies" and "Arkies." Why? Read John Steinbeck's novel *The Grapes of Wrath* for a great story about their plight.

**In 1932,** a wagon full of oats didn't pay for a pair of shoes. In Illinois in 1933, a bushel of corn sold for 10 cents. If there are 56 pounds in a bushel, how much does 25 cents' worth of corn weigh? Can you see why farmers had problems? Can you see why some talked about the failure of democracy and capitalism?

big change for people used to farm life.) This was the first major *urban* depression. City people have a terrible time without jobs or income.

Farmers don't have an easy time of it either, but at least they can usually feed themselves. America's farmers, as you remember, had not done well during the '20s. They didn't prosper with the rest of the nation. Crop prices stayed low. So the farmer's income was low, too. In 1929, most farms still didn't have electricity or indoor toilets. During the '30s, things got worse. The price of wheat and other grains dropped so low that it was sometimes below what it cost to grow it. Dairy farmers dumped thousands of gallons of milk onto the land to protest the low price of milk. Other farmers destroyed their own crops. All this waste was happening at a time when city children were hungry. Clearly, something was terribly wrong with our economic system.

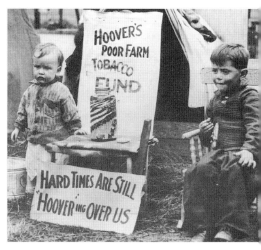

Some public relief money for the destitute was organized under Hoover—but how did a family of four manage on $5.50 a week?

84

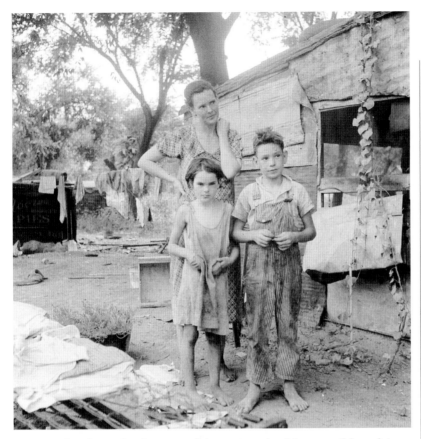

Photographer Dorothea Lange took this picture in Elm Grove, Oklahoma, in 1936 (see page 200 for another of her images). It was originally captioned: "People living in miserable poverty."

## Farmers' income

in 1932 was one-third what it had been in 1929. Even farmers who could feed themselves were often unable to pay their mortages, loans, or taxes. So tens of thousands lost their farms. How would they feed themselves now? By 1932 a million people roamed the country—walking, hitchhiking, or riding boxcars. Starvation was rare, but hunger wasn't. Nor was shame and despair.

To ***abuse*** means to "hurt or to treat carelessly."

Many bankers, brokers, and investors had been wild and irresponsible in the '20s. That irresponsibility caused great hardship in the decade that followed. The American farmer had been irresponsible for generations. Mostly, he hadn't known better, although he should have: European farmers had been practicing crop rotation for over a century.

But, beginning in Jamestown, American farmers had abused land. Farmers used up the fertile land and moved on. They cut down trees and cut up the sod. It didn't have to happen. With careful farming, land can be preserved

## Dust Bowl Days

The Dust Bowl is the name given to the region that was devastated by drought during the Depression years. It went from western Arkansas to the Oklahoma and Texas panhandles to New Mexico, Kansas, Colorado, and into Missouri. That area has little rainfall, light soil, and high winds. During World War I (when grain prices were high), farmers had plowed up thousands of acres of natural grassland to plant wheat. When drought struck (from 1934 to 1937), the soil lacked a grassy root system to hold it. Winds picked up the topsoil and turned it into black blizzards. Cattle choked and people fled. The government formed the Soil Conservation Service (in 1935) to teach farmers to terrace the land (to hold rainwater) and to plant trees and grass (to anchor the soil). Artists and writers such as Dorothea Lange, John Steinbeck, and Woody Guthrie photographed, wrote, and sang of the tragedy.

Alexander Hogue saw the awful effects of drought combined with dust and painted *Drought Stricken Area (above).* Woody Guthrie walked the highways of the Dust Bowl and wrote a song called "So Long, It's Been Good to Know Yuh." Here's one stanza: *A dust storm hit, and it hit like thunder/ It dusted us over, and it covered us under/ Blocked out the traffic and blocked out the sun/ Straight for home all the people did run.*

and enriched. For generations, however, there had seemed to be so much land that few people in America worried. They weren't prepared for nature's tricks: for the droughts and wind storms that came, dried up the land, and turned it to desert. Soil—good, rich topsoil—became dust. Much of the Great Plains just blew away. It was so bad that sailors at sea, 20 miles off the Atlantic coast, swept Oklahoma dust from the decks of their ships. For drought-stricken farmers, there was nothing to do but leave the land, head for a city, and hope to find a job.

But there were no jobs to be found in the cities. City people were moving in with relatives on family farms. It was a time of national calamity.

Now, back to you. Remember, everyone in your family is out of work. How are you going to pay the rent? If you don't have any money, you can't do it. That means you're going to get evicted—

thrown out—from your apartment. (If you live in a house and can't pay the mortgage, the bank will take your house.)

What are you going to do? Well, you're lucky: you happen to have a nice aunt and uncle, and they have jobs. So you move in with them. Things are crowded, and everyone gets a bit irritable, but you'll make it.

The family of your best friend—the girl who lives next door—isn't as lucky. They have no relatives to take them in and no place to go. The only thing they can think to do is to build a shack of old boxes and boards on some land near a garbage dump. They are not alone; hundreds of others are camped in that same unhealthy place. Those shanty towns—where people keep warm around open fires—spring up all over the nation. People call them "Hoovervilles," after the president, who says he is trying hard to solve the problem of the homeless and hungry. But nothing he does seems to help. By 1933, a million people in America are living in Hoovervilles.

*Above:* a glimpse of the fate of the American dream during the Depression. *Below:* This Hooverville in Seattle was home to thousands of "forgotten" men, women, and children.

# 18 Economic Disaster

**When** Herbert Hoover is inaugurated, he says, "We in America today are nearer to the final triumph over poverty than ever before in the history of the land."

Mellon pulled the whistle
Hoover rang the bell,
Wall Street gave the signal,
And the country went to hell.
—ANONYMOUS DITTY

Herbert and Lou Henry Hoover in 1929.

President Hoover thought the Depression was over. At least that is what he said, and he seems to have believed it. He said the economy was "fundamentally sound." And he said no one was starving in America.

Well, he was wrong about all those things. All he had to do was look out the windows of the White House and he would have seen hungry people. Thousands of veterans of the First World War were camped in the center of Washington, D.C. They were without jobs. Congress had voted them a bonus for their war service. The bonus was not due to be paid until 1945, but these were difficult times. The men needed the bonus now.

So they marched to Washington to see the president. Some brought their families. They built a Hooverville in Washington, D.C. They had no jobs or money, so they slept in tents, in empty buildings, in shacks on public grass. There were said to be 20,000 of

General MacArthur was helped in his breakup of the Bonus Army by another war hero to be, a Major Eisenhower. Hoover's public image got even worse.

them. They were called the "Bonus Army." Most carried American flags. Some were Medal of Honor winners; some had lost arms or legs in the services. Hoover wouldn't see any of them.

The police asked them to leave. They wouldn't go. So President Hoover sent the army. When the former soldiers first saw the army patrols and tanks and cavalry, they cheered. They thought the troops were parading for them. That was a mistake. The troops came with tear gas, guns, and bayonets. Their leader, General Douglas MacArthur, went farther than the president wished. His troops tore down the shacks; they used tear gas and billy clubs. People were hurt; a baby died. When it was over, Hoover said he saved the country from mob action. But many Americans hung their heads in shame.

**What do** popular songs tell you about a country? During the Depression people sang a song called "Brother, Can You Spare a Dime?" But the next presidential candidate campaigned with a song called "Happy Days Are Here Again."

The Bonus Marchers' shantytown burns down within sight of the Capitol. Millions watched it on movie newsreels.

In many cities, public employees such as teachers had to give up part of their already lean salaries to help pay for soup kitchens.

Mrs. Hoover *(right)* gives Christmas presents to poor families at the Central Union Mission in Washington, in 1932, to illustrate the virtue of private charity.

Hoover never understood. Each night he and Mrs. Hoover dressed formally for dinner—in tuxedo and long gown—and were served seven-course dinners by a large staff. Soldiers stood at attention around the table. Hoover thought about cutting down on White House expenditures, he said, but then decided that it would not be good for the people's morale. (Do you think the people agreed?)

Hoover was scared, and so were many other leaders. Democracy and capitalism seemed to be failing. Some people—who were considered to be sound thinkers—were saying that our system was finished. A new day was dawning, they said, and American democracy was out of date. All over the world the disruptions of war and depression were making people turn to dictators. Mussolini had taken control in Italy; Adolf Hitler was gaining power in Germany; and Joseph Stalin was in control in Soviet Russia. Some people in the United States thought those leaders were great men. We now know that they were terrible, bloodthirsty tyrants, but we are historians. We have the advantage of hindsight. We know how things came out. People in 1932 didn't know that.

Charles Lindbergh went to Germany and reported that Hitler was a fine leader. Wisconsin's governor, Philip LaFollette, was an admirer of Mussolini. Many intellectuals were fascinated with communism. They weren't the only ones. Senator Theodore Bilbo of Mississippi said, "I'm getting a little pink [communist] myself." The nation's favorite humorist, Will Rogers, said, "Those rascals in Russia...have got mighty good ideas... just think of everybody in a country going to work."

Could capitalism be saved? Were the democratic ideals of George Washington, Thomas Jefferson, and Abraham Lincoln old-fashioned? Mussolini said, "Democracy is sand driven by the wind." The writer William Manchester said that if Hoover had been reelected, "the United States would have followed seven Latin American countries whose governments had been overthrown by Depression victims." That may be going a bit far. You don't have to agree with every historian. We in the United States have a strong Constitution and we value it. Still, this was a revolutionary age. Hoover, who was a brilliant engineer, was not the man for the times. He didn't understand the needs of ordinary people.

In 1930, when many Americans were going to bed hungry, he said: "The lesson should be constantly enforced that though the people support the government, the government should not support the people."

What Hoover meant was that no government money should be spent on relief programs. He thought people could help themselves. If government money was spent it should go to business. That would strengthen the economy, he said,

*Of course* WE CAN DO IT!

**But how could we do it? We couldn't roll up our sleeves and get down to work when there was no work to be had.**

and business money would "trickle down" to the people. Many economists believed as he did.

Hoover didn't realize there was a need for new thinking. People were starving in the land of plenty. The gap between rich and poor had grown big as a chasm. Hoover believed in *voluntarism;* he thought individuals should help each other. It was a good idea, and there was a lot of neighborliness during the Depression, but it wasn't enough. More needed to be done, much more, or there might be a revolution.

Henry Ford, who was a pacifist (he didn't believe in fighting wars), bought a gun.

The poet Stephen Spender (who came from England for a visit) wrote about our country:

> Despite its...amazing civilization, the social organization is right back in the Victorian Age....She has no pensions for her old people; no medical benefits for her workers; no unemployment insurance for any trade.

We Americans had clung to the wrong parts of our economic past. No major industrial nation was so unprepared for calamity.

The United States needed a strong leader, someone who would be open to new ideas. Someone who would take charge. And that was just what we got. Fortunately, that strong leader loved America's democracy. He had been taught that being a good citizen means serving your country.

His name was Franklin Delano Roosevelt, and he became the most loved president since Abraham Lincoln—and also the most hated president since Abraham Lincoln. He was one of the most dynamic, active men in all of American history. And that is amazing, because he could hardly stand up by himself.

**The Depression** was a terrible spiral. Many people were so poor that they stopped buying goods altogether. If people didn't buy goods, manufacturers couldn't make them. So workers couldn't get work, and they, too, couldn't buy anything. So more and more people became poorer and poorer.

Franklin Delano Roosevelt campaigning for the presidency. He traveled all over the country to talk to people.

91

# 19 A Boy Who Loved History

James Roosevelt and his son, Franklin. Baby boys wore dresses in the 19th century.

**As a boy** he was called Frank. As an adult he was Franklin or FDR.

All of our people all over the country—except the pure-blooded Indians—are immigrants or descendants of immigrants, including even those who came over on the Mayflower.

—FRANKLIN DELANO ROOSEVELT, IN A SPEECH GIVEN IN BOSTON, 1944

"I think families are the most interesting things in the world," said Franklin Delano Roosevelt. His wife agreed. She said, "In the story of every family is the stuff from which both novels and eventually history is written."

They were right. Every family—rich or poor, famous or little known—has stories. If you don't know your family stories, start asking questions. You are sure to hear some interesting things.

Franklin Roosevelt's family was full of stories, and all his life he listened to them. His father, James Roosevelt, could remember the Civil War. He told Frank stories of Abraham Lincoln and of the general who gave Lincoln a hard time, James's friend General George B. McClellan.

Franklin Delano Roosevelt loved history. He loved the way history can connect you to past times. His own family connections went way back into early American history. The first American Roosevelt was a Dutch farmer named Claes. He arrived in New York about 1650. One of Claes's grandsons started the branch of the family that led to Franklin. Another grandson had descendants who included Theodore Roosevelt and Eleanor Roosevelt (we'll get to her soon).

When Franklin was growing up, his

Franklin, age three, with his dog Budgy and his pet donkey.

Hyde Park, where FDR grew up, is a big, comfortable house, but it is homey, not a palace like the neighboring Vanderbilt mansion.

father liked to show him a teapot that had belonged to Franklin's great-great-grandfather, Isaac Roosevelt. Isaac was a banker and a Patriot during the Revolutionary War and a friend of Alexander Hamilton. But it was Hamilton's rival, Thomas Jefferson, whom young Roosevelt really admired. He tried to find some connection between Isaac and Jefferson, but he never could. (Years later, when Franklin Roosevelt became president, he tried to be like Jefferson and concern himself with the average citizen, whom he called "the forgotten man." However, he also believed, like Alexander Hamilton, in the importance of a strong federal government.)

Franklin's father wasn't the only one with stories to tell. His mother talked of her family, the Delanos. The first American Delano was French, and a Huguenot, and he arrived at the Plymouth Colony in 1621. (He missed the *Mayflower* by a year.) It was love that brought him to America. He was in love with Priscilla Mullins. She must have been special; Myles Standish and John Alden loved her, too. She married Alden and rejected the Frenchman, Philippe de la Noye, who, some years later, married an Englishwoman named Hester. Then he dropped the *ye* from his name and became Delano.

The Roosevelts and Delanos prospered in America. Most of them, like Theodore Roosevelt, became Republicans. But James Roosevelt, Franklin's father, was a Democrat.

When Frank was five years old, in 1887, his father took him to meet President Grover Cleveland. Cleveland was the first Democrat to be president in 28 years. James Roosevelt had contributed money to help get him elected. But being president is no easy job; the day young FDR visited, the chief executive was tired. "My little man," said the huge president to the small boy dressed in a sailor suit standing in front of him, "I am making a strange wish for you. It is that you may never be president of the United States."

Well, you know how kids are. Just tell them what you don't want them to do, and that is what they will go for. So it may have been that day that Franklin Delano Roosevelt first got the idea that he would like to be president.

Franklin, at age 11, with his mother, Sara. She smothered him with love, advice, and overprotection.

I am interested in and have respect for whatever people believe, even if I cannot understand their beliefs or share their experiences.
—FRANKLIN DELANO ROOSEVELT

# 20 How About This?

**Franklin with the family dog, Monk. He did not go to school until he was 14. Instead he was tutored with the children of other local estate owners.**

**The Roosevelt house at Campobello in New Brunswick, Canada, near the coast of Maine.**

How would you like this: a house in New York City, a country house overlooking the Hudson River at Hyde Park, New York, and a summer house in Campobello, New Brunswick, by the sea? Now, just for variety you'll take plenty of trips: Paris this year, England the next. You'll be surrounded by servants: cooks, drivers, gardeners, a laundress, and your own private teachers. You'll have a pony and dogs and just about everything you want. In addition, you'll have loving parents who adore you and see that children come to play with you. When you finally go off to school—at age 14—your parents will take you in their own railroad car; it has a bedroom and living room.

Sounds pretty terrific? Well, it wasn't bad—and that was what Franklin Delano Roosevelt's childhood was like. No, he wasn't a prince; he just lived like one. So did other children of the wealthy American upper class in the late 19th century. That was at a time when 11 million of the 12 million families in America had an average income of $380 a year. Only a few thousand families could be called rich. And, compared with the really wealthy Vanderbilts or Astors, the Roosevelts were no big deal.

How do you think you would turn out if you had everything you wanted? Do you think you might be vain, arrogant, spoiled, and worthless? Well, that is just how some of those rich kids turned out. (Some poor kids probably turned out that way, too.) But not Frank Roosevelt.

His parents gave him good values. They expected him to behave like a gentleman: to be kind, considerate, and honest. They gave him a strong religious faith. (He was an Episcopalian.) That faith gave him courage when he needed it.

He needed courage many times in his life. First, when he went away to Groton. Groton was a rich boys' school (and still is, mostly), but the headmaster didn't believe in pampering. Every boy was expected to take a cold shower each morning. That wasn't really hard, if you gritted your teeth and showered fast; it was much harder trying to be just one of the group when you had always been the center of attention. Franklin was handsome, charming, and friendly—but he never got along with people his age as well as he did with those older and younger. At Groton, he didn't get picked for awards and teams he really wanted, and that hurt; but he had been taught not to complain.

It became a part of his character, not complaining. He would be enthusiastic and act as if everything was fine, even if it wasn't. It made him pleasant to be around, but it also made some of his friends uneasy. They never knew how he really felt.

Franklin in a school play. He loved to have fun and play practical jokes.

Franklin went to Harvard, as his parents expected him to do, and to Columbia Law School. His mother intended him to live the comfortable life of a country squire, as his father had before him. After all, with the family money, he had no need to work hard. He didn't have to concern himself with others, but he did. When he was a student himself he wrote to segregated southern colleges appealing to them to do as Harvard did and accept black students.

Franklin, age 20, now a big man on campus at Harvard.

He may have been concerned with those who were less fortunate than himself because of an important influence in his life, a man he admired more than anyone else. A man who cared about people and wanted to make the world better than he had found it. It was the president of the United States, his cousin Theodore.

When Frank was a child he loved to visit Sagamore Hill, TR's Long Island home in Oyster Bay. There he could romp and run with energetic, fun-loving Teddy and his five children. Frank decided that someday he, too, would have a big family and play with his family as TR did.

One day early that first term [at Groton] a group of older boys...trapped him in a corner of the corridor and ordered him to dance, jabbing hard at his ankles with hockey sticks to make sure he stepped fast enough.... Refusing ever to seem a victim, even to himself, he pirouetted and toe-danced in apparent high spirits as if he were part of the fun instead of its object. No one sensed his fear. "He did what he was told," one eyewitness recalled, "with such good grace that the class soon let him go."

—GEOFFREY C. WARD, *BEFORE THE TRUMPET*

He also decided he would serve his country—and he set out to do it. First he became a New York state senator. Then Woodrow Wilson made him assistant secretary of the navy. (TR had held that job.) In 1920, he ran for vice president with James Cox against Warren Harding and Calvin Coolidge. He lost, but people began to talk of him as a politician to watch.

He soon had a fine family: a busy wife, a daughter, and four sons. He was an energetic father, full of good spirits, who loved to sail and hike. Yale's football coach watched him exercise and said, "Mr. Roosevelt is a beautifully built man with the long muscles of an athlete."

But what he wanted most of all was to be president. He told that to a classmate while he was still in college. And it looked as if he had a good chance to fulfill his ambition.

Then tragedy struck. He went to bed one night, not feeling well; the next morning, he couldn't move. He was 39 and he had a dreaded disease: *poliomyelitis* (PO-lee-o-my-uh-LY-tiss). Usually it struck children: its common name was *infantile paralysis.* It was especially hard on adult victims. (Later, Jonas Salk and Albert Sabin developed vaccines to prevent polio; but that was still 20 years in the future.)

Imagine you're an active man, father of five children, with big ideas. Then, overnight, you're crippled. At first Roosevelt couldn't move at all. Slowly, with painful therapy and concentration, he regained the use of his upper body. He would never run again. When he walked it was in heavy braces with agonizing steps. Would you have the courage to go on with your plans? Would you feel sorry for yourself? Would you take it easy and let people wait on you?

At first, everyone was sure his career was finished. Franklin's mother expected him to live the life of a wealthy invalid. But Franklin was determined to live normally. He was a cheerful man, and an optimist. Where others saw problems, he saw challenges.

His parents had trained him not to complain, and, even when he was in great pain, he didn't. As it turned out, he gained something from his terrible illness. It taught him patience and made him more determined. It made him know frustration, and sorrow, and anguish. He—the boy who had had everything—learned to understand those who had troubles.

On top of all that, he was married to a very unusual woman. She, too, was determined that he should not change his goals. Her name was Eleanor.

FDR held his job as assistant navy secretary for seven years. He loved the work, and was disappointed that the navy didn't see much action in the First World War.

# 21 A Lonely Little Girl

*I knew a child once who adored her father. She was an ugly little thing, keenly conscious of her deficiencies, and her father, the only person who really cared for her, was away much of the time; but he never criticized her or blamed her, instead he wrote her letters and stories, telling her how much he dreamed of her growing up and what they would do together in the future, but she must be truthful, loyal, brave, well-educated, or the woman he dreamed of would not be there when the wonderful day came for them to fare forth together. The child was full of fears and because of them lying was easy; she had no intellectual stimulus at that time and yet she made herself as the years went on into a fairly good copy of the picture he had painted.*

Elliott and Anna Hall Roosevelt, Eleanor's father and mother. Her mother was a great society beauty, but cold to her daughter. When she died Eleanor seemed to hardly feel the loss. But when Elliott died, two years later, she refused to believe it. After that he was always alive for her.

Eleanor Roosevelt was writing about herself. She wasn't ugly, but she thought she was, perhaps because her mother was a great beauty. Eleanor had long blond hair, blue eyes, a plain face, and teeth that seemed too big for her mouth. She was shy, easily frightened, and serious. Sometimes she told little lies because she was afraid people would not want to hear the truth.

Her father, Theodore Roosevelt's handsome brother Elliott, was a daredevil horseman and a man-about-town. Everyone who knew Elliott loved him. He was sweet-natured and charming. He became an alcoholic. It ruined his life, and his family's life, too.

But he loved his sad-eyed daughter. He called her "little Nell," and told her that he wanted her to grow up to be good, brave, kind,

Even at three Eleanor was lonely. Her mother called her "Granny," because she was "old-fashioned" and not pretty.

Eleanor at her grandmother's. She loved her horse and hated the childish short dresses her grandmother made her wear.

## Eleanor's Other Mother

Marie Souvestre was the principal of the school that Eleanor attended in England. She was a strong, proud Frenchwoman, and the girls at Allenswood had to speak French. She taught Eleanor to think for herself, and she taught her that women could become something without the help of men.

and honest. And she did. She always remembered those things that were fine in Elliott Roosevelt and forgave him his shortcomings. All her life she kept his letters, read them and reread them, and tried to be the kind of woman who would have made him proud. That wasn't easy.

She had a dreadful childhood. Not an ordinary unhappy childhood; a horrible, awful, terribly lonely one.

She adored her father, but most of the time he wasn't there. She lived for his visits. Sometimes there were wonderful carriage rides with her father driving the horses fast and little Eleanor holding him tightly. Sometimes he promised to see her and then, perhaps because he was drunk, he disappointed his child. Once he took her and his prize terriers for a walk. They stopped at his men's club and he left Eleanor and the dogs with the doorkeeper while he went inside "for just a minute." Hours later he was carried out—drunk; the little girl was sent home in a taxi.

When she was eight her mother died. When she was nine her brother died. When she was ten her father died.

Is this too sad to read? It is all true. Eleanor and her younger brother, Hall, went to live with their grandmother. The grandmother didn't know anything about bringing up children. She lived in a big, spooky house. The noise of children playing bothered her. A governess took care of Eleanor and Hall. The governess didn't like Eleanor. She was mean to her.

Then Eleanor was sent away to school in England. Finally, her life took a happy turn. The principal of the school realized that Eleanor had a good mind and a generous, kind nature. Eleanor became her favorite student. Eleanor soon became everyone's favorite. She had a talent for leadership. She was able to inspire others to do their best.

The child who had not always told the truth, who had struggled against the demons that make people lie, was becoming the kind of person her father had wished her to be. For the rest of her life, Eleanor Roosevelt would be known for her truthfulness.

**Eleanor smartly dressed for European travel on a school vacation.**

# 22 First Lady of the World

Eleanor in her wedding dress. FDR's mother made them wait a year to announce the engagement.

When Eleanor came home from England she was tall and willowy. She still thought she was ugly, but other people didn't. Especially her cousin, Franklin, the most dashing of the young Roosevelts. Like Eleanor's uncle Theodore, Franklin had energy and ambition. Like Elliott Roosevelt, he had charm. He and Eleanor fell deeply in love.

They were soon married. Before long, Eleanor found herself with five children, three houses that needed managing, and a husband with a busy political career.

Then her husband fell ill with polio. She had had experience with tragedy. Maybe that was why she handled it so well. Her husband's legs would never carry him again. She said that needn't stop him. There was no reason to change his goals. She could become his legs—and his eyes and ears, too.

They were a team, one of the greatest political teams in history. He became president, but she was his link to the people. He stayed in the White House; she went to coal mines and factories and workers' meetings. Then she told the president what people were thinking.

The first time she spoke before an audience her knees shook. Soon she was one of the most successful speakers of her day. She wrote a newspaper column and a magazine column and books. She was the first First Lady to hold regular press conferences. She served food to needy people, read stories to poor children, visited

Eleanor and Franklin at a friend's house in Scotland on their European honeymoon.

Eleanor as First Lady was usually out and about. Here she is visiting an Ohio coal mine.

**99**

Eleanor fought against racial discrimination. Here, she talks to Aubrey Williams, executive director of the National Youth Administration, and Mary McLeod Bethune, the NYA's Director of Negro Activities, at a conference.

**The Bonus Army** returned to Washington when Roosevelt was president. It was called the "Second Bonus Army." He offered the veterans the use of an army camp, sent food, coffee, a convention tent, and doctors, and then added a navy band to entertain them. Mrs. Roosevelt came to visit. "Hoover sent the army," said one Bonus Army man. "Roosevelt sent his wife." Roosevelt did not pay the bonuses, but he did offer the veterans jobs in the Civilian Conservation Corps (CCC), planting trees, creating parks, and so forth. Many went to work.

hospitals, and spoke out for minority rights when few others did.

It is hard for a president—any president—to take time to check out government projects. Besides, everyone knows when a president is coming to visit, so things can be made to look good beforehand. But no one ever knew where Eleanor Roosevelt would pop up. The Secret Service had a code name for her: they called her "Rover." She checked up on government projects and told the president the truth about what was happening. If someone wrote to the president complaining about a problem, Eleanor made sure the letter got answered. Sometimes she invited the letter writer to dinner at the White House. She invited all kinds of people to White House meals: young and old, rich and poor, people of every race and religion.

Always, she fought for the underdog—for those who were persecuted, or treated unfairly. She wanted to see that all people were given an equal opportunity. She worked for women's rights. She worked for minority rights. She stood on the side of truth and justice.

When a women's organization refused to let Marian Anderson, a renowned black singer, use its auditorium, Mrs. Roosevelt resigned from the organization. She encouraged Marian Anderson to sing on the steps of the Lincoln Memorial in Washington, D.C. Marian Anderson sang "America," and more people heard her than could have fit in any auditorium.

Shy, insecure, ugly-duckling Eleanor had grown up to be a strong, sensitive, capable person. She had a kind of no-nonsense wisdom that made her admired around the world. She has been called the outstanding woman of the 20th century. Eleanor Roosevelt became everything her father wanted her to be—and more.

Marian Anderson sings "America" on the steps of the Lincoln Memorial.

**Eleanor's press conferences were generally only for women writers. That got newspapers to hire more female journalists.**

# 23 Handicap or Character Builder?

FDR's wheelchair, built from an ordinary kitchen chair.

When Franklin Roosevelt first entered politics he was wealthy, charming, astoundingly good-natured, ambitious, and optimistic—but not very serious. Perhaps everything had come to him too easily. In his boyhood and youth and early manhood he had not known suffering. Now he knew. Now there were steel braces on his legs and a current of steel in his veins.

He had gone through a testing time of great pain when he could hardly move at all. He would never stand by himself again—he always had to call on others for help. Sometimes he crawled to the bathroom. For a proud man it must have been very hard. But if he felt sorry for himself he didn't show it. Even at first, when he was very sick, he made those who came to see him feel good. Everyone remarked on his good spirits, his lighthearted manner, and his great courage.

He was determined to conquer polio, so he worked hard exercising and swimming and learning to manipulate the seven-pound leg braces. His slim, boyish torso became strong, muscular, and powerful. For seven years he stayed away from active political life, trying to learn to

"How marvelous it feels!" Roosevelt said, the first time he slid into the pool at Warm Springs. "I don't think I'll ever get out!"

**101**

He was brave, that Roosevelt. O Lordy he was brave. He must have known that he would never be whole, but he was brave. A clear-cut nothing-from-the-waist-down case, and yet he forced himself to walk. With steel and fire, he forced his arms to take him across the room, across the lawn, down the steps. He knew, some part of him knew he would never be walking at the head of the Labor Day Parade again, but he kept on pouring his will into what was left of his muscles, trying to walk that walk again.

—LORENZO MILAM,
*THE CRIPPLE LIBERATION FRONT MARCHING BAND BLUES*

**Exuberance** is "joyful enthusiasm."

## Keeping It Simple

Roosevelt knew that good writing is clear and direct. In 1942, during the Second World War, there was fear that we might be attacked by air. It was important that lights not show at night and help enemy pilots spot targets. So a government official wrote this blackout order for Washington, D.C.:

*Such preparations shall be made as will completely obscure all Federal buildings and non-Federal buildings occupied by the Federal government during an air raid for any period of time from visibility by reason of internal or external illumination.*

Roosevelt rewrote the blackout order. "Tell them," he said, "that in buildings where they have to keep the work going to put something across the windows."

An aide wrote: "We are trying to construct a more inclusive society." Roosevelt changed that to: "We are going to make a country where no one is left out."

Roosevelt had to work tremendously hard to learn to walk with leg braces and crutches. But, said Eleanor, "It gave him strength and courage he had not had before."

walk again, but his weak legs would not respond. If he despaired, if he was sorrowful, he didn't let anyone see it.

He refused to act like an invalid. And so he sailed and went to dances and did everything anyone else would have done. Only he did it with more energy and exuberance than most people. At a square dance—where he called the dances—others remarked at what a good time he seemed to be having. This was a man who had always loved to dance. How do you think he really felt?

Perhaps, by not showing his inner feelings, he convinced himself, as he convinced others, that he wasn't hurting.

A man whose office was next door to Roosevelt's mother's house in New York wrote this:

*Our staff used to watch him from the windows*

102

*as he got out of his car, clicking the brace on one leg into place, then the other. Pulling himself erect by his powerful arms, he would then make his way slowly up the inclined boardwalk which covered one side of the steps. He never failed to pause, grin and wave a greeting to the girls in our windows...as always, every move was a test of courage, met as a matter of course with dignity; he simply would not allow bodily disability to defeat his will.*

**FDR had a Model A Ford built with hand controls. He loved to go out driving; in a car he could feel as physically independent as the next man.**

It would have been easier to become president if he had not had polio. And it probably would have happened. After all, he had the Roosevelt name, that incredible energy, and determination. But his disease changed everything. It made the goal harder to achieve; it made the victory sweeter.

And it made the man different. He had been called a political *dilettante* (DILL-uh-tont), which means an "amateur": someone who dabbles, who plays the game for sport, as just one of many interests. There was something to the accusation.

William Phillips, a friend who knew him when he first entered politics, described him as "brilliant, lovable, and somewhat happy-go-lucky...always amusing, always the life of the party." But serious, or focused in his beliefs? No one thought that. "He was not a heavyweight...not particularly steady in his views."

Did his crippling disease make him a stronger, more sensitive, more serious person? There are many who believe it did.

**Roosevelt collected and built model boats and ships. For a very busy man, he had a lot of hobbies.**

# 24 Candidate Roosevelt

Hunger marchers in Washington, D.C. In 1932, the year FDR was elected president, one out of four Americans belonged to a family in which no one had full-time work.

The little plane tossed about in the heavy wind. The pilot, looking down, followed the path of the old Erie Canal; he was flying from Albany to Chicago. Twice he landed for more fuel. In the backseat, the plane's violent swaying was too much for young John Roosevelt. He threw up.

But John didn't even tell his parents. They were busy. His father was polishing a speech he was soon to deliver. FDR was on his way to the Democratic National Convention to personally accept that party's nomination for president of the United States. No candidate had done that before.

In the old horse-and-buggy days, before telephones, it sometimes took a week or more for a messenger to tell a candidate he had been chosen by his party to run for president. Only then was the candidate expected to make an acceptance

## A New Deal—Deal Us In!

When Roosevelt accepted the Democratic Party's nomination for president, he pledged a "new deal for the American people." A cartoonist picked up the phrase, and *New Deal* was the name soon given to President Roosevelt's domestic (home) policies. The ideas of the New Deal were firmly in the American tradition. They were based on Progressive ideas: on opposition to mo-

nopoly; on a belief that government should help regulate the economy; and on the conviction that no one wants to be poor and that most poverty is the result of social problems. The New Deal's methods were experimental; some worked, some didn't. The Progressive Party was important at the end of the 19th and beginning of the 20th century. Theodore Roosevelt was a Progressive.

speech. That time gap had been continued for tradition's sake. Roosevelt saw no reason to stick with the old ways.

Besides, Roosevelt wanted people to know he would be an active candidate and president. If anyone was worried that his weak legs would slow him down, he would show them: they would not. So he flew to Chicago, locked the braces on his legs, and stood before the delegates.

Hyde Park's front porch on election night: left to right, daughter Anna, son John, mother Sara, FDR, son Franklin Jr., and Eleanor.

"I pledge you, I pledge myself, to a new deal for the American people," said FDR in his captivating, mellifluous voice. To a nation that had suffered three years of devastating depression, the words *new deal* sounded very good. The Republican candidate, Herbert Hoover, didn't have a chance.

Whether he deserved it or not, Hoover was blamed for the Depression. Roosevelt campaigned hard, but he didn't have to. People wanted a change. The election was a landslide. Forty-two of forty-eight states went Democratic.

Today, because of the 20th Amendment (adopted in 1933), a candidate elected in November becomes president in January.

**Mellifluous** (muh-LIFF-floo-us) means "flowing and sweet as honey." It is from the same roots as *mellow* and *fluid*.

"I DID"

"BUT WHY DIDN'T YOU SAVE SOME MONEY FOR THE FUTURE, WHEN TIMES WERE GOOD?"

It wasn't only speculators who lost money in the Great Crash. A lot of banks failed, and many people lost all their savings; there was no banking insurance then.

In 1932, the delay was longer. Roosevelt did not take office until March. Between Election Day in November 1932 and Inauguration Day in March 1933, the economic situation got worse and worse.

By March, the U.S. economy seemed close to collapse. Every day more and more banks closed. Those who had gold were hoarding it. There was even a question as to whether the government had enough money to meet its payroll. A newspaper reporter described the mood of the people in Washington, D.C., as like "a beleaguered capital in wartime." General Douglas MacArthur prepared his troops for a possible riot. Capitalism, said many experts, was too sick to recover.

As the black crows of hard times come flying over the horizon, this cartoon mocks Hoover's attempts to scare them off with a straw man.

**Beleaguered** means "under siege."

# 25 President Roosevelt

Over the airwaves, FDR sounded warm, not like a speechmaking politician. He always began a radio talk with the words "My friends."

The patient seems to be dying. Dr. Leave Alone is in the sickroom. Leave Alone is a distinguished man. He wears a dark suit and a dark manner. He has been telling the patient that there is nothing wrong. But the patient is gasping for breath. He screams in pain. The doctor attempts to be calm. "Pull down the shades, keep your voices low, and don't disturb the patient," he tells the family. "Medical science has never encountered an illness like this. We will hope for a miracle." The family weeps, the patient groans. Dr. Leave Alone says, "We have done everything we can," and departs.

Desperate, the family turns to another doctor. A big, hearty man, he comes into the sickroom, pulls up the shades, lets in the sunshine, and in a booming voice tells the patient, "You're going to get well." Then he adds, "The

Dr. New Deal brings an alphabet soup of medicines for sick Uncle Sam. If a remedy didn't work, he would try another.

only thing you have to fear is fear itself."

"Medical science may not know how to treat this illness," says confident Dr. New Deal, "but that won't stop us. We'll find a way. First we'll try one method, then another, then another. We'll throw out what doesn't work, we'll keep what does. Start smiling, everybody—you're going to see some action—we'll lick this disease!"

Dr. New Deal, of course, was Franklin D. Roosevelt. The sick patient was the economy of the United States. Almost everyone thought it was dying and would have to be replaced. But not FDR. He was a man of action. Besides that, he was a *pragmatist*. That means someone who believes in whatever will work. Someone who has practical intelligence. That was FDR. He also had energy and enthusiasm, and that gave people confidence. They believed in him. Here are some words to describe FDR:

FORCEFUL
DYNAMIC
RESOURCEFUL
OPTIMISTIC
OUTGOING
SENSITIVE
ENERGETIC
VIVACIOUS
ENTHUSIASTIC
LIKABLE
TIRELESS

When former president Calvin Coolidge was asked for his ideas on how to lick the Depression, he said:

*In other periods of depression it has always been possible to see some things which were solid and upon which you could base hope, but as I look about me I see nothing to give ground for hope—nothing of man.*

A group of prominent bankers was called to Washington to see what suggestions they had for solving the banking crisis. They had none.

President Herbert Hoover said, "We are at the end of our string. There is nothing more we can do."

That gives you an idea of the gloom and pessimism

At the Democratic convention in 1932, comedian Will Rogers *(right)* introduced FDR *(far left)*. He certainly managed to make the candidate laugh uproariously.

Inauguration Day 1933. "America hasn't been as happy in three years as they are today," said Will Rogers (ungrammatically but cheerfully). "They know they got a man in there who is wise to Congress....If he burned down the Capitol, we would cheer and say, 'Well, at least we got a fire started anyhow.'"

**Thomas Corcoran**, a New Deal official, said, "Without bloodshed, the New Deal defanged our most dangerous internal crisis since the crisis of 1861." What did he mean? Do you agree?

"THE ONLY THING WE HAVE TO FEAR IS FEAR ITSELF--"

This seems to be a photograph, but look closely: it's really a collage (a paste-up) put together from several photos by an anonymous artist to honor FDR.

THIS IS ONE RABBIT THAT NEVER FAILED ME!

SPENDING

OLD RELIABLE!

One senator said, "The admirable trait about Roosevelt is that he has the guts to try." His opponents said programs such as Social Security (right) could be paid for only by raising taxes and spending too much money.

OLD AGE INSURANCE PROGRAM

in Washington the day Hoover packed his bags and left the White House.

The next day, March 4, 1933, Franklin Roosevelt stood, bareheaded, in front of the Capitol, holding tightly to a lectern. It was his inauguration day. Some small boys perched in nearby tree limbs; dignitaries sat in special seats; but most of the crowd stood and shivered in the cold wind. When the new president spoke, his strong voice cut through the gloom. All across the land, people clustered around radios to hear what he had to say.

"This nation asks for action, and action now," said President Roosevelt. "We must act quickly."

And that was exactly what he did: act quickly. The first 100 days of his presidency are famous for all the things that got done. Congress was on vacation when Roosevelt took office. He called Congress back into session. He began to act. Soon new programs and laws were pouring out of Washington. "It is common sense to take a method and try it," said Roosevelt. "If it fails, admit it frankly and try another. But above all, try something."

And he also said, "The only thing we have to fear is fear itself."

FDR put together a group of advisers. Newspaper reporters called them "the brain trust." Many were college professors. They were new to government, but they had ideas, intelligence, and a desire to help their country. They worked hard. Washington became an exciting place for idealistic, energetic citizen workers.

Roosevelt's ideas really were a "New Deal." He changed America profoundly. He probably saved American capitalism, but he changed some of its habits. The New Deal did away with most child labor, regulated the stock market, made bank deposits safe, helped make employers pay fair wages to employees, encouraged workers' unions, limited hours of work, helped farmers, brought electricity into rural areas, and gave Americans an old-age pension policy called "Social Security." The New Deal made the government an active participant in citizens' lives. Yet most of the ideas of the New Deal were not really new. They were the old Progressive ideas in a new package. They had already been tried in Europe. America was behind the times when it came to social welfare.

In order to put people to work, the New Deal sent young people out of doors and paid them to plant trees, build parks, and fight fires. It paid painters to paint murals, writers to write books, and musicians to play and create music. Needy people were given money for food and shelter.

Civilian Conservation Corps members planting seedlings in Oregon. Young men between ages 18 and 25 whose families were on relief got room and board for a year and were paid $30 a month, $25 of which went straight to their families.

## New Ideas for a New Deal

*Here are some of the best-known New Deal programs (a star means the program still exists today):*

• * The SECURITIES AND EXCHANGE COMMISSION (SEC) was formed to regulate the stock market.

• * The FEDERAL DEPOSIT INSURANCE CORPORATION (FDIC) insured bank deposits. We no longer had to fear bank failures.

• The CIVILIAN CONSERVATION CORPS (CCC) gave jobs to more than 2 million out-of-work young men in the nation's parklands: building roads, trails, cabins, and campgrounds. Many are still in use today.

• The PUBLIC WORKS ADMINISTRATION (PWA) built New York's Triborough Bridge and Lincoln Tunnel; Oregon's Coastal Highway; Texas's port of Brownsville; the road between Key West and mainland Florida; and the University of New Mexico's library.

• The CIVILIAN WORKS ADMINISTRATION (CWA) lasted less than a year, but employed more than 4 million men and women. Opera singers were sent to the Ozark mountains (where none had ever sung before); teachers kept rural schools open; Native Americans restocked the Kodiak Islands with snowshoe rabbits.

• * The TENNESSEE VALLEY AUTHORITY (TVA) began as a federally directed experiment in regional planning. The TVA built five dams along the Tennessee River and provided cheap electric power, flood control, and irrigation water to seven states.

• * The SOCIAL SECURITY ACT established old-age pensions, unemployment benefits, and welfare benefits for the elderly, children, and the handicapped.

• The WORKS PROGRESS ADMINISTRATION (WPA) provided useful jobs. WPA workers built highways, cleared slums, and labored in rural areas. Writers were paid to write regional guidebooks and compile oral histories. Painters painted murals in public buildings; musicians organized orchestras; actors brought plays to communities that had never experienced live theater. Between 1935 and 1939, the WPA gave work to 8.5 million people.

This cartoon caption says, "Come along. We're going to the Trans-Lux to hiss Roosevelt." The Trans-Lux was a newsreel theater (this was before TV). Who are those people, and why are they going to hiss Roosevelt?

Critics of the New Deal saw the government diving gaily into an ocean of spending and debt and taking the drowning taxpayer with it.

Roosevelt did something else. Something that was really new and innovative. Something that people in power almost never do without a battle. He shared power with those who had never held it before.

From the country's earliest days, the leaders of the United States had mostly been drawn from one group: white Protestant men of northern European descent.

Franklin Roosevelt was part of that white-Protestant-male traditional aristocracy of privilege. But he opened its doors. He included in positions of government power those who had been excluded: women, blacks, eastern Europeans, southern Europeans, American Indians, Catholics, and Jews. He began a process that soon added Muslims, Buddhists, Hindus, and all who are citizens. He rejected the idea of an aristocracy of birth and replaced it with the goal of an aristocracy of talent.

There were those who hated him for doing it. It is hard for us today to imagine how much some people hated him. He was called "a traitor to his class." Some who had gone to school with him refused to speak his name.

Some, in the business world, hated him, too. Business leaders had been the heroes of the Roaring Twenties. Calvin Coolidge had said, "The business of America is business." The Depression changed all that. Now Roosevelt was the popular hero, and the American people were demanding that business be regulated for the public good.

But the Supreme Court began vetoing New Deal legislation. FDR, fighting back, tried to add extra justices to the bench (justices friendly to him). That court-packing plan was a poor idea that cost the New Deal support and slowed its momentum.

Before the New Deal, government had been expected to provide conditions that would help business. But government was expected to do nothing for the workers who made business profits possible. With Roosevelt, many laws were passed to help workers, farmers and ordinary citizens. Government money was spent on the poor. Some people didn't like that idea. But others understood that, if it was done wisely, the nation would be stronger and better for it.

110

# 26 Twentieth-Century Monsters

A magazine portrayed Hitler as the strong man come to deliver the German damsel in distress.

On the very day of Franklin Delano Roosevelt's first inauguration, the day he told America that "the only thing we have to fear is fear itself," something fearful was happening in Germany. It would change the fate of the world. The Reichstag (RIKES-tahg)—Germany's congress—was deciding to give absolute government power to the German chancellor, Adolf Hitler.

Imagine a country letting its meanest, worst people take charge. Imagine giving those kinds of people the power of life and death over the whole nation. Imagine a nation where children are taught to be tattletales and tell the secret police about anyone who protests—even their parents. Imagine a nation that burns the books of its greatest writers because it fears and hates ideas and truth. Imagine a nation that kills people because it doesn't like their religion or their ideas, or because they are handicapped. That's what happened in Germany in the 1930s.

Germany no longer even attempted to be a democracy. It willingly became a dictatorship—the most evil dictatorship in recorded history. (Although the dictatorship in Soviet Russia was almost as bad.) The Germans used their intelligence and skill to create factories of death. They allowed their government to do unspeakable deeds. Some Germans did not approve, but few spoke out. To do so meant risking their lives.

But in that March of 1933, most people in America paid no attention to what was happening in Germany.

**In the Weimar** Republic in Germany, the chancellor was chosen (like the prime minister in Great Britain) by his party's leaders—not by direct election. The head of the party with the most seats in the Reichstag became chancellor. Hitler's party was the National Socialist (Nazi) Party.

German industry and transportation collapsed after the Great War. In 1922, these women and children, desperate for fuel, were gleaning coal scraps on a mine dump heap.

In October 1922, 4,500 German marks bought one U.S. dollar. In November 1923, the exchange rate was 4.2 *trillion* marks to the dollar. One woman lit the fire with marks; children played blocks with bundles of bills.

The Depression seemed more important. Adolf Hitler? He was a little man with a black brush mustache and dark straight hair that fell into his face. He strutted about raising his arm in a straight salute and shrieking his speeches. He didn't seem evil; he seemed silly.

The German people didn't find him silly. They were still angry about the war they had lost. Their leaders and historians had misled them about the causes of the Great War. They had been told that Germany was no more to blame for the start of the First World War than any other nation. That wasn't true. But the Germans believed it; they thought the rest of the world had picked on them. They thought the Versailles Treaty—the treaty that had ended the Great War—was unfair. They were humiliated by the terms of peace. Germany was not allowed to have a large army, navy, or air force. Germany was to make large cash payments—called "reparations" (rep-uh-RAY-shuns)—to the winners to help pay back the costs of the war. Germany was made to say that it was totally to blame for the war.

Since most Germans thought they were no more to blame for the war than others, they were furious, especially about those payments. As it turned out, we lent Germany much more than they ever paid. But most German citizens didn't know that.

Germany's citizens were angry and unhappy. Their country was in awful shape economically. Soon after the war, Germany suffered a time of incredible inflation. The government began printing lots of money (partly to pay those reparations). Printing presses ran day and night. When you print a lot of currency, soon none of it is worth much. Prices in Germany rose beyond belief. In 1923, a Hershey chocolate bar cost 150,000 German marks (in the United States the same chocolate bar cost a nickel). German money was almost worthless. Buying a loaf of bread might take a bucketful of bills. People lost all their savings. They had to use up everything they had just to pay the rent. Then, after they had finally got the inflation under control, the Great Depression set in worldwide. Unemployment became a big problem.

**During** the Great War, the German leaders kept telling their people that Germany was winning. So it was a real shock when those same leaders surrendered. Somehow the Germans couldn't believe they had really lost. They felt betrayed.

**The Versailles** Treaty was harsh; but in 1918, the Germans had forced their own harsh peace treaty on Russia at a place in Poland called Brest-Litovsk.

112

What the German people wanted was a leader: someone who could lead them out of the economic mess, someone who could make them feel good about themselves. During this Depression era people in other countries were looking for strong leaders, too. The Americans chose Franklin Delano Roosevelt. The Germans turned to Adolf Hitler.

They made a big mistake. That mistake would cost

Adolf Hitler, in 1938, being greeted by thousands of supporters.

them and the rest of the world grief beyond imagining. Their leader was an evil genius who captured his countrymen and women in a web of words and convinced them that he could solve all their problems. He told them that others were to blame for Germany's troubles. He told them that Germany was greater than any other nation and meant to rule the world. He told them that other peoples should be their slaves. He told them that they must love their "fatherland"—Germany—before all else. He told them that they must not worry about right and wrong, because anything Germany did would be right. He told them that *might makes right*—and most believed him.

Hitler wasn't the only one who preached the gospel of nationalism—that loving your nation was more important than loving truth and right actions. Militant nationalism was a 20th-century disease.

In Japan, a military dictatorship took control of the nation and began stomping on its neighbors. The Japanese, too, were suffering from economic depression. They thought they needed more room for their growing population.

**113**

# GERMAN AGGRESSION by 1941

NORWAY 1940

FINLAND

SWEDEN

ESTONIA

LATVIA

LITHUANIA

GER.

DENMARK 1940

IRELAND

GREAT BRITAIN

U.S.S.R.

NETHERLANDS 1940

1939

GERMANY

POLAND

1940 BELGIUM

ATLANTIC OCEAN

1936 RHINELAND

1938-39 CZECHOSLOVAKIA

FRANCE 1940

SWITZ. AUSTRIA 1938

HUNGARY

ROMANIA

PORTUGAL

SPAIN

ITALY

YUGOSLAVIA 1941

BULGARIA

ALBANIA

GREECE 1940

TURKEY

Mediterranean Sea

GERMAN-CONTROLLED TERRITORIES, NOV., 1941

They began by attacking China with a ferocity that is still hard to believe. In a massive campaign of terror, millions of civilians were tortured and killed. Just as in Germany, the Japanese rulers told the people they were a superior race and destined to rule others.

In Spain, a strongman named Francisco Franco muscled his way to power, although many Spaniards (and other Europeans, and some Americans, too) fought against him.

In Italy, a pompous dictator named Benito Mussolini took control of the government. Mussolini was a bully, and, like all bullies, he picked on those who were weak. He sent Italian forces to Ethiopia. There, Italian tanks, machine guns, and airplanes attacked brave Ethiopians, who fought back with spears and lances.

**After** the Bolshevik Revolution in 1917, the old Russian empire became a collection of republics called the Union of Soviet Socialist Republics—the U.S.S.R., or Soviet Union. The republics were not all Russian—they included Central Asian Muslim peoples such as the Uzbeks, the Tadjiks, and the Azerbaijanis; Caucasian peoples such as the Georgians and Armenians; and Baltic peoples such as Latvians and Estonians. These countries were supposed to be independent, but they were not. They were controlled by Russia, the Soviet Union's largest and most powerful republic. Many in America referred to the U.S.S.R. as Russia, or Soviet Russia.

**Francisco Franco**

**Benito Mussolini**

Russia's dictator, Joseph Stalin, killed millions of his own people—anyone who he believed might threaten his rule. His

**Joseph Stalin**

kind of government, he said, would soon conquer the world.

Mussolini called his political movement *Fascism.* Hitler named his *Nazism,* for National Socialism. In Russia, the forces of evil took charge in the name of *communism.* These were all *totalitarian* forms of government. They were the opposite of democracy. In a totalitarian state, individual people don't matter—only the state is important.

Why did good people listen to these terrible leaders? Why did some modern nations become gangster nations? Those are questions that are hard to answer. It didn't happen here; it didn't happen in England. Were we just lucky, or did our democratic tradition give us the strength to resist the evil thinkers?

The Depression brought grave problems to the people of the United States. In 1933, hogs were selling for only $2\frac{1}{2}$ cents a pound in the Midwest. One farmer had to sell all his hogs to pay his rent for a month. Another farmer sold a wagonload of oats to buy a pair of shoes. Hunger and malnutrition were serious problems in the '30s. Many Americans were angry and desperate. It is not surprising that some of them, too, listened to horrid voices. They needed to blame someone for their problems, so they paid attention to: the Ku Klux Klan; the German-American Bund (BOONT), which was inspired by the Nazis; a radio preacher, Father Coughlin, who spewed out a message of hate; and others. A few Americans no longer believed that "all men are created equal." A few wanted to throw out the Bill of Rights. But most Americans rejected the philosophies of wickedness.

Why did we escape the 20th-century virus of totalitarianism? Was it New Deal leadership? Was it our tradition of liberty and democracy? What do you think? Could it happen here?

The Bund combined Hitler worship—its salutes, rallies, and brown shirts—with perverted patriotism: Washington was the "first Fascist."

**Charles** Lindbergh urged Americans not to fight Hitler. He let his anti-war feelings make him do and say things he would later regret. He allowed himself to be used by the Nazis. The America First Committee that he supported got financial aid from Nazi Germany.

**Communism** is an economic system, and as such it is not evil. It just doesn't seem to work efficiently. When combined with a harsh political system, as it was in Soviet Russia, it was evil.

**Father Coughlin**

# 27 A Final Solution

On arrival in a Nazi camp, new inmates' clothes and belongings were taken away, their heads shaved, and identification numbers tattooed on their arms.

In Germany, as soon as the Nazis came to power, Jews were persecuted for no reason except their religion. Jews who weren't even religious were persecuted. A Jewish grandparent was enough to get you into trouble.

There was an evil disease in the world that had been around for a very long time. It was called "anti-Semitism." It was hatred of Jews. No one was quite sure where it came from—although the subject was studied endlessly.

No question about it, Jews have been troublesome to some kings and priests. Jews believe that every person is equal before God, which, if you think about it, means that a king is no different from a peasant. Now that is a nonconforming idea. It must have been maddening to some authorities. Imagine where it might lead if everyone thought that way. (Just where might it lead? To democracy, eventually?)

The Jews are people with a powerful book. It is a freedom document, written in Hebrew, and called a "bible." It tells stories that make people think and ask questions. It tells how, a long time ago, the Jews escaped from Egypt, where they were slaves of the pharaoh. It tells of Queen Esther and how she saved the Jews when they refused to bow to the king's agent, wicked Haman (HAY-mun).

Using principles based on "scientific" ideas, Nazis subjected people to absurd tests of their ethnic origins, such as measuring the size of a nose.

Berlin, the morning after *Kristallnacht*, November 10, 1938—the "Night of Broken Glass," when the windows of Jewish businesses were shattered by yelling mobs.

That Bible became the starting point for a new religion called Christianity, and for another, called Islam.

At first, Christians were persecuted. Then, in the 4th century C.E., the Roman emperor Constantine became a Christian. Before long, most Europeans were Christians. But not the Jews. The Jews stayed with their beliefs. They wouldn't change their religion even for the emperor or the pope. It was frustrating to those in charge. Others might catch their independent ideas. So some of those in power hated them, and blamed them for whatever was wrong at the time. If there was a plague, it was the Jews' fault; if there was an economic disaster, it was the Jews' fault. Finally, many of Europe's Christians went on religious wars called "Crusades." The crusaders' aim was to recapture Jerusalem from the Muslims; but anyone not a Christian was considered an *infidel*—a heretic—and was liable to be murdered. Thousands of Jews died, and Jewish property was up for grabs among the crusaders.

In Spain, in 1492, Jews were told they had to leave the country (Jews had already been expelled from many other parts of Europe). They couldn't take their possessions with them. It was a windfall for the rest of the Spaniards. Jews who converted to Christianity were able to stay in Spain, but some were tried by a religious court called the "Inquisition," and, if they were found guilty of not being sincere Christians, they were burned alive. That was the opposite of what real Christianity stands for, but most people didn't question the rulers and priests who were in command.

So anti-Semitism stayed in the air. It was still mainly about that nonconformism. Then, in 1517, Martin Luther came into conflict with the Catholic Church and things got complicated. The Catholics, and each of the new Protestant sects, seemed to believe that they alone had the only true religion; that led to centuries of religious wars. Christians were killing Christians—as well as Jews. Hatred and killing in the name of God shouldn't make sense, but it seemed to to some

## Freedom of Conscience

In Virginia's Statute for Religious Freedom, Thomas Jefferson wrote: *Be it enacted by the General Assembly, that no man shall...suffer on account of his religious opinions or belief.*

John Adams, discussing the subject of religion and government was, as usual, blunt: *Congress shall never meddle with religion other than to say their own prayers.*

And James Madison said: *Religion and government will both exist in greater purity, the less they are mixed together.* The Founding Fathers were clear: ours was to be a nation founded on the idea of separation of church and state. There are no religious restrictions on citizenship in the Constitution.

## In the Name of Science

That pseudo-science of race led to another "science" called "eugenics," based on the idea that races should keep their blood pure by getting rid of problems. In the 1880s, Pennsylvania began sterilizing children who were said to be "feeble-minded." (*Sterilizing* means they were "made unable to have children themselves.") Indiana was the first state to pass a law forcing the sterilization of certain people who were thought undesirable. (That usually meant the retarded, or criminals, or, often, sexually active teenagers.) Another 31 states followed with sterilization laws. In California, some 17,000 people were sterilized, most of them immigrants. In Virginia, a 1924 sterilization law was challenged, taken to the U.S. Supreme Court—and upheld. In that case, *Buck* v. *Bell,* Carrie Buck had been sterilized because she was said to be retarded. Recent evidence suggests that was not even true. The Nazis used Virginia's law as a model. Under their sterilization act, thousands were made unable to have children.

GERMANS! DEFEND YOURSELVES! DO NOT BUY FROM JEWS! says the sign on this Jewish-owned store in Berlin. The Nazi boycott of Jewish businesses began on April 1, 1933. Shops were marked with a yellow Star of David. After 1939, German Jews had to wear the yellow star sewn onto their clothes, too.

**Troops force Polish Jews out of the Warsaw ghetto.**

people (who couldn't have been thinking deeply).

There was another factor that produced anti-Semitism. It was economic. Jews were often successful and provided competition. That may have made some people jealous or annoyed.

Then, toward the end of the 18th century, things began to change. After the French Revolution (in 1789), Jews, in one nation after another, were emancipated. They entered Europe's mainstream. People who had been locked in ghettoes were suddenly let out and began a period of great achievement. Especially in Germany, Austria, and Hungary, Jews flocked to the universities, and soon many of them were doctors, lawyers, bankers, store owners, newspaper writers, musicians, teachers, and political leaders. Although Jews made up only about 1 percent of the German population, they won one-quarter of all Germany's Nobel prizes in the first third of the 20th century. Some Germans were proud of that achievement, but others saw it as a problem.

There was something else. It had to do with a science—at least, some people thought it was a science. It was racism, and today we think of it as a false, or pseudo- (SU-doe) science. But, in the 19th century, some thinkers (who believed in what they were doing) divided the world's peoples into races and then said that some races were better than others. They even said that race determines blood, and character, and brain size. They said that the Jews were an evil race that was polluting Aryan (white northern European) blood. They said that people of color were inferior to whites. Since this theory was supposed to be scientific, there were many who believed them.

Hitler used that idea of racism, and bad blood, and the old anti-Semitic virus to explain Germany's problems. It was convenient. Whatever was wrong must be the fault of the Jews. Inflation? Depression? The Treaty of Versailles? It was all because of the Jews, said Hitler. He was an astonishing speaker. People were swept up by his words; they believed

The start of the journey for most eastern European Jews, like these people from Cracow in Poland, was a filthy, crowded train journey in a boxcar. The luckier ones ended up in camps where they had to work for the German war effort, such as at this airfield.

him. It was easier than blaming themselves.

Besides, many Jews had good jobs and nice homes. All their property was inviting. Hitler was soon giving it away.

Germany went farther down the road of wickedness than any nation in history. The Nazis used the technology of the modern world for purposes of murder. They built factories for killing. Then they hunted down the Jews of Europe, packed them in railroad cars, and sent them to be slaughtered. They didn't just kill Jews. Hitler hated Slavs (who lived in eastern Europe), gypsies, people who were crippled, and anyone who didn't agree with him. The Nazis killed as many of those people as they could. They enslaved others. It made Hitler and his terror troops feel powerful (and it set an example for other dictators in the future). Because of what was happening to the Jews and Hitler's other victims, all of Europe shivered. People knew that after the Jews were gone it could happen to them.

"The removal and transportation of Europe's Jews was a fact known to every inhabitant of the continent," says John Keegan, a historian of the Second World War. "Their disappearance defined the barbaric ruthlessness of Nazi rule…and warned that what had been done to one people might be done to another."

## Guests or Prisoners?

After 1943 (until war's end), no Jews entered the United States except for 874 "guests of the president" who were denied visas, sent to an internment camp in Oswego, New York, kept behind barbed wire, and told they would have to leave the country as soon as the war was over. Some had close relatives in the U.S. One refugee, whose paralyzed wife lived on Long Island, could not visit her even at holiday time.

More than 55,000 immigrant quota spots for eastern Europeans went unfilled in 1944. During the war years, about 100,000 German prisoners of war—mostly Nazi soldiers—were safe in the United States.

*Visiting through the barbed wire at Oswego.*

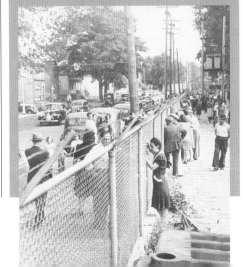

# Arrival in Auschwitz

Auschwitz (OWSH-vits) had been a Polish military barracks, but in 1940 it was turned into a concentration camp. Two years later, gas chambers and furnaces (for killing purposes) were added at a section of the camp called Birkenau. By this time Hitler was frantically rounding up Jews from across Europe; Auschwitz, because it was on a major railroad line between Cracow (in Poland) and Vienna (in Austria), was where most were sent. Day and night, sealed trains arrived from Holland, France, Austria, Czechoslovakia, Yugoslavia, Italy, and other European countries. Auschwitz grew to encompass 40 square miles.

The Wiesels arrived in 1944 on a train from Hungary. One of the family survived: a son named Elie. He wrote a book called Night that tells what happened to him. Here is some of it.

The cherished objects we had brought with us thus far were left behind in the train, and with them, at last, our illusions.

Every two yards or so an SS man held his tommy gun trained on us. Hand in hand we followed the crowd.

An SS noncommissioned officer came to meet us, a truncheon in his hand. He gave the order:

"Men to the left! Women to the right!"

Eight words spoken quietly, indifferently, without emotion. Eight short, simple words. Yet that was the moment when I parted from my mother. I had not had time to think, but already I felt the pressure of my father's hand: we were alone. For a part of a second I glimpsed my mother and my sisters moving away to the right. Tzipora held Mother's hand. I saw them disappear into my distance; my mother was stroking my sister's fair hair, as though to protect her, while I walked on with my father and the other men. And I did not know that in that place, at that moment, I was parting from my mother and Tzipora forever. I went on walking. My father held on to my hand.

Children at the camps were photographed in prison uniform so they could be identified if they escaped. Few lived long enough to try.

Behind me, an old man fell to the ground. Near him was an SS man, putting his revolver back in its holster.

My hand shifted to my father's arm. I had one thought—not to lose him. Not to be left alone.

The SS officers gave the order: "Form fives!"

Commotion. At all costs we must keep together.

"Here, kid, how old are you?"

It was one of the prisoners who asked me this. I could not see his face, but his voice was tense and weary.

"I'm not quite fifteen yet."

"No. Eighteen."

"But I'm not," I said. "Fifteen."

"Fool. Listen to what I say."

Then he questioned my father, who replied: "Fifty."

The other grew more furious than ever.

"No, not fifty. Forty. Do you understand? Eighteen and forty."

He disappeared into the night shadows. A second man came up, spitting oaths at us.

"What have you come here for, you sons of bitches? What are you doing here, eh?"

Someone dared to answer him. "What do you think? Do you suppose we've come here for our pleasure? Do you think we asked to come?"

A little more, and the man would have killed him.

"You shut your trap, you filthy swine, or I'll squash you right now! You'd have done better to have hanged yourselves where you were than to come here. Didn't you know what was in store for you at Auschwitz? Haven't you heard about it? In 1944?"

No, we had not heard. No one had told us.

Did all this have anything to do with the United States?

That is a good question.

Suppose you see someone beating up someone else. Really beating her up. She is going to end up in the hospital, or maybe dead.

What do you do? This isn't your fight. If you try to break it up you almost certainly will get slugged. Should you call the police? Should you stay out of it? If someone is killed it won't be your fault. Or will it?

Are we responsible for others? Do you agree that "He who permits evil, commits evil"?

In 1939, 20,000 children—all under 14—were in danger in Germany. Hitler wished to get rid of them. He was willing to let them leave the country. Many were Jewish; some were not. Quakers, Jews, Catholics, and members of other American church

groups agreed to take responsibility for them. It would not cost the government any money. Surely America would accept them.

This is the land of promise. The land built on a spirit of generosity. The land that, from the days of the Pilgrims, has been a place of refuge for the persecuted of other nations.

*Top left:* laborers at the camp at Buchenwald. Many starved to death or were killed when too weak to work. *Top right:* inmates in an Austrian camp where the Nazis were said to perform "scientific" experiments on human beings. *Center:* a gas chamber at Maidanek, in Poland. New arrivals were told to undress for showers; poison gas came out of the showerheads. *Left:* a box full of the wedding rings that all were made to remove.

121

Many Jews and opponents of the Nazis did escape, some to the United States. Among them were pianist Rudolf Serkin *(below)* and philosopher and writer Hannah Arendt *(above),* who wrote an important book about Hitler and fascism called *The Banality of Evil.*

**The League** of Nations gave Jews the right to buy land in Palestine, but the British wouldn't let them in. In 1942, the ship *Struma,* with 769 Jewish refugees aboard, was turned away. It sank in the Bosphorus (a Turkish waterway separating Europe and Asia); only one passenger survived.

Those who had founded this nation, and written its Constitution, had been clear about it. Although they were much alike—white, male, Protestant, and of English descent—the Founders didn't limit the nation to people like themselves. For they were unselfish in spirit and very wise. They believed they were creating something new on earth, a generous nation that would find strength in diversity. A nation that would take peoples from all over the world and allow them to become a new people—an American people—more varied in its roots than any before it.

The Founders offered the gift of citizenship, not just to their kinsmen, not just to the strong, or the handsome, or the rich, but fully and equally to all who came here to live.

The nation grew, and its citizens understood what was intended. Under the Statue of Liberty they carved the words *Give me your tired, your poor, your huddled masses yearning to breathe free.* Men, women, and children—from all over the world—came to this "promised land." Many were *refugees*—people fleeing tyranny and persecution.

Of course the children Hitler was threatening with death would be welcome in America. Or would they?

There was another tradition here. It was not the tradition of Jefferson, Washington, and Madison. It was a spirit of greed and selfishness.

It was that selfish spirit that had caused Alien and Sedition acts to be passed soon after the nation was founded. It was that spirit that had caused men to rise in Congress and say that slavery was a "positive good." It was the spirit behind the Know-Nothing Party and the nativists. It was the spirit of the Ku Klux Klan and the only-one-race-allowed country club. It was mean-spirited. It was anti-American, but it was there.

Here is what Abraham Lincoln wrote in 1855:

> As a nation we began by declaring that "all men are created equal." We now practically read it, "all men are created equal except Negroes." When the Know-Nothings get control, it will read "all men are created equal except Negroes and foreigners and Catholics." When it comes to this, I shall prefer emigrating to some country where they make no pretense of loving liberty.

The Imperial Wizard of the Ku Klux Klan, in 1923, said: *Negroes, Catholics, and Jews are the undesirable elements in America.* The Imperial Wizard was a bigot, but some people listened to him. They didn't know their history. Maybe they hadn't read the famous letter George Washington wrote the Jews of Newport, Rhode Island. In it, he said: *The government of the United States…gives to bigotry no sanction, to persecution no assistance.*

In 1924, Congress passed a racist immigration bill. Its aim was to keep Asians, Jews, blacks, and people who can't speak English out of America.

Anti-Semitism and xenophobia (zen-uh-FO-bee-ya—"anti-foreign-ism") had infected some Americans. Some of the people with the disease were in Congress, the State Department, and other government offices. Did they realize they were being un-American?

Most Americans are hospitable. Eighty-five newspapers wrote editorials urging Congress to pass a bill letting in those 20,000 children from Germany. Citizens offered their homes to the young refugees. Leaders of church, labor, and social organizations spoke out. But not loudly enough.

The head of a powerful group, the American Coalition of Patriotic Societies, told Congress to "protect the youth of America from this foreign invasion." He shouted the message of the racists. There was fear in the world, and a depression, and Congress listened.

Does this have anything to do with you? Isn't anti-Semitism a Jewish problem? No. It is a human problem. People who hate become hateful. A nation that allows bigotry and persecution is diminished by it. In 1939, the U.S. government gave sanction to bigotry and assistance to persecution. Those children were not allowed into the United States.

Hitler now knew that no one would rescue the children. He felt free to build death camps. That is where most of those 20,000 children—and a girl named Anne Frank—ended their lives.

## The *St. Louis* Is Turned Back

Liane Reif-Lehrer, pictured here *(left)* in 1938 with her mother and brother, was born in Vienna, Austria, in 1934. These are her words:

*I should have been a normal little girl, happy with my special doll, my big brother (who thought me a noisy nuisance but loved me anyway), and my doting parents. But the world around me was going mad, and the life I should have had was not to be.*

Liane's father was a dentist, but the Nazis would not let him or other Jews work. One day he was found dead at the bottom of a stairwell. Did he commit suicide or was he murdered? Liane has never been quite sure.

She was not yet five when she, her mother, her brother, and 934 other Jewish passengers set sail for Cuba from the port of Hamburg, Germany, on the luxury liner *St. Louis*. The passengers all had Cuban entry permits, and most had quota numbers that would have let them into the United States eventually. But while they were at sea, Cuba changed its immigration policy. Most of the passengers were not allowed off the ship.

After days of frantic negotiations, the *St. Louis* was forced to leave Cuba. The captain didn't want to take the Jewish passengers back to Germany; he knew what would happen to them there. He headed for Miami. Telegrams were sent to President Roosevelt asking him to grant asylum to the refugees. The telegrams were not answered. A U.S. Coast Guard boat stayed close to the *St. Louis* to make sure no passengers jumped overboard and tried to swim ashore. Finally, the captain could do nothing; he headed back to Europe. Here are Liane's words again:

*My mother and brother and I were among the passengers who survived—about a fourth of those on the ship. We were sent back to Europe and given haven in France, only to find the Nazis at our doorstep again a few months later. But somehow we managed to get to the U.S. in 1941. I was seven, a wide-eyed, bewildered girl, greeted by New York children playing street games to wartime hate ditties. I remember a particularly popular one: "Whistle while you work, Hitler is a jerk, Mussolini is a meanie, and the Japs are worse."*

*I tried to explain that some Germans were good and some bad. On more than one occasion my "non-groupy" response earned me the wrath of the parents, who did not hesitate to suggest that I "go back to where I came from." It hurts even now when I remember the tone with which those words were delivered.*

Dr. Liane Reif-Lehrer moved to Massachusetts and became a research scientist, a mother, and an American.

# 28 War and the Scientists

**Albert Einstein** was a theoretical physicist who ranks with Galileo and Newton as one of the great thinkers who have helped us understand the universe. He published his theories of relativity in 1905 and 1916. In 1921 he won a Nobel prize. In 1933 he wrote *Why War?* with Sigmund Freud (the father of psychoanalysis, and also a Jew).

Einstein sought U.S. citizenship in 1935; immigration laws forced him to leave the country and then reenter it. So Einstein spent nine days in Bermuda with his family. He used this photo on his new immigration visa.

In California in 1933, Einstein mused that on a bike you have to keep moving or you lose your balance, just as in life.

A. D. 1939

Immigrant identification card No. 831234 issued

There were some people who felt they had to see Roosevelt. But the president couldn't see everyone who wanted to see him—especially with a war on.

It was a group of scientists. They had something very important to tell the president. How could they get to him? If they had gone to Mrs. Roosevelt they might have had no problem. But they didn't think of that. They met and planned and worried.

Then someone got a bright idea. There was one scientist whom Roosevelt would listen to. Almost anyone in the world would listen to him. He was Albert Einstein, and he was the greatest scientist of the 20th century and one of the greatest scientists of all time. He had discovered the theory of relativity. That theory changed the way science looks at the world.

Einstein was born in Germany. Because he was Jewish he had to escape from that country, and he did. He became a fellow of the Institute for Advanced Study in Princeton, New Jersey, and an American citizen. Other scientists fled the evil regimes in Germany and Italy, too. Hitler lost their fine minds and talents. Britain and the United States gained them.

Some of those scientists knew that the Germans were working on a secret weapon. It was more powerful than anything the world had ever known. If the Germans developed it, they would probably win the war and rule the world. Roosevelt had to be told.

Italian American physicist Enrico Fermi with ceramic artist Maria Martinez, at San Ildefonso near Los Alamos in New Mexico, where the secret research took place.

Leo Szilard (SILL-ard), a Hungarian-born physicist, figured out that when a nucleus breaks apart it can start a chain reaction splitting other nuclei and setting off an enormous explosion. That's called nuclear fission.

But scientists who talked of secret weapons sounded like dreamers. Roosevelt was busy with important practical matters. He needed to strengthen the army and navy. He needed warships and carriers and tanks and planes. He had a depression to fight, too. Secret weapons? Super bombs? Wasn't that the stuff of science fiction?

Einstein's friend, Leo Szilard, urged him to write a letter to the president. Then Szilard convinced Alexander Sachs, a businessman and New Deal advisor, to deliver the letter. Sachs told FDR about the Germans' secret weapon. The president didn't seem to be paying attention. He must have had all those other things on his mind. Sachs was desperate. How could he get the president to pay attention?

Finally Sachs remembered that Roosevelt loved history. He used that knowledge. He told Roosevelt that the French emperor Napoleon was fighting the British when he was told about an American inventor, Robert Fulton, who had built a ship powered by steam. It could carry troops. Napoleon didn't pay attention. Steam power? All he knew about was sails. Roosevelt realized that if Napoleon had listened he might have been able to invade England and win his war.

Roosevelt didn't want to make the mistake Napoleon had made. He was ready to listen to Sachs. He was ready to read Einstein's letter. He decided that the United States should work on the secret weapon and try to develop it before the Germans did.

It was an enormous decision. It would be very costly. It was a race against time. The scientists told Roosevelt that they intended to split tiny particles of matter—the nuclei of atoms—and that would release vast amounts of energy.

They could use that energy to make the most powerful weapon the world had ever seen.

Roosevelt was convinced. The president made the decision to let the scientists go ahead with their plans. The project was top secret. Not even the vice president knew about it.

J. Robert Oppenheimer led the Manhattan Project, based on an isolated mesa in New Mexico.

**Einstein** regretted his part in the atom bomb's development. "I made one great mistake in my life," he said, "when I signed the letter to President Roosevelt recommending that atom bombs be made… but there was some justification—the danger that the Germans would make them." Chapter 43 has some clues as to why he changed his mind.

Not Yummy: In a squash court under a grandstand at the University of Chicago, Enrico Fermi, Leo Szilard, and some other physicists layered uranium and graphite into a 24-foot high sandwich. In 1942 it produced the world's first controlled nuclear chain reaction. That was a mighty powerful sandwich!

125

# 29 Fighting Wolves

In an illustration for an anti-Axis propaganda film, *The Fruits of Aggression,* Hitler, Mussolini, and Tojo lick their lips and slice up a juicy watermelon world.

You are probably wondering how three nations— Germany, Italy, and Japan—could be a threat to the whole world. Have you ever thought about how a wolf terrorizes a flock of sheep? A lone wolf doesn't attack a big flock. He picks them off one by one. Give him enough time and he can kill them all.

Germany, Italy, and Japan were wolves. They were powerful. They thought they could devour the world's nations, one by one. They believed most other countries—especially the democracies—were weaklings.

They had good reason to believe that. In a democracy, everyone's ideas are heard. Sometimes democracies have a hard time acting quickly, because so many individuals and groups are debating each other. In the 1930s there were strong *isolationist* voices in America. They said that the oceans—the Pacific and the Atlantic—protected us from danger. They said we didn't

*Isolate* means to "separate from others." Isolationists believe a nation should stay out of world affairs. Some of the World War II isolationists were the same people who prevented the United States from joining the League of Nations after the Great War.

War in Europe suddenly made the Atlantic seem narrower. When the Germans invaded Poland, FDR said, "It has come at last. God help us all."

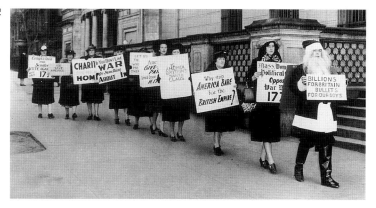

need to pay attention to what was going on in the rest of the world. Some of the isolationists were selfish. They didn't even want to help victims of the war.

Others who were *pacifists* didn't think it right to fight any war. They believed that if we behaved peacefully others might do the same.

Still others—in the military—were attached to old ways of thinking. They thought that battleships could protect us. Our battleships were huge. Some were 800 feet long. Imagine three football fields. (A football field is 300 feet long, so chop off a bit.) Float that picture, and add a crew of about 2,800 men, and guns that fire shells 20 miles or more, which was farther than any other weapon of the time. Battleships were much feared.

A few voices disagreed. They said that air power had changed all the rules of war. The oceans were no longer enough protection. Colonel William ("Billy") Mitchell of the U.S. Army said we needed to build up our air force. He said we needed to build aircraft carriers for our navy. An aircraft carrier is a floating airfield that carries its own airplanes. It is really big. (A bit longer than a battleship, and much wider.)

Mitchell pestered everyone: congressmen, army officers, naval officers, newspapermen. They got annoyed. Only a few people thought air power was important. Because he criticized his superiors in public, Mitchell was finally court-martialed and thrown out of the army. Some people said his ideas were laughable.

The official program of the Army–Navy football game, in November of 1941, showed a picture of the battleship *Arizona* with this caption: *Despite the claims of air enthusiasts no battleship has yet been sunk by bombs.* (That was meant as a slap at Billy Mitchell and those who agreed with him.)

**American mothers protest Lend-Lease, a program to lend equipment and raw materials to help the Allies fight the war in Europe. The mothers feared a war that might include their sons. But there was no escape from this war.**

*Top:* **Billy Mitchell was General Pershing's chief of air services in the Great War. He tried to prove the effects of air power by bombing obsolete warships (*right,* the *Alabama* in 1921), but no one was interested. They said it would cost too much.**

**In 1942, a young architect named Albert Speer took control of German industry. Arms and munitions production, until then feeble and inefficient, increased hugely.**

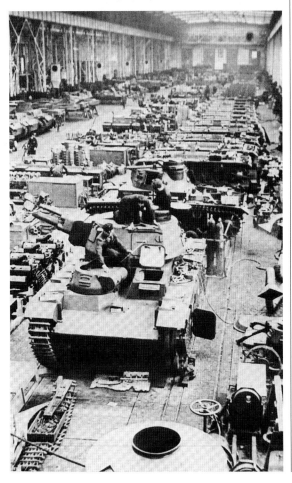

The United States had become weak militarily. We listened to the isolationists. It was partly for a good reason: we hated war. In 1941, our military force ranked 19th in the world, smaller than that of Belgium. At the same time, the armies and navies of Germany, Italy, and Japan had become strong.

Once its economy had recovered from the terrible effects of the Great War, Germany ignored the Versailles Treaty. It built a powerful army and air force. It turned out hundreds of submarines. Japan's naval fleet was awesome. Only a few people seemed concerned. "War could have been prevented," said a British statesman named Winston Churchill. "The malice of the wicked was reinforced by the weakness of the virtuous."

Roosevelt understood that the totalitarian powers were dangerous. He knew they hoped to rule the world. He took them seriously. The president wanted to build up our armed forces. It wasn't easy to fight the isolationists in Congress. He began by sending war supplies to England. That got our factories going. But we were still behind most other nations, and way behind Germany, Italy, and Japan, who were making plans to divide the world among themselves, and were known collectively as the *Axis*.

Militarily, we were weaklings. However, we had an advantage that the Axis powers didn't consider. It was the very thing they thought gave us a disadvantage. We were a democracy—a nation of free people. When free people set their minds to something, they become a powerful force. It took some time, but we became astonishingly strong.

Whether we wanted it or not, war was coming. We would win this war in our science laboratories and factories as well as on battlefields. The American people had been through a testing period that toughened them for a fight. The testing period was the Depression. We were used to tightening our belts and working hard. All of that, and more, was going to be necessary to win this war. It would be the most awful war in all of history.

# 30 Pearl Harbor

German tanks enter Czechoslovakia. Having to salute the invader was only the start of a conquered people's humiliation.

It is Sunday, December 7, 1941, and the sun is shining in Washington, D.C. To the morning churchgoers it seems just another bright winter day. At the White House, 31 guests are expected for lunch. There will be guests for dinner, too. None of that is unusual. The White House has become an informal, busy place since the Roosevelts moved in. That was more than eight years ago. FDR was reelected in 1936 and again in 1940. No other president has served more than two terms.

The American people (or most of them, anyway) have great faith in their president. These are dangerous times, and alarming things are happening all around the world. It is important to have a leader who can be trusted.

Hitler has steamrollered his way to some astounding victories. He has taken Austria, and Czechoslovakia, and Poland, and Denmark, and Norway, and Holland, and Belgium. One by one he picked off all those countries. The democracies let him do it. The democratic nations are so sick of war that they are willing to do anything to try to avoid it. What they have actually done is to make the war much worse than it would have been if they had stopped Hitler earlier.

It was when the Nazis marched into Poland that Britain and France finally responded. (Both nations had pledged their help to Poland if it was attacked.) Britain and France went to war.

German troops arrive in Prague, March 15, 1939, the day Hitler announced, "Czechoslovakia has ceased to exist."

The Polish army was hopelessly under-equipped and outdated; what could cavalry with lances do against a tank?

**129**

The Germans swept into Belgium and Holland at the same time. The Dutch city of Rotterdam resisted so strongly that Hitler bombed it to pieces out of spite. *Below:* a Belgian family stumbles through air-raid rubble. *Above:* the incredible sea rescue on the beaches of Dunkirk.

What they faced was something called *blitzkrieg*. That was the German word for "lightning war," which was a good description. The Germans sped their troops, tanks, and artillery across nations, obliterating them almost before they knew what was happening.

When superbly trained, well-equipped German forces raced into France, the country was overwhelmed. A large British–French army was trapped at Dunkirk, on the English Channel. It looked as if the soldiers were doomed. Then the British government sent out an appeal for boats. Soon fishermen, dentists, grocers, tugboat captains—anyone with a boat that could make it across the Channel—were sailing, back and forth, back and forth, ferrying soldiers to England. They saved an army, but they couldn't save France. On June 14, 1940, German tanks rolled into Paris.

Now almost the only European democracy left is Britain. And Britain is under attack. German bombers are pounding that small island. It looks as if it will go next. Everyone knows that the Nazis plan to invade England. Hitler's goal is world conquest. Americans have plenty of reason to worry.

In Asia, Japan has earlier occupied Manchuria (in 1931) and other parts of China (in 1937), and has just invaded French Indochina (now Vietnam, Laos, and Kampuchea) in July 1941. Japan is also threatening Thailand, the Philippines, and other Pacific nations. The United States sends letters to Japan objecting to this aggressive behavior, and finally imposes a total trade embargo and freezes Japanese funds in U.S. banks. Inside Japan there is a power struggle between civilian and military leaders. In the summer, Prime Minister Prince Fumimaro Konoe offers to meet with Roosevelt. The president doesn't understand the importance of the request. He refuses the meeting. Konoe resigns, and is replaced by army minister General Hideki Tojo. In Japan, the military is now supreme.

This very day, December 7, Secretary of State Cordell Hull receives a call from two Japanese diplomats. They ask for an emergency meeting. Hull expects to be given the Japanese government's answer to an American peace letter. At the White House, after lunch, the president works on his stamp collection (he began collecting stamps as a boy). His good friend Harry Hopkins is with him; so is his Scottie dog, Fala. They are relaxing. The phone rings. It is close to 2 P.M., Eastern time.

Secretary of the Navy Frank Knox is on the line. His voice is quivering. A message has just been received from Hawaii. This is what it says: AIR RAID ON PEARL HARBOR—THIS IS NOT A DRILL.

Pearl Harbor, in the Hawaiian Islands, is where the Pacific Fleet is headquartered! On Sunday morning ships were lined up in the harbor; their crews were having breakfast, or relaxing, or sleeping. At 7:02 A.M. Hawaiian time, a radar operator saw some blips on his screen. The operator didn't pay attention to them. He thought they were bombers he was expecting from the West Coast.

By 7:55 A.M. he knew better. That was when the first dive bombers—with the red Japanese sun painted on their sides—let their bombs

One week after France surrendered, Hitler was in Paris.

**Japan's** prime minister, General Hideki Tojo, called the attack on Pearl Harbor "a blow for the liberation of Asia."

The U.S.S. *Shaw* explodes during the Japanese raid on Pearl Harbor.

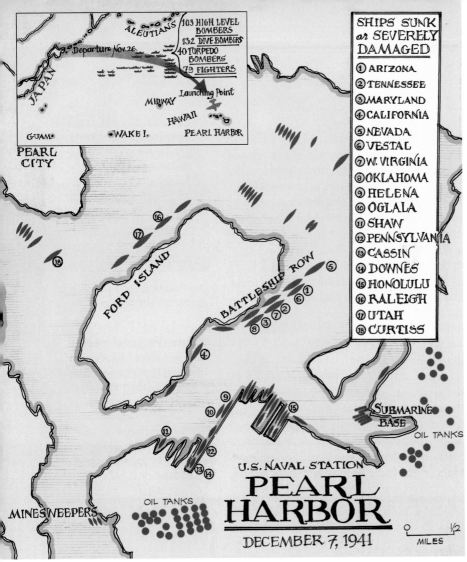

## SHIPS SUNK or SEVERELY DAMAGED

1. ARIZONA
2. TENNESSEE
3. MARYLAND
4. CALIFORNIA
5. NEVADA
6. VESTAL
7. W. VIRGINIA
8. OKLAHOMA
9. HELENA
10. OGLALA
11. SHAW
12. PENNSYLVANIA
13. CASSIN
14. DOWNES
15. HONOLULU
16. RALEIGH
17. UTAH
18. CURTISS

**103 HIGH LEVEL BOMBERS**
**132 DIVE BOMBERS**
**40 TORPEDO BOMBERS**
**79 FIGHTERS**

Departure Nov. 26.

Launching Point

MIDWAY
HAWAII
PEARL HARBOR

GUAM • WAKE I.

ALEUTIANS
JAPAN

PEARL CITY

FORD ISLAND

BATTLESHIP ROW

SUBMARINE BASE

OIL TANKS

OIL TANKS

MINESWEEPERS

## U.S. NAVAL STATION
# PEARL HARBOR
### DECEMBER 7, 1941

0    ½
MILES

loose on Battleship Row. The battleship *Arizona* gave off a tremendous roar, split in two, and slipped to the bottom of the harbor. That was just the beginning. Almost all the American planes on the island were damaged or destroyed. Most of the warships were crippled or sunk. And more than 2,400 soldiers, sailors, and civilians were killed.

At 2:05 P.M. Washington time (which is 8:05 A.M. Hawaiian time), the Japanese envoys arrive at Secretary of State Cordell Hull's door. They are part of an elaborate Japanese plan of deception, but their timing is off. Before the secretary can see them, his phone rings. It is the president, with the awful news of the Japanese attack. Now, Hull is from Tennessee, and he claims he has a Tennessee temper. The stories of what he says to those envoys will differ, but it is known that they leave quickly, with their heads down.

Hull is soon at the White House. So are many government and military officials. Newspaper reporters begin arriving. At 2:25 P.M. the story goes out on news wires to the American people. The reports from Pearl Harbor are humiliating, but that isn't the only bad news. This same day, the Japanese have attacked American and British bases at Midway, Wake Island, Guam, Hong Kong, Singapore, and the Philippines.

It is an astonishing act of aggression. But this president is at his best in a crisis. His advisers are angry, fearful, and frustrated. The president remains calm. He came into office during the nation's worst economic crisis. This is worse: the free world is fighting for survival.

**Nationalist China's** old walled capital city, Nanking, was captured by the Japanese in December of 1937. What happened is told in a book by an American writer, Iris Chang, called *The Rape of Nanking*. It's a story of the unspeakable horrors of war and of heroism, too.

Pearl Harbor is a disaster, but it may also be a lucky break. It unites the nation. There are no more isolationists. Everyone joins the war effort. Pearl Harbor shows the damage that air power can do. It changes people's thinking on that subject.

The next day the president goes before Congress. The Japanese have launched an "unprovoked and dastardly attack," he says. December 7 is "a date which will live in infamy." He asks Congress to declare war on Japan. Three days later, Japan's allies—Germany and Italy—declare war on the United States. It is World War II. It will make the awful First World War seem like a fire drill. The United States will fight this war against the wolves, maintain its democracy (as it did during the terrible Depression), and remain, as Abraham Lincoln said, the last best hope of earth.

*Infamy* (IN-fuh-me): it means "evil reputation."

Secretary Hull with Japanese ambassador Nomura *(left)* and special envoy Kurusu on their way to the White House, three weeks before the bombs fall on Pearl Harbor.

## Two Great Leaders Speak and Inspire

*Winston Churchill was an orator who could, and did, inspire a nation. This is part of what he said to the British people on June 4, 1940:*

"We shall go on to the end. . .we shall fight on the beaches, we shall fight on the landing grounds, we shall fight in the fields and in the streets, we shall fight in the hills; we shall never surrender. . . until in God's good time, the new world, with all its power and might, steps forth to the rescue and the liberation of the old."

*When it came to oratory, Franklin Delano Roosevelt was a match for Churchill or anyone. He liked to talk to the American people—as if he were a friend sitting in their living rooms—in radio broadcasts called "fireside chats." Usually those chats were filled with humor, but on February 9, 1942 he didn't have anything funny to say:*

"We are now in this war. We are all in it—all the way. Every single man, woman, and child is a partner in the most tremendous undertaking of our American history....On the road ahead there lies hard work—grueling work—day and night, every hour and every minute. I was about to add that ahead there lies sacrifice for all of us. But it is not correct to use that word. The United States does not consider it a sacrifice to do all one can, to give one's best to our nation, when the nation is fighting for its existence and its future life....

"The true goal we seek is far above and beyond the ugly field of battle. When we resort to force, as now we must, we are determined that this force shall be directed toward the ultimate good as well as against immediate evil. *We Americans are not destroyers; we are builders.*

"We are now in the midst of a war, not for conquest, not for vengeance, but for a world in which this nation, and all that this nation represents, will be safe for our children....We are going to win the war and we are going to win the peace that follows.

"And in the dark hours of this day—and through dark days that may be yet to come—we will know that the vast majority of the members of the human race are on our side. Many of them are fighting with us. All of them are praying for us. For, in representing our case, we represent theirs as well—our hope and their hope for liberty under God."

133

# 31 Taking Sides

President Roosevelt said Four Freedoms were essential for world peace: Freedom of speech, Freedom of religion, Freedom from want, and Freedom from fear.

**After their first meeting, Churchill got a cable from FDR: "It is fun to be in the same decade with you."**

**FDR smoked** cigarettes through an extra-long cigarette holder, and Winston Churchill puffed on an ever-present cigar. Few people then knew that smoking shortens lives and increases the risk of disease.

*Berlin, Rome, and Tokyo are the capitals of which nations?*

This is how the war was fought:

On one side was the Berlin–Rome–Tokyo Axis led by Adolf Hitler, Benito Mussolini, and Japan's premier, General Hideki Tojo.

On the other side were three major Allied forces. Who were they? Who were their leaders?

President Franklin Delano Roosevelt represented the United States. His was already a voice of freedom respected all over the world.

Britain, the second Allied power, was led by a man with a pudgy baby face. His name was Winston Churchill, and, like Roosevelt, he had a powerful voice and was inspiring when he spoke.

Churchill had an American mother and a father who was a British lord. When he was young he was a poor student, but he got better. He went to Sandhurst—the British West Point—and became an army officer, a good one. He got medals for bravery. Then he became a newspaper reporter, learned to pilot a plane, wrote history books, entered politics, and became a member of Britain's Parliament. He was one of the first Englishmen to see the danger of Hitler's Nazi Party and to speak against it. That was when most people in England and America were

**The Russians were stunned when Hitler invaded. The Nazi–Soviet Pact was dead, and they had a new role as Allies.**

134

acting like ostriches. They buried their heads in the sand, closed their ears, and didn't want to hear anything about war.

The third Allied power? Was it France? No. France was under German control. (However, as you know, a free French army was saved at Dunkirk. It was led by General Charles de Gaulle, and it did fight with the Allies.) How about China? Was China the third power? No. China was fighting Japan. And China was in turmoil. Civil war between the Communists and the Nationalists had broken out in China in the 1930s. That war wouldn't be finally decided until 1949: the Communists would win.

You may have a hard time believing who the third Allied power was, but here it is: Soviet Russia (the U.S.S.R.). Russia's leader, in 1941, was dictator Joseph Stalin. He was head of the Soviet Communist Party. He ruled Russia using secret police and terror. Many of his own people hated him. But others were fooled by Stalin. Roosevelt may have been one of them. Dictators often have charm, and Joe Stalin had a lot of charm—when he wanted. But what mattered was that he was fighting Hitler and so were we. As Winston Churchill said, "If Hitler invaded Hell I would make at least a favorable reference to the Devil in the House of Commons."

Russia, however, didn't start out on the Allied team. Here is some background.

In 1939, Hitler and Stalin signed a friendship pact. They said they would not fight each other. They made plans together to march into Poland—one from the east, the other from the west—and to gobble up that nation. They did it. Poland was squashed and divided.

Before the Nazi army marched into Poland, Hitler told his generals:

*The victor will not be asked afterward whether or not he told the truth. In starting and waging war it is not right that matters but victory. Close your hearts to pity! Act brutally!…The stronger is in the right.*

His generals did as they were told.

That was when France and England finally realized that they couldn't avoid war—although now it would be a difficult one. They had let Germany build a huge military force. At the same time, the free nations had cut their armies and navies. There wasn't a lot anyone could do when Germany marched armies into Belgium, Holland, Luxembourg, and France. The Nazis were winning everywhere.

The German air force—the Luftwaffe (LOOFT-vah-fuh)—soon began dropping bombs on England—tons and tons of bombs.

FDR couldn't stand the French leader Charles de Gaulle. He called him "a nut." But De Gaulle was a good general and kept underground resistance going in France throughout the German occupation.

In August 1940, the first German bombs fell on London. Night bombing of London—"the Blitz"—began in September and went on until June. Londoners, led by tough, resolute Churchill, stuck it out through the "Battle of Britain."

Then Hitler made some stupid moves. First, he went into Greece and Yugoslavia, where his forces faced some heroic fighters. That stopped Germany for a while. Then Hitler double-crossed Stalin. He decided to invade Russia. That had been his plan all along. He had even written a book, called *Mein Kampf* (it means "my struggle" in German), that told all about his goal of world domination. "No human being has ever declared or recorded what he wanted to do more often than me," he said.

Anyone who read Hitler's writings knew what he had planned. He said that Germans were the "master race," and that they needed more room, and other nations to serve them as slaves. Churchill and Roosevelt paid attention. They knew Hitler was capable and effective, as well as evil. For a long time, most other politicians just didn't take him seriously.

But Hitler didn't intend to share power. The Russians were a threat to his goal of world domination. So, when some of his generals told him not to go into Russia, he didn't listen. He needed oil and wheat and other resources from Russia. Besides, he thought Russia would be an easy victim. So did experts everywhere. The American secretary of war predicted that it would take Germany three months to conquer Russia.

Look at the map at the back of this book. The Germans prepared the most massive army ever assembled. Their

The damage done in London by the fires the bombs caused was as bad as their explosive effect. The great cathedral of St. Paul's, seen here during the worst raid of the Blitz, survived intact.

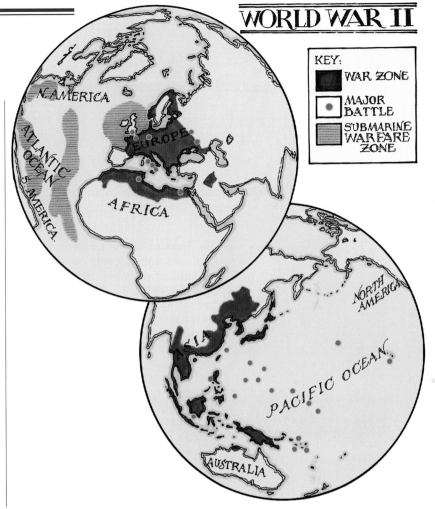

KEY:
- WAR ZONE
- MAJOR BATTLE
- SUBMARINE WARFARE ZONE

forces stretched from Finland to the Black Sea. They attacked with the latest in military equipment: tanks, bombs, and artillery.

At first, the Germans had an easy time of it. The Russians weren't prepared; much of their military equipment was out of date. Hitler instructed the German army to turn Russia into a slave nation. The Nazis murdered millions of Russians.

Now look at the map again. Notice the size of Russia. Look at Moscow and Leningrad (which today is called by its old name, St. Petersburg). Those cities are very far north. They are cold places. Winter came early in the fall of 1941. The first snow fell in Moscow on October 2. The Germans weren't prepared for the cold. They got stuck in a Russian

*Left:* children outside what is left of their London home. Many city kids like these were "evacuated"—taken in by families in the country. Their white bags hold gas masks.

The Second World War was a truly global conflict, involving several continents and many nations and peoples (unlike World War I, which was fought largely in Europe and around the Mediterranean Sea).

**Russia's** winter had stopped Napoleon, too. Hitler should have remembered that.

137

Even the cleated caterpillar tracks of the German tanks *(above)* bogged down in the snow. One of the victors in Russia was winter.

**The Russian city of Leningrad was almost totally cut off from September 1941 until January 1943. People had no electricity or heat; water was contaminated because mains burst *(below:* collecting water from a broken main). Leningraders ate dogs and rats and Vaseline and made soup from the glue in furniture or wallpaper. Many died of hunger anyway.**

winter. It happened to be the coldest winter in 30 years. The temperature dropped to 60° below zero. The German army was far from home, and having a hard time getting supplies and food. German soldiers froze. German soldiers starved. So did Russians. It was a disaster for both sides. But the Russians were at home, and able to outlast the hungry, discouraged German army.

FDR sent his friend Harry Hopkins to Russia. "Give us anti-aircraft guns and aluminum and we can fight for three or four years," said Stalin. He was right. We sent guns, aluminum, food, tanks, planes, and more. The Russians gave their lives.

The Russians went all out in their fight against Nazi Germany. No nation fought harder.

No one knows how many Russians died in World War II. Some say 15 million. Some say more. No other country has ever suffered such war losses. Russia was our ally and friend during the world war. But Russia under Soviet communism was a dreadful place. Stalin was a vicious dictator. Stalin expected something for fighting Hitler. What he expected, and got, was domination over the other countries of eastern Europe. Could Hitler have been destroyed without Stalin's help? Perhaps not. Certainly it would have taken many, many more American and British lives.

# 32 World War

One officer mans the periscope in the control room of a U.S. submarine, about 1942.

**Sailors load machine-gun cartridge belts for dive bombers at Norfolk, Virginia.**

Billy Mitchell was right: air power changed war. In World War II more people were killed by bombs or pieces of shells (called "shrapnel") than by bullets. In World War II cities were bombed; huge civilian populations were massacred.

There was something else about air war: it made killing a mechanical act. Imagine being in the infantry. You see the enemy eye to eye; it makes you realize the enemy is just like you—human. Officers know that some soldiers are never able to pull their triggers. They are never able to murder—even to save themselves. But a bomber pilot doesn't see his victims. A bomb can't tell the difference between an enemy soldier and a child on her way to school. It will kill them both.

An enormous number of bombs were dropped—by both sides—during World War II. Billy Mitchell thought air power would eliminate the need for foot soldiers. He was wrong about that. There was still plenty of old-fashioned infantry fighting.

Look at the world map on page 137. World War II was truly a world war. Here are just a few of the places where American troops fought; see if you can find them in an atlas.

*France, Germany, Tunisia, Sicily, Italy, Morocco, Burma, Guam, Malaysia, Philippine Islands, Wake Island*

Now imagine you are a general and you are

**The United States drafted black men, but segregated them—and often assigned them to service jobs instead of combat units. These Negro Seabees were members of the Navy's construction battalions, volunteers chosen for their skill in building or engineering. They are shown here in training near Norfolk, Virginia, practicing landing tactics, around 1942.**

*Above left:* parachutes fill the sky as waves of paratroopers land in Holland during operations by the 1st Allied Airborne in September 1944. *Right:* one method of getting soldiers—along with their trucks and all their ammunition and supplies—across a river is with a kind of barge. This one in Burma is powered by ordinary outboard motors.

**U-boat** is the abbreviation for the German word *Unterseeboot*— "undersea boat."

A **torpedo** is like a giant bullet with a propeller that travels through water and can sink a ship.

planning a battle on a Pacific island. Suppose you want to get 15,000 men onto the island and surprise the enemy. How are you going to do it?

A parachute drop?

Maybe, but remember, parachutes make great targets. You'd be better off bringing them in by boat. Many of those islands don't have deep harbors, though. Big ships can't come in close.

Can the soldiers swim in?

Not with their guns and artillery and trucks and tanks and food and ammunition and medical supplies.

We're going to have to invent and develop new kinds of landing equipment and war gear. And we're going to have to do it very fast. We'll design huge landing craft that have big rooms—called "holds"— that can be flooded to form miniature lakes so that boats can zoom out. We'll design other landing ships that will carry tanks and trucks as well as men. We'll design *amphibious* (am-FIB-ee-us) vehicles that will go on land or water. One of the most useful—a truck that swims— will be called a "duck." Another new, tough vehicle—which can handle rough roads, mountain passes, and rutted fields—we'll call a "jeep."

We'll design superb submarines that can stay under water for months at a time. Then we'll design torpedoes and depth charges to destroy submarines. The Axis nations will be doing the same thing. Submarine warfare will be very important in this war. German subs are called "U-boats," and the Atlantic Ocean is full of them.

We're going to do amazing things in medical science so that disease and infection will no longer be the major causes of wartime deaths. The lives of many badly wounded men will be saved.

All through the war we will keep improving our weapons, planes, tanks, and armored vehicles. The Germans and Japanese have a head start on us. They have fine scientists and technicians. This war will become a race to see who can produce the best weapons fastest. The Germans are working on rockets—called V-1s and V-2s—that are devastating. Luckily, it will take most of the war to get them perfected. When they start shooting rockets at England there will be many, many deaths. (The V-2 rockets are being designed to hit the United States.) We are behind on rocket development. After the war, German rocket engineers will tell us they got many of their ideas by studying the work of our rocket expert Robert Goddard.

We know something that they don't suspect we know. They think they are smarter than we are. They are wrong. We have learned to read their most difficult codes. That will prove more valuable than almost anything else we do.

Have you ever tried writing in code? It's easy. Just put numbers in place of letters and you have a code. Armies have always needed codes. Suppose a general wants to tell a faraway commander to attack. He sends a messenger. But he wants his orders in code in case the messenger is caught. He certainly doesn't want the enemy to know his plans.

In George Washington's day, a screen was sometimes put over a piece of paper. There were holes in the screen. The secret message was the words that showed through the holes. Everything else was there to fool you.

During World War II, both sides moved huge armies and navies and tried to do it secretly. Most orders were sent by telegraph.

Getting from A to B. *Top left:* lowering a jeep from a Coast Guard assault transport into a landing craft. *Top right:* each of these tiny cars carries a real bomb. *Above:* an aerial photo of U.S. troops wading ashore from landing craft onto Morotai Island, between New Guinea and the Philippines.

**141**

A V-2 rocket prepared for launching. Nazi Germany's V-1 and V-2 rockets were the first long-range missiles—deadly and terrifying.

**Germany's** racial policies have caused many of its best scientists to flee the country. That helps the Allies and slows Germany's progress.

**When American** naval forces capture a German submarine off the coast of West Africa, they find a newly developed torpedo and a secret radio code on board. They pretend they have sunk the sub, so the Germans won't change the code.

Anyone could listen. So codes were vital. They became very complicated. The Germans and Japanese thought no one could possibly figure out their complex codes.

We cracked the Japanese secret code even before the war began. Solving the German military code was much harder. German coded messages were sent and received on special machines. Then a German tank was captured in Poland. It had a code machine inside. The machine was smuggled out of Poland to England. When it got to England no one could figure out how to work it. The English called the code machine "Enigma." An *enigma* is a puzzle. They put some of their best scientific and mathematical minds on the job of solving the puzzle. It was incredibly difficult. How they did it is a fascinating story. Several books have been written about it. You can find them in the library.

Once the code was broken, we knew almost everything the Axis powers were planning to do. Now we Allies had to pretend that we didn't know some things. We didn't want the codes to be changed.

## Cryptography Means Code Making

In World War II, code makers (who all seemed to be geniuses) created extraordinary code machines in order to write secret languages that would baffle the enemy. But code breakers were, if anything, even smarter than the code makers. Just about all the codes did get broken—except for one that stumped all the geniuses. No one could figure it out. Maybe that's because it happened to be a real language, spoken by real people, who were faster than any of the fancy machines.

The language was Navajo, and it was spoken by 420 marines who called themselves *Dineh*—the People. In western movies, Indians are usually known for their silence. These Native Americans did plenty of talking. They made up their own code using their own words: Hitler was *Daghailchiih* (mustache smeller), bombers were *jaysho* (buzzards), and bombs, *ayeshi* (eggs). Navajos landed on every major island in the Pacific. Major Howard Conner said, "Without the Navajos the marines would never have taken Iwo Jima." They were a secret weapon in the Pacific.

Two Navajo code breakers at work.

# 33 A Two-Front War

Tarawa, in the Gilbert Islands, where marines put up this lonely signpost, was a tiny spot in the Pacific. Yet it took bitter fighting to capture it.

**Western Europe** and the Far East (East Asia) were named by people who considered Jerusalem to be the center of the world. Western Europe is indeed west of Israel, and East Asia east of Israel—but to us they are the opposite. That is because the earth is a ball—which does make things confusing. As Robert Frost said of Christopher Columbus:

*Remember he had made the test*
*Finding the East by sailing West.*

Did you ever hear of Janus, the two-faced god of Roman mythology? *January* was named for Janus; he was the god of doorways and gates who looked in two directions at the same time.

During World War II the United States was like Janus. We had to look in two directions at the same time. We were fighting a two-ocean war. That was a terrible problem for our generals and admirals. How do you divide your forces? How do you protect two huge coasts from attack?

***Simultaneously*** (sy–mul-TAY-nee-us-lee) means "at the same time."

Looking west (to East Asia), the view was frightening. In the Pacific Theater the Japanese moved like lightning. (Military officers call a war region a "theater." Strange, but that's the way it is.) Their forces were well trained and well equipped. At the start, Japan's aggressive strategy seemed to work. Remember, on December 7 they didn't just bomb Pearl Harbor—they attacked a whole string of strategic spots, almost simultaneously! In just a few months the Japanese captured Thailand, the Philippine Islands, the Malay peninsula, Java, Burma,

In the first six months of war, under General Tojo *(left),* Japanese forces such as this machine-gun crew *(right)* overran more territory than any army since Napoleon's.

In May 1942, in the battle of the Coral Sea, both the U.S. and Japan suffered heavy losses: here the crew of the sinking aircraft carrier U.S.S. *Lexington* bail out frantically. But the Japanese lost two of their carriers and had to retreat.

## Black and White Blood

Charles R. Drew was uncommonly gifted. He was a star athlete (in football, basketball, baseball, and track!), a brilliant student at Amherst College, an outstanding doctor (he was a professor of medicine at Howard University), and the man who developed the idea of a blood bank for storing blood plasma (during World War II). In 1942, he organized the blood-bank programs for both the U.S. and Britain, and supervised the Red Cross's blood-donor program. Besides all that, he had an amiable personality—people liked him. But he was enraged that black blood and white blood were segregated in blood banks, and he spoke out against that absurdity. He was killed in a car accident. A myth has grown that because of his color, he was refused treatment at an all-white hospital. That is not true. What is true is that his talents were often frustrated by the idiocy of prejudice.

Dr. Charles R. Drew

Guam, Wake Island, the Gilbert Islands, Singapore, and Hong Kong. Check those places on a map and you'll see: the Japanese controlled East Asia. People in India and Australia were trembling. They thought they were next.

The European Theater wasn't any better. As you know, the Nazis controlled most of Europe. They even had troops in North Africa; the Mediterranean was a kind of Nazi sea.

So was the Atlantic Ocean. That was because of the German U-boats. England and Russia were desperate for help. The United States had to ship weapons, tanks, oil, and men across the Atlantic to Europe. But the U-boats seemed to be everywhere. In the first four months of 1942, almost 200 of our ships were sunk. One summer day, people in Virginia Beach, Virginia, watched in horror as a ship was torpedoed and sunk in sight of the beach. Ships were being sunk faster than they could be built. Each time a ship was torpedoed, American men drowned.

Somehow, people in this country didn't get discouraged. We were convinced we could win this war and we set about doing it. Dr. New Deal turned into Dr. Win the War. He became a great war president. No matter how gloomy things seemed, President Roosevelt remained confident and optimistic. He gave courage to the nation.

He had good people to work with. General George C. Marshall, his chief of staff, was a superb general, and modest. Someone said he had the wisdom of George Washington and the strategic sense of Robert E. Lee.

Before and after a U-boat sneak attack: targets sighted through the periscope *(right);* an Allied freighter, split in two by a torpedo *(above).*

**Dwight D. Eisenhower**

Tough and experienced Admiral Ernest J. King, chief of naval operations, did his job well. So did Admiral Chester W. Nimitz and generals Dwight D. Eisenhower, H. H. "Hap" Arnold, Douglas MacArthur, and others. Remember all the trouble Abraham Lincoln had with his generals? Roosevelt was lucky; the nation was lucky, too.

**Chester W. Nimitz**

But the first battles were grim. Admiral King warned, "The way to victory is long; the going will be hard." He was right. We started out as losers. Then things began to change. Maybe it was

*Above:* a water buffalo assault vessel near Guam. *Right:* the 165th Infantry reaches Makin atoll in 1943 (Tarawa was captured at the same time). The coral bottom makes for very hard wading.

**145**

U. S. S. R.

MONGOLIA

CHINA

MANCHURIA
1931-32

1936
1933

1937-38
1944

KOREA
1910

SAKHALIN
1905

KISKA
1942

ALEUTIAN
ISLANDS

JAPAN

MIDWAY
ISLAND

*Pacific Ocean*

CANTON
1944 1938

BURMA
1942

FORMOSA
1895

HONG KONG
HAINAN 1941
1939

FR. INDOCHINA 1941

WAKE
1941

PHILIPPINES
1942

GUAM
1941

THAILAND
1941

MALAYA
1942

EXTENT of JAPANESE EXPANSION 1942

NETHERLANDS EAST INDIES
1942

NEW GUINEA

EQUATOR

EXPANSION 1942

EXTENT of JAPANESE

KEY:
*Dates show year
conquered.*

GUADALCANAL

*Indian Ocean*

AUSTRALIA

JAPANESE EXPANSION

**1943:** An American PT (propeller-torpedo) boat (like the one above) is rammed by a Japanese destroyer. Two Americans are killed. Eleven others cling to the boat and then swim to a nearby island. Their commander carves a message in a coconut and gives it to friendly islanders, who bring help. The commander's name is John F. Kennedy.

because the Japanese got greedy. They didn't know when to stop. They thought they were invincible—which means "unbeatable." Nobody is unbeatable. We had been taking a pounding in the Pacific. But when we won three big victories, the Japanese learned to respect our fighting ability. The victories were in the Coral Sea, at Midway Island, and at Guadalcanal (all in 1942).

The Coral Sea battle wasn't exactly a victory. There was a series of mistakes on both sides—big mistakes. Our losses were heavier

146

than the enemy's. But we prevented them from capturing a strategic base in New Guinea, and that may have saved Australia from invasion.

The Japanese expected an easy win at tiny Midway Island. If they controlled that island they would control the air over Hawaii. Then, perhaps, they could attack our West Coast. In addition, they intended to destroy the ships in our fleet that had escaped Pearl Harbor—especially our aircraft carriers. Their plan was to lure us into a trap and surprise us. What they didn't know was that we could decode their secret messages. We knew of their plans. Still, they almost won. The battle over Midway was ferocious.

At first, things were awful for us. Forty-one of our torpedo bombers took off after the Japanese ships, and most were shot down. Then our dive bombers arrived, and destroyed four massive Japanese aircraft carriers. It was the first defeat the Japanese navy had suffered. And it was a battle that proved that air power would be the key to this war.

The battle for Guadalcanal was something else. If you hold on for a chapter I'll tell you about it. But before that you need to learn about something going on at home.

The battle of *Midway* lasted for two days in June of 1942. U.S. Navy bombers, like the one below (called a "hell diver" by the Japanese), sank a number of ships, including the cruiser *Mikuma* (*bottom*), caught refueling.

# 34 Forgetting the Constitution

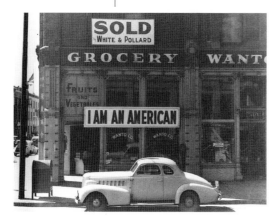

The American citizen who owned this store put up the sign the day after Pearl Harbor was bombed. Like so many others, he had to sell his business at a sacrifice price and go to a camp.

**All four** of the photographs on pages 148 and 149 are by Dorothea Lange, as are those on pages 85 and 200. What do you think Lange is saying in her work?

**The Japanese** internment camps on the West Coast, and the internment camp for Jews in Oswego, New York, were run by the same government agency. Even the food was the same.

Haruko Obata lived in a house in lovely, tree-shaded Berkeley, California. Her father was a professor at the University of California. Haruko was an American citizen. Like most Japanese Americans, she was proud of her Asian heritage, but she didn't approve of the ways of the warlords who ruled the Japanese empire. In school she studied the Constitution and its guarantees. She was happy to live in the land of liberty.

Then, one day, Haruko's world changed. Her father came home and told the family they were moving. They had just a few days to get ready. They could take only as much as they could carry. They might never again see the things they would leave behind. They were going to live—against their wishes—in a prisonlike camp.

What had they done? Just a minute, and I'll get to that. But first, imagine that you are Haruko. You have some hard decisions to make, and you need to make them quickly. What will you choose to take with you? Sorry, your dog can't go. You'll have to give her away. Books? Games? Toys? Not if

One girl was seven when her family was taken to a camp in the California desert. "Someone tied a numbered tag to my collar and to the duffel bag," she wrote. Nobody explained why they suddenly had to move.

they are heavy. No one knows exactly where this camp is. It may be very cold. Or hot. You won't be able to take much besides clothes. Your parents must sell the car, the house, and almost all their possessions; because they do it so quickly, they will get hardly anything for them.

You and your family are going to a camp that is surrounded by a barbed-wire fence. Armed guards stand in watchtowers. If someone tries to walk out into the desert he will be shot. What have you done that is so terrible? Why are you and your family in this prison camp?

You have not done anything wrong. Yes, you read that right. The Obatas have done nothing at all. They have been fine citizens.

But they are of Japanese descent, and the United States is at war with Japan. There is anti-Japanese hysteria in America, especially in California. Some of it is understandable. War is terrible. The Japanese government is horrible. But the Japanese in America have nothing to do with that. Some people don't understand that. Many authorities expect the Japanese to attack the West Coast. A Japanese submarine fires shells that land—harmlessly—near Los Angeles. People are terrified. There are rumors that Japanese-American fishermen are sending signals to Japanese ships and planes. There is no evidence for this, but in wartime, how can anyone be sure?

Reports of Japanese atrocities in Nanking, China, and elsewhere are horrible (and turn out to be true). But Japanese Americans have nothing to

A young woman named Miné Okubo was interned at Tanforan and then in Topaz, Utah. She drew pictures for a book about her life called *Citizen 13660*. The clothes the camps supplied never fit; the Utah mosquitoes were fierce; and the walls were so thin and badly built that quiet and privacy were impossible.

do with that, just as German Americans have nothing to do with the savagery in Nazi Germany.

Most Japanese Americans feel anguish. They love the United States, its opportunities and its inspiring vision. But they also take pride in their ancient Japanese heritage. For them, World War II is like a civil war.

In addition, the Japanese in America face a special problem. It is an old problem. It is racism. A racist law prevents Japanese immigrants from becoming citizens. However, anyone born here is automatically an American citizen. Two-thirds of the Japanese Americans are *Nisei*—the Japanese word for those born in America—and they are citizens. Racism has been part of America's history from the time of the first contact of Europeans and Native Americans. But so has the fight against racism. That clash—between bigotry and decency—is found in the human drama in every culture (and perhaps in every human heart).

Now the racists have something important on their side: it is the very real fear that war brings. There is something else here, too. It is greed. Japanese Americans have been industrious; their property is valuable. If they are put behind barbed wire, their property will have to be sold, and quickly, for much less than it is worth. Some people will profit mightily.

The first calls for internment (putting the Japanese in camps) come from newspaper columnists. Then a group of West Coast politicians join in. They include Earl Warren, who will later become chief justice of the Supreme Court. J. Edgar Hoover, head of the FBI, says quietly that internment is unnecessary; the FBI can handle surveillance of suspects. But Norman Thomas, leader of the American Socialist Party, is a lonely political figure when he speaks out forcefully, opposing internment.

The attorney general reminds the secretary of war that the Fourth Amendment protects citizens from "unreasonable searches and seizures." The 14th Amendment says "nor shall any State deprive any person of life, liberty or property without the due process of law." But we are at war, and the War Department is worried about "national security." The right of habeas corpus has been shelved in wartime before.

President Roosevelt issues Executive Order 9102. One hundred and twenty thousand Japanese Americans have a few days to get ready. They will be sent to 10 different internment camps.

Here is how Haruko Obata described her arrival at the Tanforan camp:

*When we arrived at Tanforan it was raining; it was so sad and depressing. The roadway was all mud, thick mud and our shoes would get stuck in mud when you walked outside. They gave us a horse stable the size of our dining room with a divided door where the horse put his head out—that was our sleeping quarters. There were two twin beds made of wood, bunk beds, and another bed on the opposite wall. It was supposed to be a couch but it was made of wood too. There was nothing else. Nothing. That one time I cried so much. That was the only time I cried; it was awful.*

There is much more to this story—much, much more. Mostly it is of a people who—as soon as they got settled—didn't cry. They did their best in a bad situation. They planted seeds and grew crops. They raised farm animals. They fed themselves and sent their surplus to support the war effort. They fixed up their sleeping quarters. They established schools, churches, recreational centers, newspapers, scout troops, baseball teams, and their own camp governments.

Some were let out of the camps to work in war factories. Many became soldiers. A Nisei regiment fighting in Europe won more commendations than any other regiment in the whole United States Army. Infantryman Harry Takagi explained:

*We were fighting for the rights of all Japanese-Americans. We set out to break every record in the army. If we failed, it would reflect discredit on all Japanese-Americans. We could not let that happen.*

More than 16,000 Nisei served in the Pacific, most in military intelligence work as interpreters. Some went behind enemy lines as American spies. Japanese-American women volunteered and served in the Woman's Army Corps, as army nurses, and in the Red Cross.

At first, people in the War Department objected to the idea of Nisei serving in the army. But, finally, President Roosevelt spoke up. He said:

*The principle on which this country was founded and by which it has always been governed is that Americanism is a matter of the mind and heart; Americanism is not, and never was, a matter of race or ancestry.*

Japanese-American soldiers, in Europe, being reviewed by Secretary of Defense James V. Forrestal.

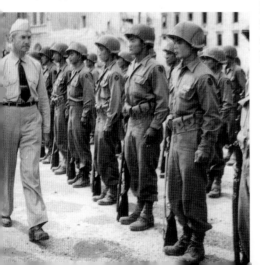

*If you don't know what habeas corpus is, see book 3 of A History of US.*

**They issued us army mess kits, the round metal kind that fold over, and plopped in scoops of canned Vienna sausage, canned string beans, steamed rice that had been cooked too long, and on top of the rice a serving of canned apricots.... Among the Japanese, of course, rice is never eaten with sweet foods, only with salty or savory foods. Few of us could eat such a mixture. But at this point no one dared protest. It would have been impolite. I was horrified when I saw the apricot syrup seeping through my little mound of rice. I opened my mouth to complain. My mother jabbed me in the back to keep quiet. We moved on through the line and joined the others squatting in the lee of half-raised walls, dabbing courteously at what was, for almost everyone there, an inedible concoction.**

**—JEANNE WAKATSUKI HOUSTON,
*FAREWELL TO MANZANAR***

**151**

The Hirano family with a photo of their other son in uniform. They were sent to Arizona.

Photographer Toyo Miyatake and his family were sent to Manzanar. He wasn't allowed a camera, so he made one and took secret pictures of life behind the barbed wire.

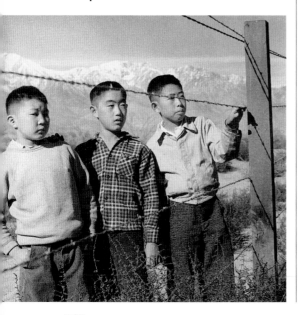

In the course of the war, 10 people were convicted of spying for Japan. All were white. Only one Japanese American was convicted of treason; she was Iva Ikuda Toguri, a graduate of UCLA, who was in Tokyo when the war began and couldn't get home. Toguri, known as Tokyo Rose, agreed to do propaganda broadcasting to avoid work in a munitions factory. She was paid $6.60 a month.

Eventually, the camps were closed and people went out and did their best to build new lives. It wasn't easy; they had lost all their possessions. Many still faced racism when they tried to find jobs and new homes.

Now, you may be thinking that racism is terrible, but that, really, it is only a problem for the people who are made to suffer. Don't be fooled. Hatred is a contagious disease; it spreads quickly. It is like the poison gas that both sides used during the First World War; when the wind changed, it blew back on the gassers.

No people is immune to the virus of hate. It is how they handle it that decides the kind of people they are. This nation was founded on the idea that *all men are created equal.* A group of women at Seneca Falls, New York, changed that to *all men and women are created equal.* That is what we believe. That is what this nation is all about.

> *We the People of the United States, in Order to form a more perfect Union, establish Justice, insure domestic Tranquillity, provide for the common defense, promote the general Welfare, and secure the Blessings of Liberty to ourselves and our Posterity, do ordain and establish this Constitution for the United States of America.*

Remember George Washington's words:

> *The government of the United States...gives to bigotry no sanction, to persecution no assistance.*

The more you read history, the more you will realize that the haters never win. Eventually, they get found out and put down. Often, unfortunately, it takes time.

Forty years after the end of the war, the American government officially apologized to the Japanese Americans for the terrible injustice done to them during World War II. Those who had been in the camps were given money in partial payment for their suffering. Today, when we Americans think back on the internment camps, we feel shame.

# 35 A Hot Island

**Admiral Ernest King was a stern, opinionated man who was hardly ever known to smile.**

General Eisenhower, who was a likable fellow, wrote in his diary in March of 1942: "One thing that might help win this war is to get someone to shoot King."

He was kidding. The King he was talking about was Admiral King. They disagreed on strategy. Do you think wars are easy to plan? Do you think the leaders all agree on how to go about it? Not often.

Most of our military leaders believed we should fight the war in Europe first and then the war in the Pacific. That made sense. Splitting your fighting forces is never a good idea. Besides, we didn't yet have enough supplies for two regions. But Admiral King said we couldn't just sit back and let the Japanese take over the Pacific. If we did, they would become so powerful that it would be almost impossible to win the war against them.

When the Japanese started building an airfield on an obscure island in the Solomon Island chain, Admiral King said that the United States needed to go on the

**Do you remember** when Thomas Jefferson wrote to James Madison about Patrick Henry? He said, "What we have to do, I think, is devotedly pray for his death." Patrick Henry was fighting some of Jefferson's ideas. Do you think Jefferson really wanted him dead?

**U.S. troops of the 160th Infantry Regiment going ashore from a landing boat at Guadalcanal. It seemed a paradise—until they got past the beach.**

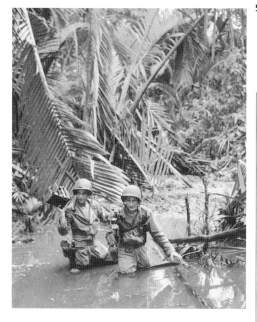

Jungle warfare can be as much of a fight with the jungle as with the enemy. Some men's clothing was damp so long, it rotted on their bodies.

U.S. Marine Raiders and their dogs, which were used for scouting and sending messages. One platoon had specially trained dogs that tracked down Japanese hiding deep in the jungle.

offensive. So far—in Europe and the Pacific—we had been defensive fighters. King insisted that we take that island from the Japanese. It was an important decision. Not everyone agreed with it. It would cost many lives—American and Japanese. It turned out to be a decision that helped win the war.

The obscure island was named Guadalcanal, and it was such an out-of-the-way place that no one even had a map of it. But it was the right spot for a war base.

Find Australia on a map. Then look north, to New Guinea. To the east of New Guinea are the Solomon Islands. Guadalcanal is one of the southernmost of the Solomons. Anyone who has an airbase on Guadalcanal can make big trouble for ships and airplanes going to Australia, New Zealand, or even Japan (which was where the American military planned to go eventually). We couldn't let the Japanese put planes on that island.

From the air, Guadalcanal looks like a heavenly place: very green, with high mountains, thick forests, and jungles filled with wild orchids and bright-feathered and beaked tropical birds. To that picture, add sandy beaches, coconut palms, and banana trees. Does it sound like a place you'd like to visit? Well, the men who fought there called it "a bloody, stinking hole."

Guadalcanal is intensely hot (note the nearness of the Equator). Its jungles are filled with monster leeches, huge scorpions, poisonous centipedes, giant ants, writhing snakes, skulking rats, snapping crocodiles, and hungry anopheles (uh-NOF-fuh-lees) mosquitoes (whose bites bring malaria).

During the Spanish–American War, Walter Reed, an American doctor, discovered that quinine (KWY-nine) cures malaria. Quinine comes from a plant found in Java. The Japanese had captured Java. Doctors were working on synthetic quinine, but not fast enough for the troops who fought on Guadalcanal.

Most of Guadalcanal is tropical rainforest—which means steamy, thick jungle, a whole lot of rain, and black, squishy mud that comes up to a man's knees. Where there isn't rainforest there is kunai (KOON-i) grass. Kunai grass blades are saw-toothed, stiff as wood, and often seven feet high. Walk through kunai grass and your arms and legs will be a mess of cuts. Do you get the picture? Does Guadalcanal sound like a great place to fight? Watch out, you can't even see the enemy hiding in the grass or behind those jungle trees.

The 1st Marine Division landed in August of 1942. Marines are trained to fight on land or sea. The 1st Marine Division was a proud division—specially trained, and tough. They needed that toughness. Guadalcanal was one of the hardest-fought battles in history. Remember the back-and-forth slugfest at Gettysburg? This one was worse. It went on for six months. It combined jungle fighting with terrible sea and air battles.

At first, things seemed easy. The marines surprised the Japanese on the island, who were mostly construction crews building an airfield. The marines captured the airfield. They named it Henderson Field, after a pilot who had been killed at Midway Island. At last, said President Roosevelt, we have a toehold in the Pacific."

*Above:* Machine gunners in the jungle. *Below:* The fight for Henderson Field, the main objective of the entire battle of Guadalcanal. By the end, Japan had lost 600 aircraft and 24 warships.

Words made up from initial letters, like SNAFU, are called "acronyms." Some other acronyms are WASP ("white Anglo-Saxon Protestant") and NOW (National Organization for Women). Do you know other acronyms?

First Lt. Thomas J. "Stumpy" Stanley became a company commander in the 1st Marine Division. "We thought highly of Stumpy and respected him greatly," wrote E. B. Sledge in a book about the Pacific war called *With the Old Breed*. Tom Stanley was my brother-in-law (and a real hero).

The Japanese were determined to knock that toe into the sea. We wanted to plant both feet on the island. To tell the story of what happened next would take a whole book. Here is some of it:

Let's begin with the military word for a mistake. It is SNAFU, a combination of letters for *Situation Normal, All Fouled Up*. It means that someone goofed.

Who goofed on Guadalcanal? Both sides. It happens all the time in warfare. The pressure and fear of battle often lead to mistakes. Most of our soldiers and even our officers were amateurs. They had not fought in a war before. They had to learn on the job.

One captain, unloading marines onto the beach, didn't want to risk a Japanese attack on his ships. So he pulled out before the loading was finished, taking supplies and U.S. marines with him. He stranded the marines already on the island. That was just one of the goofs.

The Japanese officers matched our snafus. They were too sure of themselves. An old Chinese proverb says, "A lion uses all his strength to fight a rabbit." The Japanese were lions in 1942, but they must not have heard of that proverb. They kept sending small forces to Guadalcanal. They thought Japanese fighters were unbeatable. They thought Americans were not good fighters. They were wrong.

When the marines wiped out the first group of Japanese soldiers, their leader was so ashamed he committed suicide. The next Japanese commander arrived on the island with a starched white uniform in his trunk. It was for the surrender ceremony he expected to conduct. After he and his men were destroyed, a marine found the trunk and dressed up in his uniform.

In six months, the marines, and the army units that came to fight with them, lost 1,598 men on Guadalcanal. Japanese war records show an incredible 23,800 deaths. Many Japanese deaths came in suicidal charges. Surrender was considered shameful. The Japanese also suffered many deaths from tropical disease. Our medical care was much better.

Most of the battle for Guadalcanal was fought at sea. There the statistics were more even. Each side lost 24 big ships and many smaller ones. The water near Guadalcanal was so full of sunken ships that it was called "Ironbottom Sound." It should have been called Graveyard Sound. About 20,000 American and Japanese sailors went down there with their ships.

The first of the sea fights—off nearby Savo Island—was the worst disaster in United States naval history. We were whipped. After that it was a seesaw of a conflict. It was bizarre: control switched every 12 hours. The Japanese were skilled fighters in the

The battles at Guadalcanal, at Bougainville, Tarawa, and in Papua and New Guinea turned marines into seasoned jungle fighters. These Raiders posed in front of a Japanese dugout on Bougainville, near Guadalcanal in the Solomon Islands.

dark; at night they were masters of water and air. During the night Japanese planes dropped bombs on Henderson Field; Japanese ships lobbed shells at the field.

In the mornings the Americans took over. Seabees (construction crews) repaired the holes in the airfield. Then our planes took off after Japanese ships and troops. Our pilots were superb during the daytime.

The battles on the island were ferocious. The Japanese were a brave foe. They had not lost a war in 400 years. But the marines outfought them. When it was all over, a doctor examining the marines wrote:

Of 36,000 Japanese soldiers who fought on Guadalcanal, only 12,000 returned home alive.

> The weight loss averaged about 20 pounds per man....Many of these patients reported being buried in foxholes, blown out of trees, blown through the air, or knocked out.

The important thing was that they didn't give up. They held Guadalcanal. The marines ended the myth that the Japanese were invincible.

Guadalcanal was a turning point in the war. We went from defense to offense. The Japanese went from offense to defense. A captured Japanese document said, "Guadalcanal Island...is the fork in the road which leads to victory for them or us." We took the right road. It would lead to Japan.

# 36 Axing the Axis

This poster of Rosie the Riveter doing war work later symbolized women's empowerment.

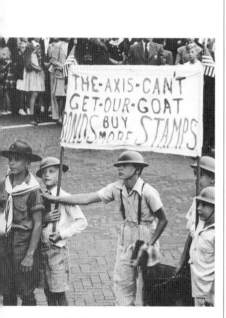

Defense stamps and war bonds were a way to lend the government money. You bought a stamp and stuck it in a book. A bookful of stamps added up to a bond. The government used your loan for war expenses; later you got the money back with interest. Here, Boy Scouts appeal to a large crowd during a parade in Ashland, Kentucky, in 1942.

"We have reached the end of the beginning," said Churchill, early in 1943. He was right.

The beginning was horrible. The Germans had perfected their *blitzkrieg* (that lightning attack with planes, tanks, and armies all charging together). The Japanese used the same tactic, and mowed down everyone in their way. The Allies were losing the war. The Axis seemed invincible. Then things began to change. This is what happened:

• In February 1943, Japan pulled out of Guadalcanal.

• That same month, we cracked the Nazi naval code, *Triton*. Now we knew where their submarines were. The Atlantic was full of U-boats,

Russian troops, in winter camouflage, advance. The Red Army pushed the Germans back from Moscow through the winter snows of 1941–1942.

American women threw them-selves into the war effort. *Left:* pol-ishing airplane nose cones at Willow Run. *Above:* Eastine Cowner, a former waitress, works as a scaler on the construction of the Liberty Ship S.S. *George Washington Carver* at the Kaiser shipyards in Richmond, California, 1943. Her job was to "scale," or clean and scrape off excess metal from the welded joints. Women also did many other non-military jobs usually held by men in peace-time—delivering mail, driving buses, and so on.

but we began sinking them. The German U-boat admiral couldn't figure out what was happening.

• We realized that the Germans must have broken our naval code. That would explain why they always seemed to know where our convoys were going. We changed our code. More ships made it to Europe. We began winning the war of the Atlantic.

• The Russians trapped a German army at Stalingrad. Then they laid siege to that army. They starved them. Finally, the German army surrendered. Then the Russians went on the offen-sive. They headed for Germany. Hitler hadn't planned on that.

• America's factories reached high gear. We began turning out guns, ships, tanks, planes, and other military equipment at an incredible rate—faster than anyone had believed possible. Picture this: a flat, sandy, empty field at a place called Willow Run (in Michigan). Now picture the same field, six months after Pearl Harbor. What you see is a vast building, half a mile long and a quarter of a mile wide. Someone described it as the "most enormous room in the history of man." Steel, rubber, and other raw materials are fed into one end of the room; airplanes emerge from the other end—almost 9,000 airplanes the first year. It is not surprising that many historians say the Second World War was won in America's factories and laboratories.

• In 1943, the Russians were fighting the Axis alone on the European continent. Stalin was crying for help. He asked his allies to land forces in Europe and take some pressure off his troops. He asked for a second front. American and British leaders agreed, and made plans for a joint landing. Its code

A *front* is a "battle line." Stalin's front was in Russia and eastern Europe. He wanted the Allies to launch a western front, so that the Germans would have to fight on two sides at once.

*Convoys* were "groups of ships." Ships carrying troops or supplies traveled together with destroyers for protection against submarines.

**159**

"The venture [in North Africa] was new," said General Eisenhower *(above, right,* with General Patton). "Up to that moment no government had ever attempted to carry out an overseas expedition involving a journey of thousands of miles from its bases and terminating in a major attack." *Right:* U.S. troops in North Africa.

In 1942, when Rommel (on the right, in Tripoli) reported to Hitler and Hermann Göring that Britain was dropping American shells on his men, Göring said, "Impossible. All the Americans can make are razor blades and refrigerators." Rommel replied, "I wish, *Herr Reichsmarschall,* that we had similar razor blades!"

name was *Operation Torch*.

But when the landing came, it was in North Africa, not Europe. That wasn't exactly what Stalin wanted, but it did help. North Africa was a good place to begin our offensive. It had been 23 years since we fought in World War I, and our troops needed combat experience. North Africa became a war school for us, with General Dwight D. Eisenhower in charge.

The Nazi forces there were led by General Erwin Rommel, who was known as the "desert fox." Rommel was intelligent, wily, and tough. His Afrika Korps had been destroying British troops. Then the British went on the offensive, heading west from Egypt. (Massive supplies helped.) Combined Allied forces headed east from Morocco and Algiers. A small French force came north from Chad. Rommel was caught in a pincer. We had managed to outfox the fox. We drove the Axis from North Africa. The Germans no longer controlled the Mediterranean Sea.

• We were now bombing Germany from the air day and night, but we needed to do more than that. We had to invade and help destroy Hitler's forces. Should we land in France and push east to Germany? Should we land in Italy and move north? Should we go through Greece? Finally, it was decided. We would start on the Mediterranean island of Sicily and go on to Italy. Look at the map at the back of this book and you'll see why Sicily was important.

• The invasion of Sicily was given the code name *Husky*. We landed by sea and air and captured the island. Amphibious ducks were used for the first time. But there was a snafu: we let an Axis army escape to Italy.

• The Italian people were now fed up with war. Our bombs were blasting Rome. Things hadn't worked out as some Italians thought they would. Their morale collapsed. They kicked Mussolini out of power. Their army went home. They got out of the war. Because of that, we thought Italy would be easy to capture. It wasn't. More snafus. The German army moved into the mountainous Italian peninsula and captured the mountaintops. Picture the enemy shooting down at you as you attempt to climb. That's what happened. The Germans were on the heights. Our soldiers faced ferocious fire. Italy was a bloody standoff.

• Planning began for *Operation Overlord*—code name for the invasion of France. It was to be the largest amphibious invasion in all of history. The Nazis knew it was coming, so they began planning to defeat it. We assembled men and materials in England. The Germans readied their defenses. They laid explosive mines all along the coast, layers and layers of mines. Then they put steel and concrete barriers in the water and on the beaches. They added barbed wire, huge steel spikes, and more mines on the beaches. They built rooms of thick concrete—called "bunkers"—and filled them with heavy antitank guns, versatile medium-size guns, deadly flamethrowers, and machine guns. They called all this the *Atlantic Wall*.

They fortified the whole coastline—from the Netherlands to the west coast of France—although they were sure they knew the exact spot where the landing would be made. Everyone knew. Look at the map on page 166, and see if you can figure it out, too.

The best route is obvious: from Dover, England, to the Pas de Calais (pah-duh-KAL-ay) in France. It is the shortest distance across the treacherous English Channel, it has gentle beaches, and it is the best place to land if you are heading for Germany's heartland. German intelligence officers decoded Allied messages that told of invasion plans for Calais. German pilots bombing England brought back photographs of tanks and trucks lined up near Dover. Spies reported on plans for a second invasion, on the same day, into Norway.

The messages were all fakes. The tanks and trucks were big balloons, designed to look real from aerial photographs. We weren't going to land at Pas de Calais. We weren't planning a Norway invasion. The German spies were double agents working secretly for us.

June 1944: Italian civilians cheer wildly as U.S. 5th Army troops and armored vehicles begin their triumphal march into Rome. Behind them looms one of Rome's great sights, the Victor Emmanuel monument, spared by Allied bombing.

*Below:* Rommel's ferocious Atlantic Wall on the beach at Pas de Calais, a regional district in France. It's leading city is Calais, an industrial port. Arras, another historic city, is its capital.

**161**

# The End of the Road

*Ernie Pyle was a war correspondent. In this excerpt from his book* Brave Men, *he is writing about the war in Italy.*

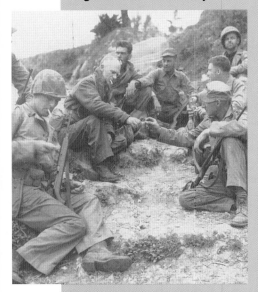

*Ernie Pyle* (center, *balding) on Iwo Jima early in 1945. He died the same year, shot on the island of Ie Shima.*

Captain Waskow was a company commander....He was very young, only in his middle twenties, but he carried in him a sincerity and gentleness that made people want to be guided by him.

"After my father, he came next," a sergeant told me.

"He always looked after us," a soldier said. "He'd go to bat for us every time."

"I've never known him to do anything unfair," another said.

I was at the foot of the mule trail the night they brought Captain Waskow down. The moon was nearly full and you could see far up the trail....Dead men had been coming down the mountain all evening, lashed onto the backs of mules. They came lying belly-down across the wooden packsaddles, their heads hanging down on one side, their stiffened legs sticking out awkwardly from the other, bobbing up and down as the mules walked.

I don't know who the first one was. You feel small in the presence of dead men, and you don't ask silly questions....We left him there beside the road, that first one, and we all went back into the cowshed and sat on water cans or lay on the straw, waiting for the next batch of mules....We talked soldier talk for an hour or more....Then a soldier came into the cowshed and said there were some more bodies outside. We went out into the road. Four mules stood there in the moonlight, in the road where the trail came down off the mountain. The soldiers who led them stood there waiting.

"This one is Captain Waskow," one of them said quietly.

Two men unlashed his body from the mule and lifted it off and laid it in the shadow beside the stone wall. Other men took the other bodies off. Finally, there were five lying end to end in a long row....The unburdened mules moved off to their olive grove. The men in the road seemed reluctant to leave. They stood around, and gradually I could sense them moving, one by one, close to Captain Waskow's body. Not so much to look, I think, as to say something in finality to him and to themselves. I stood close by and I could hear.

One soldier came and looked down, and he said out loud, "God damn it!" That's all he said, and then he walked away.....

Another man came. I think he was an officer. It was hard to tell officers from men in the dim light, for everybody was bearded and grimy. The man looked down into the dead captain's face and then spoke directly to him, as though he were alive, "I'm sorry, old man."

Then a soldier came and stood beside the officer and bent over, and he too spoke to his dead captain, not in a whisper but awfully tenderly, and he said, "I sure am sorry, sir."

Then the first man squatted down, and he reached down and took the captain's hand, and he sat there for a full five minutes holding the dead hand in his own and looking intently into the dead face. And he never uttered a sound all the time he sat there.

Finally he put the hand down. He reached over and gently straightened the points of the captain's shirt collar, and then he sort of rearranged the tattered edges of the uniform around the wound, and then he got up and walked away down the road in the moonlight, all alone.

The rest of us went back into the cowshed, leaving the five dead men lying in a line end to end in the shadow of the low stone wall. We lay down on the straw in the cowshed, and pretty soon we were all asleep.

# 37 Going for D-Day

June 6, 1944, England: Eisenhower gives paratroopers leaving for Normandy the orders for D-Day—to go all-out for a full victory.

General Erwin Rommel, Germany's brilliant desert warrior, looked at the skies and decided to take a two-day trip home to Germany. It was his wife Lucie's 50th birthday (he had bought her a gift—shoes from Paris); he also wanted to see the Führer and ask for more troops. The weather was too rough for an invasion, he said.

General Eisenhower looked at the same skies and decided to go for it. The English Channel was in turmoil, but the moon was full and the tides were low.

The invasion began at night, when paratroopers dropped behind enemy lines. They captured bridges and lit flares to guide the gliders that followed. With all the sophisticated equipment available, it was a tiny child's toy—a snapper that made a sound like a cricket—that the paratroopers used as a signal during the night so they could find each other.

Then, at daybreak, the sky filled with airplanes—wingtip to wingtip—9,000 of them. Two submarines raised flags to mark a landing area. The largest armada ever assembled appeared off the French coast: landing vehicles, minesweepers, attack transports, tankers, cruisers, battleships, ocean liners, yachts, hospital ships and puffing tugs—all the

Hitler was known in Germany as *Der Führer* (FEW-rur), which means "the leader" in German.

Troops plunge down their Coast Guard landing barge ramp and wade for the beach. Behind the clouds loom the Normandy cliffs they will climb.

**General Rommel** had good reasons for taking time off. He intended to see Hitler and ask for more men to beef up the beach defenses. He also wanted to see Manfred, his 14-year-old son, who had been drafted into the army. Some of the other officers who took time off got together to practice war games.

Anti-aircraft barrage balloons over Omaha Beach. Among the arrivals on June 7, D-Day-plus-1, are a group of hulks that will be sunk off the beach as the foundations for temporary artificial harbors. The Allies need a base from which their invading troops can be easily landed and their equipment and supplies handled.

**The rains** are ferocious, but General Eisenhower's weatherman—tall, serious-faced Captain James Stagg—gets reports from five weather stations in the Atlantic. They indicate that there will be a 16-hour "window" in the bad weather. Ike entered Europe through that window.

boats and ships that could be found. They made an awesome fleet 20 miles wide. Giant military barrage balloons floated above, to interfere with enemy planes.

It was June 6, 1944, and forever it would be known as *D-Day*. The Allies were heading for the treacherous, mine-strewn beaches of Normandy in France, 100 miles from the nearest English port across the turbulent Channel. Enemy soldiers, in bunkers on top of the Normandy cliffs, some of them 150 feet high, waited behind formidable heavy guns. But most were asleep. No one was expecting an attack in this weather. Rommel wasn't the only officer on vacation. Most of the German leaders had taken the weekend off.

Soldiers are supplied with assault equipment suited to their landing area. Those on the cliffs have ropes and ladders; these men have bikes.

164

General Omar Bradley *(right),* U.S. 1st Army commander, and British General Bernard Montgomery discussing maneuvers in a field near Omaha Beach.

What happened next? The landing had been planned with the precision of a ballet. Everyone had a place and time in the drama. And, at four of the five landing beaches, things went more or less on schedule. But on Omaha Beach (one of two beaches where Americans landed), everything seemed snafued. The first men ashore couldn't secure the beach. What was supposed to take minutes took hours. Of 32 tanks, with collars that were supposed to keep them afloat, 27 sank in the choppy water with men inside. Allied planes, sent to bomb the enemy's gun-filled bunkers, went too far, missed the guns, and dropped their bombs on French cows. Immense traffic jams of men and supplies backed up in the water and on the beaches. Mines and shells were exploding everywhere. Gliders dropped men and supplies behind the beaches into swampland, where many sank. "Our men simply could not get past the beach. They were pinned down right on the water's edge by an inhuman wall of fire....Our first waves were on the beach for hours, instead of a few minutes, before they could begin working inland," wrote war correspondent Ernie Pyle, who was there.

General Omar Bradley, on the command ship *Augusta,* thought about calling off the landing. Then a destroyer came up into the shallow water and lobbed a shell right inside a main bunker. When other ships added their firepower, the Nazi gunners in the concrete emplacements were in big trouble. The Navy had opened a crack in the German defenses and the Yanks were on their way.

American troops injured while storming Omaha Beach wait below the chalk cliffs for transport to a field hospital.

## A Great War Photographer

*Most of Robert Capa's Normandy photographs were never published; they were accidentally ruined by a Life magazine darkroom technician.*

**R**obert Capa was one of the war's great photographers. He took part in the D-Day invasion:

*The sea was rough and we were wet before our barge pushed away from the mother ship. It was already clear that General Eisenhower would not lead his people across the Channel with dry feet or dry anything else. In no time, the men started to puke. But this was a polite as well as a carefully prepared invasion, and little paper bags had been provided for the purpose. [There weren't enough of the bags; most men used their helmets.]*

**Emplacements** are the areas where heavy artillery (guns) are positioned.

165

ENGLAND

LONDON

DOVER

SOUTHAMPTON

1ST ARMY

2ND ARMY

Strait of Dover

CAL

PLYMOUTH

MINEFIELD

ENGLISH CHANNEL

MINEFIELD
CHERBOURG

GERMAN ATLANTIC WALL

LE HAVRE

NORMANDY

SEINE R

FRANCE

PAR

■ GERMAN FORT

D~DAY

W        E

N

S

0        50 MILES

GERMAN ATLANTIC WALL

UTAH

U.S.A.

U.S.A.

UNITED
KINGDOM

CANADA

UNITED
KINGDOM

OMAHA

GERMAN
GUN BATTERY
✚ ALLIED GLIDER LANDING
PARATROOPERS

GOLD

JUNO

SWORD

NORMANDY

BAYEUX

The BEACHES on D~DAY

Slowly at first, but then steadily, soldiers and medical personnel began to land and head inland, into the fierce guns on top of the bluffs. No word is big enough to describe their effort. *Heroic* will have to do.

The operation had been brilliantly planned. Troops and officers had trained for a year; it paid off. Equipment specially designed for this invasion worked superbly. Tanks unrolled reels of steel matting that made roadways across the sand. Other tanks, with flailing chain arms, detonated mines and began to make the beach safe. Some tanks carried small bridges. Naval engineers had built huge floating harbors; they were towed into place.

In the midst of the fighting, over the noise of battle, a British major shouted out words from Shakespeare's play *Henry V*, about another invasion of France.

> *We few, we happy few, we band of brothers;*
> *For he today that sheds his blood with me*
> *Shall be my brother; be he ne'er so vile,*
> *This day shall gentle his condition.*
> *And gentlemen in England now a-bed,*
> *Shall think themselves accursed they were not here;*
> *And hold their manhoods cheap whiles any speaks*
> *That fought with us upon Saint Crispin's day.*

It was D-Day, not St. Crispin's, but poets would write of this day, too: of heroism, of achievement, and of the waste of war. It was there to see on the beaches. They were littered with tanks and bodies and the leftovers of men's lives: socks, Bibles, toothbrushes, diaries, mirrors, letters, first-aid kits, photographs, and food rations. From Ernie Pyle:

> *There was a dog...on the water's edge, near a boat that lay twisted and half sunk at the waterline. He barked appealingly to every soldier who approached, trotted eagerly along with him for a few feet, and then, sensing himself unwanted in all the haste, he would run back to wait in vain for his own people at his own empty boat.*

By nightfall, Allied troops—American, British, Canadian, Free French, Polish—were holding French soil. We had made it. We were on our way to Berlin.

For the Axis, it was the beginning of the end.

The Allies liberate France. *Above:* U.S. infantrymen march through a town in Normandy past a wrecked German truck still in its camouflage. *Below:* An American tank rolls through the Arc de Triomphe in Paris, August 1944. **"We couldn't stick around long though,"** said one soldier. **"The Jerries were on the run and we wanted to keep them that way."**

***Flailing*** means to move wildly.

# 38 A Wartime Diary

*Find the Black Sea—above Turkey and below Russia—and you'll find the Crimean peninsula and Yalta.*

The Battle of the Bulge was Hitler's last gamble on the western front. Much of it was fought in bad, snowy conditions. *Above:* G.I.s in a chow line

*You are a newspaper writer, a war correspondent, covering this world war. When it ends you will write a book about the times you have lived through, so you have been keeping a diary to record events. It is 1945. Here are some excerpts from your journal, and some notes from this author:*

**JANUARY 1:** Allied forces are beginning to turn back a powerful German army in Belgium. Soldiers are calling this the Battle of the Bulge. *A strong German offensive created a bulge in the Allied defensive line.* Whatever you want to call this battle, it is fierce. Still, it looks as if this will be a good year for the Allies. Germany's armies are being battered on the ground, its cities pounded from the air.

**JANUARY 20:** FDR is inaugurated for a fourth term as president. No other president has served more than twice.

**JANUARY 24:** Russian soldiers have crossed the Oder River and, for the first time, are on German soil.

**JANUARY 27:** Today, in Poland, Soviet forces liberated a German concentration camp. It is named Auschwitz. People in the camp were used as slaves by a German industrial chemical company. The company has left charts of the costs and profits of slave labor. But the camp was built primarily for another purpose. It was built to kill people. The horror and evil of it all are

Christmas Eve, 1944: an 82nd Airborne Division infantryman on a one-man sortie through the lines during the Battle of the Bulge. The bump on the horizon is the head of the sniper covering him.

*Left:* the Big Three at Yalta. But their unity did not go far beyond beating Hitler, as this cartoon, showing Stalin with "secret plans," suggested.

more than anyone wants to believe. *Three million people were murdered at Auschwitz, most of them Jews.*

**FEBRUARY 1:** The sky is thick with planes—an incredible sight! One thousand airplanes are flying over Europe on their way to bomb Berlin.

**FEBRUARY 4–11:** President Roosevelt has flown to Yalta, in the Crimea, to meet with England's Winston Churchill and Russia's Joseph Stalin. They are said to be planning for the final battles of the war. They agree to call a meeting of the world's nations in San Francisco in April, to form a peacekeeping organization called the United Nations.

**FEBRUARY 14:** John D. Rockefeller, Jr., donates $8.5 million to buy land in New York City as a permanent home for the United Nations. Woodrow Wilson's idea of a league of nations may finally be achieved.

*Above:* Two days before the German army surrenders, U.S. troops force German citizens to inspect the bodies of victims of a Nazi concentration camp near their town.

January 1945: Red Army soldiers, now only 50 miles from Berlin, struggle to get a field gun across the river Oder.

**169**

*Above:* In this carefully staged photograph MacArthur wades ashore during initial landings at Leyte in the Philippines, October 1944. MacArthur liked wading, rather than having himself rowed in, because it looked grander. He sometimes had a photographer shoot the same picture many times, until he got it just right.

*Above:* U.S. firebombs fall on Kobe, Japan. *Right:* In the war's most famous photograph, G.I.s raise the flag on Mt. Suribachi after the capture of the island of Iwo Jima. This photo was actually a posed shot taken after the battle. A small flag had been raised during the fighting, hours earlier.

**FEBRUARY 19:** American marines have landed on Iwo Jima, an island in the Pacific. Reports tell of incredibly hard fighting and great losses on both sides.

**FEBRUARY 24:** General Douglas MacArthur promised to return to the Philippines—and he has done it.

**MARCH 7:** The U.S. 1st Army has crossed the river Rhine and is inside Germany. All German armies have been pushed back into the Fatherland.

**MARCH 9:** Today, 325 low-flying bombers dropped incendiary bombs on Tokyo. The bombs are filled with jellied gasoline meant to set fires. The Japanese capital became so hot that the water in its canals boiled. Still the Japanese refuse to surrender. *Later reports list 267,000 Tokyo buildings burned to the ground; 89,000 persons dead.*

**MARCH 21:** Today we watched an enormous air armada fly overhead on its way to Germany. *There were 7,000 Allied planes.* Until now, most bombing raids have been at night, to make it difficult for the anti-aircraft guns and fighter planes to see the bombers. Now Germany has little firepower left; the bombers fly at will. Bomb damage there is said to be devastating.

*The Axis powers now have no hope of winning and yet neither Germany nor Japan will give up. Those who began this insane engine of war have cut out the brakes. They can't seem to stop. It is their own people who are suffering most. Do the warlords care?*

# 39 April in Georgia

Much wartime propaganda, like this American postcard, was meant to reassure the troops, and the folks at home, that their efforts were succeeding and the war was worth fighting.

*Where is Tokyo? Where is Dresden?*

**This statue seems to be contemplating the firestorm set off in Dresden, Germany, by Allied bombing in February 1945.**

The madmen who run Japan and Germany refuse to give up. They talk of leading their nations in a fight to the death. Terrible fire-bombs are dropping on Tokyo and Dresden. Hundreds of thousands of people are dying. Just as a fist squeezes its contents, so British, American, and Russian troops are squeezing Germany. In the Pacific theater we are making plans to invade Japan. Everyone expects that invasion to be bloodier than the one in Normandy.

The Allies will win this war—that now seems clear—but the German and Japanese leaders are making it very difficult. Like ancient rulers who had their followers killed and buried in their tombs, these leaders seem determined to kill their own people.

The president knows of something that might end the war quickly. It is that secret weapon that almost no one else knows about. Partly because of this, he feels he can relax and catch up on some paperwork. He is exhausted. He has just turned 63, but he looks much older. The war has been a terrible strain: he has traveled around the world, he has run for a fourth term

The exhaustion brought on by the war years shows plainly in FDR's face as he arrives in the Crimea for the Yalta conference. He was a sick man.

**On the island** of Okinawa, the U.S. Army suffers some 80,000 casualties. Japanese losses total 120,000.

**Roosevelt** is planning to attend a Jefferson's birthday celebration. Do you remember another famous party for that occasion? It was attended by Andrew Jackson and John Calhoun. (See book 6 of *A History of US* for details.)

as president, he has been active as commander in chief of the armed services, he has been an inspiring leader. He needs to take it easy for a few days. He makes plans to go to Warm Springs, Georgia. He first visited Warm Springs years earlier, when he was recovering from polio. The waters are healing. He has been back many times, and has grown to love the slow-paced gentleness of the South.

In Georgia, wild violets are blooming; so are purple-blue wisteria and sweet-smelling honeysuckle. It is springtime—April 12, 1945—and, at Warm Springs, cooks are preparing a picnic. The smells of barbecued beef and chicken fill the air. As the president works, an artist sits nearby, making sketches for a watercolor portrait.

Almost exactly 80 years earlier, another American president had decided to relax and go to the theater, knowing that a terrible war was coming to an end.

Like that other president, Roosevelt is concerned about the peace that is to come. He wants this war to have meaning. Soon after the war began, he met with Winston Churchill and signed a document called the *Atlantic Charter*. It says that after the war, nations will be free to choose their own forms of government. That is

The president on the porch of his home in Warm Springs, known as the Little White House. It is still there.

called "self-determination." Roosevelt wants to end the old, before-the-war imperialist ways. Then, a few European nations ruled much of the world. Sometimes they ruled well; sometimes not well. To Roosevelt, that doesn't matter now. People should be free to govern themselves. Great Britain still controls India and Burma. France expects to regain control of Indochina (which includes Vietnam). Japan has attempted to become an empire. The United States rules the Philippine Islands.

Roosevelt thinks imperialism—even well-meaning imperialism— is wrong. He will show the world: America has no desire for other lands. We will begin by granting independence to the Philippines. He is planning to go to the independence ceremonies himself.

Russia is a worry. The Russian people have fought magnificently. They have been brave allies. But they aren't a free people. Stalin is a dictator. Winston Churchill believes that Stalin cannot be trusted.

Roosevelt is beginning to have worries about Stalin, too.

At Warm Springs he works on a speech to be given at the dinner to honor Jefferson's memory. This is part of what Roosevelt writes:

> The once powerful, malignant Nazi state is crumbling. The Japanese war lords are receiving, in their own homeland, the retribution for which they asked when they attacked Pearl Harbor.
>
> But the mere conquest of our enemies is not enough.
>
> We must go on to do all in our power to conquer the doubts and the fears, the ignorance and the greed, which made this horror possible....If civilization is to survive, we must cultivate the science of human relationships—the ability of all peoples, of all kinds, to live together and work together, in the same world, at peace....
>
> The work, my friends, is peace. More than an end of this war—an end to the beginnings of all wars. Yes, an end, forever, to this impractical, unrealistic settlement of the differences between governments by the mass killing of peoples.

The president is sitting in a leather armchair; he turns to the artist. "We've got just 15 minutes more," he says. Some cousins of his and a friend are in the room. They are quiet. The president is studying papers. The 15 minutes are almost up when he raises a hand to his temple. "I have a terrific headache," he says. They are the last words he will ever speak.

The August 1941 meeting between Roosevelt and Churchill aboard the U.S.S. *Augusta* that paved the way for America's entry into World War II.

*Malignant* means "harmful."
*Retribution* is "punishment."

Our only hope will lie in the frail web of understanding of one person for the pain of another.
—JOHN DOS PASSOS, DECEMBER 1940

*What do you think Dos Passos means by that? Do you agree?*

The last family photo taken before Roosevelt's death: FDR, Eleanor, and their 13 grandchildren at the White House on Inauguration Day, 1945.

# 40 President HST

In 1918 Captain Harry Truman commanded a field-artillery battery in France, where he saw active combat.

**Truman** was asked to be vice president by Democratic National Chairman Robert Hannegan, but he refused—said he wasn't a candidate. Just then the phone rang. It was FDR. He asked Hannegan if he had "got that fellow lined up yet."

"He is the contrariest Missouri mule I've ever dealt with," said Hannegan.

"Well, you tell him," FDR shouted, and Truman could hear him, "that if he wants to break up the Democratic Party in the middle of a war, that's his responsibility."

The solidly built, gray-haired man with metal-rimmed glasses sat at a high desk facing the Senate floor. A gold-bordered blue velvet drape hung behind him and made a frame for his chair. Vice President Harry S. Truman was presiding over the Senate. At least that was what he seemed to be doing. Actually, he was bored and was writing a letter to his mother and sister, who were back in his hometown of Independence, Missouri. This is part of what he wrote:

*Dear Mama & Mary: I am trying to write you a letter today from the desk of the President of the Senate while a windy Senator…is making a speech on a subject with which he is in no way familiar.…Turn on your radio tomorrow night at 9:30 your time.…I think I'll be on all the networks.…I'll be followed by the President, whom I'll introduce.*

It had amazed almost everyone—including Truman—when he was asked to be vice president. He hardly knew FDR. Some said it was the Democratic National Committee that selected Harry Truman; that the other candidates considered were all controversial.

Truman with friends in Kansas City, Missouri, in his haberdashery (men's clothing store), around 1920.

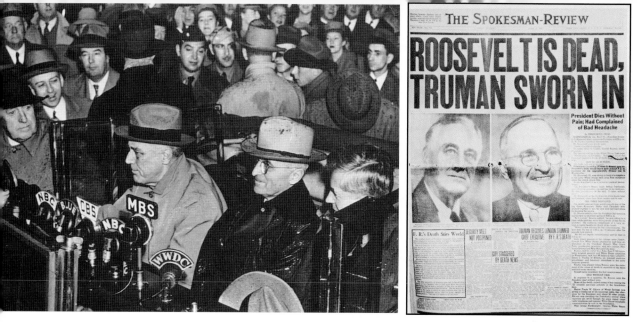

THE SPOKESMAN-REVIEW

# ROOSEVELT IS DEAD, TRUMAN SWORN IN

### President Dies Without Pain; Had Complained of Bad Headache

F. R.'s Death Stirs World | SECURITY MEET NOT POSTPONED | TRUMAN BECOMES CHIEF EXECUTIVE; BY F. R.'S DEATH | LONDON STUNNED

CITY STAGGERED BY DEATH NEWS

Truman didn't seem to have any enemies. But he didn't have many enthusiasts either. He had become a senator at age 50. He'd fought in the Great War, and had tried a number of jobs—he'd been a farmer and a men's store owner—but the store failed, and he wasn't very successful at anything until he got into politics, first as a postmaster and then as a county official. He was a bookish sort, with an astounding knowledge of history: quiet, honest, likable, and fair-minded, although he sometimes lost his temper. It was as head of a Senate committee investigating military contracts that he had impressed people—including Roosevelt. His committee probably saved the government billions of dollars.

When the windy senator finally finished, Truman went to visit his old friend, the speaker of the House of Representatives, Texan Sam Rayburn. Rayburn's office was a gathering place where congressmen relaxed and gossiped. It was called—in jest—the Board of Education. It was there that Truman got a call from the president's press secretary, Steve Early. He was to come to the White House at once. Early's voice had an urgent tone.

Truman headed through the underground passage to the Senate Office building—there his Secret Service agents lost track of him. But his car and driver were waiting. As he drove the 15 long blocks to the White House, he guessed that the president had flown in from Georgia and wanted him for something ceremonial.

Upstairs at the White House, he learned differently. Eleanor Roosevelt put her hand on his shoulder and said softly, "Harry, the president is dead." For a moment he could say nothing. Then he asked if there was anything he could do for her.

"Is there anything we can do for you?" she answered. "You are the one in trouble now."

Election night in 1944. *Above left:* FDR *(left),* returning for a fourth term as president, with Henry Wallace *(right,* bareheaded), and the man taking over Wallace's job, vice president–elect Harry Truman *(center).* Truman would serve as vice president for only four months. *Below:* Truman, in his trademark round glasses and bow tie, is sworn in as the country's 33rd president. Truman's wife, Bess, and their daughter, Margaret, look on.

# 41 A Final Journey

"Mr. Roosevelt was great," a Harvard professor said to his students, "because he, like Lincoln, restored men's faith."

**The poem** Eleanor Roosevelt remembered was written by Millard Lampell.

It was as if a member of the family had died. He had been a world-dominating figure for 12 years—strong, witty, compassionate, able. Young people could remember no other president. The nation was in a state of shock.

Those who had felt left out by government before—the poor and disadvantaged—were especially grieved. This was a president who had done more than talk about fairness and opportunity; he had acted to begin to make them reality. And, while he had broken precedent by running for office four times, he had not forgotten that as president he was the servant of the people. He had never assumed kingly trappings. He had never lost his sense of humor or his easy informality.

In Warm Springs, the flag-draped coffin began its long, sad train journey—to Washington first, and then to Hyde Park, where the president was to be buried. Sitting inside the train, Eleanor Roosevelt kept remembering a poem about Lincoln's death. It wouldn't leave her mind:

*A lonesome train on a lonesome track*
*Seven coaches painted black,*
*A slow train, a quiet train*
*Carrying Lincoln home again.*

On April 13, 1945, a hearse rolled into Warm Springs train station. Franklin Delano Roosevelt, 32nd president of the United States, was going home to Hyde Park for the last time.

At night, unable to sleep, she said:

*I lay in my berth…with the window shade up, looking out at the countryside he had loved and watching the faces of the people at stations, and even at the crossroads, who had come to pay their last tribute all through the night….I was truly surprised by the people along the way; not only at the stops but at every crossing.*

In the train's press car, reporters looking out the window saw black sharecroppers on their knees, hands outstretched in prayer. As the train slowed in a South Carolina city, members of a Boy Scout troop began singing "Onward, Christian Soldiers"; then others joined in, and soon, according to one who was there, "eight or ten thousand voices were singing like an organ." Everywhere people cried. The sobs continued as the coffin was carried, by horse-drawn caisson, through Washington to the White House. Then, during the memorial service, the whole grieving nation came to a halt and paid its respects.

Airplanes sat on runways; radios were silent; telephone service was cut off—there was not even a dial tone; news-service teletypes typed the word *silence* and went dead; movie theaters closed; cars and buses pulled to the curb; 505 New York subway trains stopped; stores shut their doors; and everywhere—in other countries, too—people put hands on hearts, or fell to their knees, or just stayed quiet. That day newspapers carried no advertisements.

Clearly he had been a great president. But how great? What would history say of him?

A poll of 50 leading historians soon ranked him just behind Lincoln and Washington as one of the three greatest presidents. Winston Churchill said that in world importance, Roosevelt was first.

And yet, as much as some loved and respected him, others hated and vilified him.

Later historians would look at him through two lenses. As an effective president, they agreed, he was like a magnificent symphony conductor who knows all the notes and just what to do with them. No question about it, they still agreed, he was a great president. But there was something that bothered many. As a human being, he was sometimes less than great. His personality was flawed. It was too bad to have to acknowledge it, but he could be devious. He could tell a person something and not mean it. He could tell a story that made him look good but wasn't quite true.

Perhaps it was that tendency to always act as if everything was fine, even when it wasn't, that some found disturbing. He was used to pretending. It was both a strength and a weakness.

Eleanor (who was more partner than wife) said:

Thousands lined the streets of Washington to watch FDR's funeral procession pass by.

**After** the president's death, Eleanor Roosevelt said that people often told her how "they missed the way the president used to talk to them…[in his radio fireside chats]. There was a real dialogue between Franklin and the people," she reflected. "That dialogue seems to have disappeared from the government since he died."

He was in a very special sense the people's president, because he made them feel that with him in the White House they shared the presidency. The sense of sharing the presidency gave even the most humble citizen a lively sense of belonging.
—JUSTICE WILLIAM O. DOUGLAS

**177**

# 42 Day by Day

April 29: U.S. troops reach Dachau concentration camp in southern Germany. An inmate writes, "First American comes through the entrance. Dachau free!!! Indescribable happiness. Insane howling."

## The Camps

*In 1945, Leon Bass was a 19-year-old soldier attached to the American 3rd Army when his unit was sent to Weimar, Germany.*

Immediately about five or six of us took off with an officer to a place called Buchenwald....Buchenwald was a concentration camp. I had no idea what kind of camp this was. I thought it might have been a prisoner-of-war camp where they kept soldiers who were captured. But on this day...I was to discover what human suffering was...about. I was going to take off the blinders that caused me to have tunnel vision. I was going to see clearly that, yes, I suffered and I was hurting because I was black in a white society, but I had also begun to understand that suffering is universal. It is not just relegated to me and mine; it touches us all.

*More from the diary that you, the newspaper reporter, are keeping.*

APRIL **12, 1945:** American soldiers enter the Nazi concentration camp at Buchenwald and find death everywhere. Germans interviewed say they didn't know anything about the concentration camps. *As camp after camp is discovered, the Allies react with cold fury. More than 10 million human beings have died in the concentration camps. In one camp American soldiers discover bins with thousands of pairs of babies' shoes.*

APRIL **13:** Everywhere there is shock and disbelief. The president is dead! It is hard to imagine the United States without FDR. The bombing of Germany continues—day and night. Germany's cities are in ruins. Mostly the bombs kill civilians. Are they to blame for this war?

*This bombing of cities is called "strategic bombing." There is something about it that is strange. The tougher the bombing, the more it makes people want to work hard and fight back. When the German Luftwaffe was bombing England, it seemed to inspire the English to fight and produce. All selfishness was forgotten. Military production went up. The same thing happened in Germany and Japan. After last year's fierce raids on Germany, there was a short lull and then aircraft production great-*

**Anne Frank**

*ly increased. The military experts don't want to believe it, but it seems to be true. The military experts say the purpose of the bombing is to destroy morale.*

APRIL **14:** The British liberate the Bergen-Belsen concentration camp. *On March 12, in this camp, a 14-year-old Dutch girl died. Her name was Anne Frank. After the war her diary is found and published.*

APRIL **20:** Hitler is 56 today. Is there anyone left who wishes him a happy birthday? *Probably. His strongman ideas had wide appeal. Democracy is difficult; it asks people to think and take part in their government. The totalitarian governments treat people like sheep—or is it dogs?*

APRIL **21:** Russian troops have entered the suburbs of Berlin, Germany's capital. The fighting is said to be fierce, although the Nazis have no hope of victory. *In less than one month, between April 16 and May 8, the Russians lose 304,887 men—killed, wounded, and missing—capturing Berlin. The total number of American deaths in the whole war, in Europe and the Pacific, is about 325,000.*

APRIL **24:** If only there were a way to end this war quickly. The deaths now seem so unnecessary. *On this day President Truman gets his first detailed briefing on the top-secret superweapon.*

APRIL **26:** Italy's dictator, Benito Mussolini, has been hanged by Italians fighting on the side of the Allies.

APRIL **30:** Hitler is dead. He has killed himself. He was living like a mole underground in a concrete bunker in Berlin.

At war's end, many German cities had been bombed to ash and rubble. Here, Germans search for usable bricks to begin to rebuild Dresden.

*Left, top:* Mussolini in death. *Bottom:* The mayor of Leipzig, Germany, and his wife and daughter have committed suicide as U.S. infantry close in on the city. *Above:* Russian soldiers approach the ruined Reichstag in Berlin. "Wherever we looked we saw desolation," said an American general.

**181**

*Left:* General Alfred Jodl signs the German surrender at Rheims, France. The war in Europe is over. None of Eisenhower's staff has a great idea for a victory statement, so the general writes his own: "The mission of this Allied force was fulfilled at 0241 local time May 7, 1945." *Right:* VE ("Victory in Europe") Day in New York.

All over Europe, in countries that had fought for the Allies and countries that had fought for the Axis, mothers like this woman in Austria wept for joy when their sons came home or for sorrow when they did not.

The aircraft carrier *Bunker Hill* blazes up after a Japanese kamikaze (suicide) pilot has crashed into it.

*Hitler boasted that his creation—the German Third Reich—would live forever. Many believed him. It lasted 12 years.*

**MAY 7:** German military leaders have surrendered to General Dwight D. Eisenhower at a school in Rheims, France. It is unconditional surrender. The war in Europe is over. It is hard to believe.

**MAY 8:** President Harry Truman proclaims this VE ("Victory in Europe") Day. It is his 61st birthday. People are cheering and hugging and crying and partying. *Maybe they should wait—the war isn't over in the Pacific.*

**MAY 11:** A Japanese pilot, trained for a suicide mission, crashes into

At the Potsdam conference, Stalin *(right)* talks of making Germany pay huge reparations to the Allied powers. When the Americans, headed by President Truman *(center;* Churchill is on the left), hear that, they threaten to leave the conference. Do you remember how Germany felt about reparations after World War I—and what came of those feelings?

the aircraft carrier *Bunker Hill*; 373 Americans are killed.

JUNE: The cities of Nagoya, Kobe, Osaka, Yokohama, and Kawasaki have been firebombed. The destruction in Japan is said to be staggering. Japan's cities are built of wood. They burn quickly. Two million buildings have been destroyed; perhaps 10 million people made homeless; hundreds of thousands are dead or injured. The Japanese warlords still won't surrender.

JULY: Japan's 60 largest cities have been burned. There is almost no food in Japan; people are starving. Four hundred Japanese have been arrested because they talked of surrender.

*In the New Mexican desert, scientists prepare to test an atomic device. No one knows if it will work. No one knows how powerful it is. They learn on July 16: it is more powerful than anything ever before devised by humans. It was "as though the earth had opened and the skies had split," said one who was there. You, and America's other citizens, are not told of the test.*

JULY 26: Truman, Churchill, and China's leader, Chiang Kai-shek, broadcasting from a peace conference at Potsdam, Germany, demand the unconditional surrender of Japan but assure the Japanese of a "new order of peace, security, and justice." Otherwise, they warn, there will be "prompt and utter destruction of the Japanese homeland." The Japanese premier Baron Suzuki says the proposal is "unworthy of public notice."

*At Potsdam, Harry Truman tells Joseph Stalin that the United States has a new and powerful weapon. The Soviet leader shows little interest. Plans for the secret weapon, stolen by spies, sit inside the Kremlin, Russia's government center. Stalin, a dictator admired by Hitler, knows all about the bomb.*

**Writer** Paul Fussell, "a badly wounded former infantry lieutenant," warns about glamorizing war. *The truth is that very few people know anything about war. In an infantry division, for example, fewer than half the troops actually fight, that is fight with rifles, mortars, machine guns, grenades and trench knives. The others, thousands upon thousands of them, are occupied with truck driving, photocopying, cooking and baking, ammunition and ration supplying and similar housekeeping tasks....For most soldiers participating in World War II, the war meant inconvenience rising sometimes to hardship....For those unlucky enough to be in the forward combat units, the war meant death or maiming, usually in extraordinarily dirty and undignified circumstances.*

183

# 43 A Little Boy

The face of Nagasaki, Japan, 24 hours after the bomb drops. This little boy is holding his emergency ration—a ball of boiled rice.

Almost no structures could withstand the two atomic bombs dropped on Japanese cities, except the shells of a few western-style buildings (made of concrete and brick). But in Nagasaki, this *torii,* the wooden gateway to a Shinto shrine, somehow survived both the blast and the firestorm that followed it.

**The U.S.S.** *Indianapolis* brings key components of Little Boy to Tinian. Three days later, the ship is torpedoed and sunk in the Indian Ocean.

The men of the 509th Composite Group of the 313th Wing of the 21st Bombing Command of the 20th Air Force have been carefully chosen from a group of ace pilots. All have volunteered for a special mission. No one tells them what the mission will be. But whatever it is, they know they will be flying B-29s, the big workhorse bombers that are known as superfortresses.

Right away, there is something strange about the training they get at an airfield in Utah. Instead of flying planes loaded with huge bombs, they train with a single bomb of moderate size. And they are trained to worry about storms, especially electrical storms. Then, when they are sent to the Pacific, to the island of Tinian in the Marianas group of islands, they just sit around. It is frustrating. From Tinian it is an easy flight to Japan. The other airmen on the island are flying B-29s and dropping big bomb loads on Japan's cities. The 509th is sent on training flights—over and over again. Sometimes they are allowed to drop one bomb. It isn't long before the other pilots on Tinian begin making fun of the 509th. Someone even writes a poem about them. Its last lines are:

> *Take it from one who knows the score,*
> *The 509th is winning the war.*

That is cruel. Everyone knows the 509th isn't winning the war; it isn't doing anything.

Meanwhile, in Washington, President Truman has come to a decision. He has called on two teams of experts: a team of scientists and a team of civilians and soldiers. They are to help him decide about

## AIR ATTACK on JAPAN

the new superweapon. Will it be used? Can anything be used in its place? Both teams agree: the weapon should be used. They believe it will bring the war to an end. Without it, the war could continue for 10 or more years. Military chiefs, who don't know about the secret weapon, are pressing Truman to let them invade Japan. If that happens, America can expect a million casualties; Japan might have 10 times that number.

# 44 Peace

VE Day had been a rehearsal. On VJ ("Victory in Japan") Day, Americans everywhere went wild (though this famous spontaneous-looking shot was, in fact, posed).

The Americans demand surrender—otherwise, they tell the Japanese, "they may expect a rain of ruin from the air." The Japanese do not respond.

On August 8 Russia enters the war against Japan. Russian forces attack Japanese armies in Manchuria and Korea. For some Japanese leaders this is more threatening than the bomb.

On August 9 a second atomic bomb is dropped. This one hits the port of Nagasaki. The nightmare of fire, wind, rain, and radiation is repeated. Has this war driven sane people to act insanely?

In Japan, the warlords and government ministers meet in stormy sessions to decide the fate of their people. They are split down the middle; most of the warriors vote to continue the fight, although everyone knows that may mean the destruction of the Japanese people. As Emperor Hirohito described it:

> There was no prospect of agreement no matter how many discussions they had....I was given the opportunity to express my own free will for the first time.

The emperor decides for his people.

From Tokyo, cables are sent to Washington, London, Moscow, and Chungking. Japan will accept the terms of the Potsdam Declaration, with one request: that the emperor remain as head of state.

"The time has come," said Emperor Hirohito (*center,* with General Tojo, *right*), "when we must bear the unbearable."

As soon as Harry Truman hears the news he calls Eleanor Roosevelt. Mrs. Roosevelt is now America's ambassador to the United Nations. President Truman tells her that he wishes her husband were alive to accept the peace proposal.

In Japan, some army officers break into the imperial palace, set fire to the home of the prime minister, and attempt to stop a broadcast of the emperor's words. They fail, and, along with the war minister, commit suicide in the public square.

The emperor, who wants to be sure that his words are exactly right, has recorded them in advance. The actual broadcast is taking place elsewhere.

It is August 15, 1945, and Hirohito's voice is heard in the first public speech an emperor has ever made. He asks the Japanese people to accept the coming of peace.

*Above:* Japanese officials arrive aboard the U.S.S. *Missouri* in Tokyo Bay to sign the surrender, September 2, 1945. *Below:* In New York City, Times Square is closed to traffic on VJ Day (August 14) as 2 million people crowd the streets, hugging and cheering.

# 45 Picturing History

George Bellows (1882–1925) called his painting of tenement-dwelling New Yorkers on a hot summer day *The Cliff Dwellers* (1913).

**Derisively** means "mockingly, scornfully, insultingly"; it comes from the verb *to deride,* which means "to ridicule."

## The Ashcan of History

I decided to end this book with some works of art for two reasons: one, I like them; and two, I want to be sure that you don't think history is just about famous people and big events. History is everything that happened yesterday and the day before. It's science and poetry; it's sporting events and fashions; it's classroom life and museum shows; it's the songs people sing and the lives they lead, rich, poor, and in between.

At the beginning of the 20th century, most American artists were painting elegant, refined portraits and scenes and showing their best work at exhibitions at the National Academy of Design. Then along came some artists who broke the rules. They painted working people. They made pictures from real life: down-to-earth, open-hearted paintings. They were following the lead of some boldly realistic 19th-century painters—especially Thomas Eakins (AY-kinz) and Winslow Homer—except that this new group concentrated on urban scenes.

Finding vitality in shabby streets and down-on-their-luck people, they were called, derisively, the "Ashcan artists." The art establishment wanted nothing to do with them. Their paintings weren't "pretty"; it was "new" art, and a threat to the old. Sir Caspar Purdon Clarke, director of the eminent Metropolitan Museum of Art in New York, made his feelings clear. "There is a state of unrest all over the world in art as in all other things. It is the same in literature, as in music, in painting, and in sculpture. And I dislike unrest."

When John Sloan sent some of his etchings to be exhibited at the National Academy, they were rejected as "vulgar." So was most of the Ashcan art. (Today it's in museums.)

The group's leader was Robert Henri (HEN-rye)—a superb teacher as well as a fine painter. Edward Hopper was one of his students. Over and over, Hopper painted the loneliness of city life with scenes of people who don't seem to be doing anything—and yet they haunt your mind. George Bellows was another of Henri's students. He, too, painted city life, but look at the difference in his vision. Do you think some of those people are lonely?

Since they couldn't exhibit at the National Academy, Robert Henri arranged for the Ashcan artists to have their own show. That revolt against the art establishment (in 1910) began a tradition of independent exhibitions. Artist Stuart Davis (1894–1964) described what happened:

> The ordinary art student in the days of the Henri school wouldn't think of having a show in a gallery because there weren't any galleries that would admit this kind of work….So the Independent Show idea developed, and this was Henri's idea, where everyone could show who had done something…then it was an amazing thing….They just hired an office building…hung up all those paintings and charged admission.
>
> [Henri] was a man with an impulse to see and know things, and was able to put that impulse into execution…and that's why instead of just an art school, it was an opening-up type of instruction….There was nothing like that in any art school in New York, in Europe, or anywhere else as far as I know.

The artist John Sloan said:

> He was a catalyst, an enthusiast….His teaching was strong stuff in an era that put "art for art's sake" on a pedestal….Henri won us with his robust love for life.

But another catalyst was also challenging the traditionalists and gathering followers around himself. He was a modernist, in contrast to the Henri realists. Both art leaders lived in New York, and, between the two of them, they dominated the avant-garde world of American art in their time.

Edward Hopper (1882–1967) sold his first painting at the Armory Show (see page 24); he didn't sell another one for 10 years. This, one of his most famous, is called *Nighthawks* (1942).

A **catalyst** is a person or thing that makes something happen, or makes something happen faster.

**Avant-garde** is a French word; it literally means "the vanguard"—the troops who move at the front of an army. In modern times, avant-garde artists are those who are in the forefront of a movement, at the cutting edge, ahead of their time.

In this 1903 portrait of New York's first skyscraper, the Flatiron building, Alfred Stieglitz used a snowy day and his camera to create a mood.

## Two Ninety-One

Robert Henri's bold realism, his strong brushstrokes, and his sensitivity to the environment seemed innovative and daring until you looked at the art that was being done in Paris. Artists there were breaking *all* the old rules. Alfred Stieglitz (STEEG-lits) brought European art to his small New York gallery at 291 Fifth Avenue even before the Armory Show scandalized the nation (see page 24 of this book to read about the shocking Armory Show). That gallery, called "291," became a center for the best in new art.

Stieglitz—a small-framed, elegant man born in fashionable Hoboken, New Jersey—had superb artistic taste, tremendous talent, and the passion to fight for his ideas. He was a photographer at a time when photography was making huge technological leaps. Stieglitz studied in Berlin and was as skilled in photographic chemistry as anyone in the world. In addition, he had the sensitivities of an artist and fierce determination. And he was determined to make people aware that great photographs can be great art.

Besides that, he cared about art in general. When he found an artist whose work he liked, he would do everything he could to be of help. And artists often need help—especially if they are breaking new ground. Modern artists were looking at the world through unusual lenses. They distorted line and shape and color playfully and didn't worry about realistic conventions. They looked for inspiration everywhere. Stieglitz's 291 gallery showed the best of their work. It held the first serious exhibition of children's art in the United States. It exhibited African-American art. And it showed some startling new paintings from Europe. Both Stieglitz and Henri helped make the Armory Show happen.

Stieglitz believed American artists were creating major works of art, and he said so in an arts magazine he published. He encouraged and exhibited works by John Marin, Marsden Hartley, Arthur Dove, Elie Nadelman, and Max Weber (never charging them a fee or profiting from any of their work). The most important of all the artists he guided and helped became his wife. She was Georgia O'Keeffe.

Have you ever known a baker who could take ordinary ingredients, mix them together, and come up with a cake that is unforgettably delicious? Georgia O'Keeffe did something like that with art. She took a single flower, or an old bone, or a mountain, used it

Alfred Stieglitz created a series of more than 400 photographs of Georgia O'Keeffe *(below):* her hands, eyes, hair, body, and face—working, resting, thinking. No other portrait record of an artist compares with it. This 1922 portrait hangs in the National Gallery of Art in Washington, D.C.

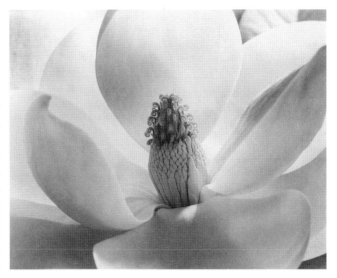

for her subject, put a rainbow of colors on her artist's palette, and created paintings that are, in their own way, as luscious as a fresh-baked cake.

O'Keeffe grew up in prairie Wisconsin, went to high school in traditional Virginia, studied art in Chicago, arrived in New York in 1914, married Stieglitz, and eventually moved to New Mexico (and fell in love with its earth and sky and mountains). "I found I could say things with color and shapes that I couldn't say in any other way—things I had no words for," wrote O'Keeffe. She was right. Check out a book of her paintings from your public library to see more of her work.

Imogen Cunningham was born in Oregon and grew up in Seattle. But to study photographic chemistry she had to go to Germany. On her way home, in 1910, she met Alfred Stieglitz. A few years later she married and had a family, and that kept her at home in San Francisco. So she went into her garden for inspiration and produced some photographs that have seldom been surpassed. She shot this photograph, *Magnolia Blossom,* in 1925.

Georgia O'Keeffe called this painting *Cow's Skull: Red, White and Blue.* She painted it in 1931. Today it is in the Metropolitan Museum in New York City.

In this abstract painting, called *Foghorns* (1929), artist Arthur Dove said the circles represent the sound of sirens in the mist. You can see this picture at the Colorado Springs Fine Arts Center. "I would like to make something that is real in itself, that does not remind anyone of any other thing, and that does not have to be explained—like the letter A, for instance," wrote Dove.

Polish-born Elie Nadelman came to America from Paris in 1914. He and his wife became major collectors of American barnyard art. They saw beauty in what many thought was junk. Do you think barnyard art influenced Nadelman's work? This wood sculpture, made around 1917, is called *Woman at the Piano*. You can see it at the Museum of Modern Art in New York City.

## Americans in Paris

In the western hemisphere, Europe was the center of the art world, and Paris was the center of Europe. After 1945, New York would take over. But in the early part of the century, Paris was the place to be if you were an artist, a writer, or a musician. Marc Chagall came from Russia, Pablo Picasso from Spain, Amadeo Modigliani from Italy, sculptor Elie Nadelman from Poland. Writer Ernest Hemingway was there, and composer Aaron Copland. Almost every American artist of significance (including Henri and Stieglitz) came, even if only for a short time. Some artists, like Henri Matisse and Paul Cézanne, didn't have to travel; they were French. If you ever find a magic wand and can put yourself in any time or place, you might consider Paris before World War I. It was as multicultural and creative as any society anywhere—ever.

Many of the Americans who went to Paris clustered around Gertrude Stein. She was a writer, but she had an eye for art, and she seemed to know everyone famous—like Picasso, who painted her portrait.

Marguerite Thompson arrived in Paris from Fresno, California, expecting to paint traditional canvases. Then she met Stein and Picasso, put pure color on her brushes, and painted boldly. Thompson was introduced to painter-sculptor William Zorach, who had come from Cleveland to Paris. They got married and became very popular figures on the art scene.

It was a learning place, but fun, too. Paris was filled with music and dance, as well as the other arts. The "modern" painters didn't attempt to copy life; they seemed to be reinventing it with color and imagination. No one could quite explain why all this was happening, but some thought it related to the new science. The ideas of James Clerk Maxwell, Charles Darwin, and Albert Einstein had turned the world upside down. Time and space were no longer what they seemed. Einstein said that what we see depends on where we are and how fast we're traveling. Everything's relative.

Some of the modern paintings were abstractions—the artist started with something real and stretched and changed and made it his own. Some paintings—called "nonobjective"—were pure color and design. They didn't try to represent anything real. Some artists looked at people and structures and painted them as if they were made of building blocks—or cubes—of color. They were called "Cubists." The Fauves (it means "wild beasts" in French) used wild, imaginative colors. The Futurists were an Italian group who said, "There is with us…chaos and the clashing of rhythms, totally opposed to one another, which we nevertheless assemble into a new harmony."

Arthur Dove was in Paris in 1910 when he painted what is said to to be the first abstract painting by an American. When he went home, he joined the Stieglitz artists at 291.

But after the Armory Show, in 1913, modernism wasn't just a European thing. It invaded America.

Stuart Davis enrolled in Robert Henri's art school at age 15. Henri had his students tramp downtown city streets and sit in saloons listening to jazz. "The big point with us was that in all of these places you could hear the blues, or tin-pan-alley tunes turned into real music, for the cost of a five-cent beer. It seems fantastic that today I can…hear this kind of music [on the radio] without taking a bus to Newark or Harlem." Davis's exposure to jazz influenced his painting. So did the Armory Show (where he exhibited some of his work). In *Landscape with Garage Lights* (1932) you can tell what he was painting, but it is an abstraction. It hangs at the University of Rochester in Rochester, New York.

Joseph Stella's *Battle of Lights, Coney Island, Mardi Gras* (1913–1914). You can see this painting at the Yale University Art Gallery in New Haven, Connecticut. It's big (about 6 x 7 feet)—a bold, exciting oil on canvas.

## Mighty Machines

In 1876, which was the year Joseph Stella (1876–1946) was born, Thomas Edison opened his "invention factory" in Menlo Park, New Jersey. Three years later he made a light bulb that shone for 45 hours. Have you ever had the power go out in your house? Can you picture a world without electric lights? Imagine how exciting lights were to people who had never had them. Now think of their reaction to an amusement park filled with lights. Coney Island, in Brooklyn (across the East River from Manhattan), was more than just an amusement park—it was a spectacular place, outlined with pulsating colored lights. How would you paint it if you were an artist? You can see how Joseph Stella did it in *Battle of Lights, Coney Island, Mardi Gras*. He was using the urban real-life subject matter of the Henri school and the futurist vision of some Italian poets and artists who wanted to do away with all traditional forms of art. (Stella studied art in Italy, Paris, and New York.)

*Coney Island* was painted in 1914, before World War I. Afterwards, things

Charles Sheeler, *American Landscape* (1930). It's in the Museum of Modern Art in New York. Can you find the man in the picture? He is just there to provide a sense of scale.

## The Great Figure

Among the rain
and lights
I saw the figure 5
in gold
on a red
firetruck
moving
tense
unheeded
to gong clangs
siren howls
and wheels rumbling
through the dark city.

—WILLIAM CARLOS WILLIAMS

were different. Paris was never quite the same for the art community; New York began its climb as an arts center. There seemed to be less light on most artists' palettes, and more cynicism. There was also more prosperity.

It was the Roaring Twenties and the judgments of the marketplace dominated. Back in 1914 (the first year of assembly-line production), Henry Ford had sold 248,000 Model Ts. By 1929, American auto makers were selling 4.8 million vehicles a year. Henry Ford and Frederick Taylor were apostles of industry. (Read Robert Kanigel's *The One Best Way* to learn about Taylor.) Their production ideas were transforming the nation's values. "The man who builds a factory builds a temple. The man who works there, worships there," said Ford.

"Our factories are our substitute for religious expression," wrote Charles Sheeler, who was hired to photograph the Ford automobile plant. He soon went from taking photographs of factories to painting them—in a style that is hard, precise, and often exquisite. Rarely did he put anything living in his paintings—no trees, no people, no animals. Those paintings are hymns to a machine-age world—a world away from the nature-inspired paintings of earlier American artists.

Sheeler described himself as a "Precisionist," thereby coining a name that other artists used, too. In 1928, Charles Demuth, from Lancaster, Pennsylvania, painted the best-known Precisionist painting—*The Figure 5 in Gold*. It has been called an

Charles Demuth, *The Figure 5 in Gold* (1928). Note the initials *W.C.W.*, and the names *Bill,* and *Carlo[s]*. This painting is at the Metropolitan Museum in New York.

**197**

An **icon** is a symbolic image (originally the word meant a religious image, such as the portrait of a saint, painted on a wood panel).

icon of American modernism. (What do you think that means?) Demuth's friend, poet William Carlos Williams, was looking out a window from an artist's studio when a big red fire truck—with the number 5 in glossy paint on its rear—roared by. Williams described it in a poem full of clear images. Demuth (who was rich, brilliant, and often ill) took the poem and painted its images. (The poem and the painting are both on the previous page.)

## Real American Art

Tom and Martha Smith, living in Kansas City, had a fine landscape hanging in the entrance hallway, and, in the parlor, Aunt Tillie gazed sternly from a portrait over the couch. What did the Smiths think of Joseph Stella or George Bellows? They'd never heard of them. But they had heard of the Armory Show and of modern art, and they associated both with the dangerous ideas that seemed to be coming from foreign lands and, sometimes, from New York. They knew of James Joyce, an Irishman whose book *Ulysses* was published in Paris and banned in the United States (that means you couldn't buy or sell it here) until 1933, when New York Federal District Judge John W. Woolsey decided in its favor in a landmark case against literary censorship.

Grant Wood, *American Gothic* (1930). Wood got his sister Nan to pose with a dentist from Cedar Rapids. Why do you think he is holding a pitchfork? The painting hangs in the Art Institute of Chicago.

**To lose caste** means "to lose social status or position."

Today many readers and critics consider *Ulysses* one of the greatest novels of the 20th century written in English. (It is not easy reading.) Joyce would influence other writers, but not be read by the Smiths, or their friends. They were bothered by the lack of tradition—and what they saw as vulgarity—in much modern art. Like many Americans, they were slow to embrace any of the new art, in books, music, or painting. But there were three contemporary artists whose work they did like: Thomas Hart Benton, John Steuart Curry, and Grant Wood. The Smiths first saw their paintings in 1933 in a show at the Kansas City Art Institute. They were presented as participants in a new regional art movement.

The three men barely knew each other, but a publicist for the museum wrote in the show's catalogue that "the shiploads of rubbish that had just been imported from the School of Paris were found to be just rubbish. The freaks...have lost caste." The artists in this show, he said, painted "real American art...which really springs from American soil and seeks to interpret American life."

When a *Time* magazine reporter saw the museum catalogue, he showed it to his boss, Henry Luce. Luce loved anything he thought was genuinely American. So he put Thomas Hart Benton on *Time*'s cover. Overnight, the three artists became stars. *Time* called them "earthy Midwesterners."

Only Iowa-born Grant Wood actually lived in the Midwest. Curry lived in

Connecticut and Benton had a studio in New York. But they all did have Midwestern roots. And they painted an idyllic America. They became known as "Regionalists." Benton (who was kin to a famous Missouri senator—see book 5 of *A History of US*) wrote of the acclaim they received, "A play was written and a stage erected for us. Grant Wood became the typical Iowa small-towner, John Curry the typical Kansas farmer, and I just an Ozark hillbilly. We accepted our roles."

So what kind of artists were they? Critic Robert Hughes says of Benton, "He was a dreadful artist most of the time." Of Curry he writes, "he was a semicompetent illustrator but an inept and formally incoherent painter." He describes Wood's "diligent and painstaking craftwork." But the Smiths loved the Regionalists. So do many Americans. And so do I.

*Above:* **John Steuart Curry, *Tornado Over Kansas* (1929), Muskegon Museum of Art, Muskegon, Michigan.**

***Semicompetent*** means "only half-able to do something"; ***inept*** means "clumsy, awkward, bungling"; ***incoherent*** means "not sticking together; falling apart."

*Left:* **Thomas Hart Benton, *Cradling Wheat* (1938), St. Louis Art Museum.**

**199**

Dorothea Lange's *Migrant Mother, Nipomo, California,* (1936). The woman is Florence Thompson; she was 32 years old and had 10 children. Lange wrote: "In a squatter camp at the edge of the pea fields. The crop froze this year and the family is destitute [penniless]. On this morning they had sold the tires from their car to pay for food."

On the facing page is Aaron Douglas's painting *Aspects of Negro Life: From Slavery Through Reconstruction* (1934). This is part of a four-panel mural in the New York Public Library's Schomburg Center for Research in Black Culture. Note the blues musician and the migrant worker. Music and religion—and the power of the Negro spiritual—inform Douglas's art.

## The Art of the Depression

In 1929, after the twenties finished roaring, another sound could be heard. Actually, it was more like a groan. The groan of hard times. Life was no longer a lark. It was grimy. The dreamy quality that characterized much of Stieglitz's fine work was replaced by stark reality in Depression-era photographs. The photographers who grappled with the Depression and the industrial era were called "social photographers." Walker Evans and Dorothea Lange were among the best of them.

Lange had polio as a child growing up in a poor section of New York City. She believed that gave her understanding of people with problems. As an adult, she lived in San Francisco with her sociologist husband and photographed city and farm life. When the Farm Security Administration went looking for photographers to document the effects of the Depression on farmers, Lange was one of six hired. Their photographs, intended for government records, turned out to be works of art as well.

William H. Johnson arrived in New York in 1918 from South Carolina and, like many African Americans, he headed for Harlem, which is north of the city's Central Park. Harlem was an exciting place to be, especially for writers and musicians who were creating important works during the Harlem Renaissance in the 1920s. Johnson studied at the National Academy and became skilled as a traditional artist. But Europe still lured Americans. So in 1926, Johnson went to Paris. From there he moved on to Denmark, where he married a potter. They went to Africa to study African art. By this time Johnson had developed his own style of painting, highly sophisticated, though it looked simple. It was based on primitive art and the work of some European artists called "Expressionists."

When Johnson returned to America, it was to the bleakness of the Depression. Like many other artists, he found work with the Works Progress Administration.

The WPA may have been the most creative idea our government has ever put into practice. Artists were especially hard hit by the Depression. When people are having difficulty finding enough money for food, they don't have any left for the arts. Franklin Roosevelt supported a program that put writers, painters, actors, sculptors, and musicians to work. This wasn't welfare. The artists had to produce work that the government then owned. They weren't paid much, but they earned respect, and they and others knew their government believed in their importance. In the eight years the program existed, 5,000 visual artists created 108,000 paintings, 18,000 pieces of sculpture, and

2,500 murals. Those works were placed in schools, libraries, post offices, and other government buildings (where you can see many of them today). They weren't all good—no one expected them to be—but many were. And the experiment of having the government value the arts was enormously encouraging to those who believe that a society without art would be a cold, sterile place. Besides, it kept a lot of artists eating.

Aaron Douglas, with a degree from the University of Nebraska, was one of the WPA muralists. His passionate work *Aspects of Negro Life* was painted for the 135th Street branch of the New York Public Library. He had been slated to be a high-school principal in Kansas City, but his friends insisted that his artistic gifts were too good to be denied. He headed for Harlem, and hard times.

But the greatest of the black artists who worked under WPA was Jacob Lawrence. He was too young, he said, for "a wall." So he didn't paint a mural. What he did paint were 60 small paintings that tell the story of black migration from South to North, from field to factory. They are among the most powerful social statements in American art (see page 40).

Sculptor Louise Nevelson said, "I got on the WPA. Now that gave me a certain kind of freedom....Our great artists like Rothko, de Kooning, Franz Kline...had that moment of peace...to continue with their work. I think it's a highlight of our American history." Jackson Pollock, from Cody, Wyoming, was a WPA artist. So was Ben Shahn (see chapter 4 and page 35), who said, "I was totally involved. It was a total commitment." Another painter wrote, "There's something that's unforgettable about that period. There was a sense of belonging to something, even if was an underprivileged and downhearted time. It was exciting."

*Above:* William H. Johnson said he would try to "tell the story of the Negro as he existed." His dignified, graceful works do just that. This painting of a child, *Li'l Sis* (1944), is in the National Museum of American Art in Washington, D.C.

# Chronology of Events

**1905:** President Theodore Roosevelt's niece Eleanor marries her fifth cousin Franklin D. Roosevelt

**1907:** Oklahoma becomes the 46th state

**1912:** New Mexico and Arizona become the 47th and 48th states

**1914:** War breaks out in Europe between the Allies (Britain, France, Italy, Russia) and the Central Powers (Germany, Austria-Hungary, Turkey)

**1916:** Woodrow Wilson is reelected president

**Apr. 1917:** The U.S. enters the war on the side of the Entente powers

**Nov. 1917:** In Russia, the revolutionary communist Bolshevik Party overthrows a more moderate regime and takes Russia out of the war

**1918:** A worldwide influenza epidemic kills nearly 500,000 Americans

**1918:** Armistice Day, November 11: the war is over; Germany accepts Wilson's Fourteen Points as the basis for peace negotiations

**1919:** Babe Ruth joins the New York Yankees and helps restore baseball's popularity after the Chicago Black Sox World Series scandal the same year

**1919:** At the Paris peace conference, Germany is humiliated and must pay punitive reparations; the Allies write a charter for a League of Nations

**1919:** Wilson asks Americans to support the League, but a stroke makes him hardly able to function

**1919:** The 18th Amendment to the Constitution prohibits making or selling alcohol in the U.S.

**1920:** The 19th Amendment gives women the vote

**1920:** Republican Warren G. Harding, advocating a "return to normalcy," becomes 29th president

**1920:** In a "red scare," thousands of immigrants are arrested on suspicion of being communist

**1920:** KDKA, the nation's first commercial radio station, begins broadcasting out of Pittsburgh

**1920:** The Census shows that for the first time more than half the United States population is urban

**1921:** Franklin D. Roosevelt is crippled by polio

**1922:** Harding ignores government corruption, which culminates in the Teapot Dome scandal

**1922:** Louis Armstrong leaves New Orleans to play for King Oliver's Creole Jazz Band in Chicago

**1922:** The era of the Harlem Renaissance in the arts among black Americans begins with the publication of Claude McKay's *Harlem Shadows*

**1923:** When Harding dies suddenly, Vice President Calvin Coolidge becomes 30th president; he is reelected the following year

**1925:** F. Scott Fitzgerald publishes *The Great Gatsby*

**1925:** A high-school teacher, John Scopes, is tried and convicted in Tennessee for teaching evolution

**1926:** Scientist Robert Goddard launches the first successful rocket powered by liquid fuel

**1927:** Charles Lindbergh makes the first solo flight across the Atlantic in the *Spirit of St. Louis*

**1927:** The first talking motion picture, *The Jazz Singer*

**1927:** In *Nixon* v. *Herndon*, the Supreme Court rules that a Texas law preventing blacks from voting in primary elections is unconstitutional

**1927:** Babe Ruth hits 60 home runs

**1928:** Walt Disney's Mickey Mouse makes his first appearance in *Steamboat Willie*

**1928:** Herbert Hoover becomes 31st president, defeating Democrat Al Smith in a landslide

**1928:** FDR is elected governor of New York

**1929:** The stock market crashes in October and hastens a worldwide economic depression

**1931:** Japan invades Manchuria

**1932:** The Bonus Army of war veterans march to Washington, asking for early payment of war benefits

**1932:** Mildred "Babe" Didrikson wins three track-and-field medals at the Olympic Games

**1932:** Depression: one in four workers in America—12 million people—are unemployed

**1932:** Democrat Franklin D. Roosevelt pledges to beat the Depression and becomes 32nd president

**1933:** Adolf Hitler, leader of the Nazi Party, becomes chancellor of Germany

**1933:** Frances Perkins becomes secretary of labor and the first woman cabinet member

**1933:** The first "100 Days" of FDR's presidency: Congress creates more agencies and passes more laws to relieve poverty than ever before

**1933:** The 21st Amendment repeals Prohibition

**1934–37:** After three years of drought, the farms of the Plains have become the Dust Bowl; 3 million victims migrate west in search of work and land

**1935:** Social Security Act introduces taxes to pay for unemployment insurance and old-age pensions

**1936:** Jesse Owens wins four gold medals in track events at the Olympic Games in Berlin

**1937:** Japan and China begin fighting in Manchuria

**1938:** Germany annexes Austria

**1939:** All German Jews made to wear yellow stars of David sewn onto their clothes for identification

**1939:** Germany occupies Czechoslovakia

**1939:** Stalin signs a nonaggression pact with Hitler

**1939:** Germany invades Poland; Allies declare war

**1939:** Physicist Albert Einstein helps convince FDR to fund the Manhattan Project to build atom bomb

**1940:** Germany rapidly overwhelms Norway, Finland, Denmark, Holland, Belgium, and France

**1940:** FDR is first president elected to three terms

**1940:** Germany tries to bomb Britain into submission

**June 1941:** Hitler ignores the Nazi–Soviet Pact, invading the Soviet Union; Russia joins the Allies

**Sep. 1941:** The siege of Leningrad begins

**1941:** FDR creates the Lend-Lease program to supply the Allies with weapons and raw materials

**1941:** Germany pushes deep into Russia and Ukraine

**Dec. 1941:** Japan bombs the U.S. fleet in Pearl Harbor, Hawaii; America enters the war

**Dec. 1941–Jan. 1942:** Japan invades Thailand, Malaya, Borneo, Burma, the Philippines, Hong Kong, Indonesia; captures Midway and Wake islands

**1942:** FDR orders 112,000 Japanese Americans into internment camps for the war's duration

**May 1942:** Heavy losses for both U.S. and Japan in battle of Coral Sea; first setback for Japan

**May 1942:** U.S. surrenders in Philippines

**June 1942:** U.S. defeats Japan at battle of Midway

**Aug. 1942:** U.S. defeats Japan at Guadalcanal

**1942:** U.S. forces join British and French to fight Germany and Italy in North Africa

**1942:** The Nazis begin systematic murder of Jews and others in concentration camps

**1942:** The Allies capture Enigma, a code machine, and begin to crack German secret codes

**Feb. 1943:** The Soviet Red Army defeats Germany at Stalingrad and begins to push Germany back

**June 1943:** Allies win battle of Atlantic

**July 1943:** Allied forces invade Sicily

**Sep. 1943:** Italian army surrenders

**Nov. 1943–Feb. 1944:** U.S. takes back numerous Pacific islands from Japanese

**June 1944:** Allied forces enter Rome

**June 1944:** Combined U.S., British, and Canadian forces invade Normandy, France, on D-Day, June 6

**Nov. 1944:** FDR wins fourth term!

**Jan. 1945:** The U.S. returns to the Philippines

**Jan. 1945:** The Allies defeat Germany in Battle of the Bulge in the Ardennes mountains in Belgium

**Feb. 1945:** Roosevelt, Churchill, and Stalin meet at Yalta in the Crimea

**Feb. 1945:** Allies firebomb Dresden, Germany

**Feb. 1945:** U.S. troops land on island of Iwo Jima

**Apr. 1945:** Hitler commits suicide in Berlin

**Apr. 1945:** President Roosevelt dies; Harry S. Truman sworn in as 33rd president

**Apr. 1945:** Soviet troops enter Berlin

**Apr. 1945:** U.S. troops liberate 32,000 prisoners in Dachau concentration camp, Germany

**May 1945:** Germany surrenders; VE Day, May 8

**June 1945:** Charter established for United Nations

**July 1945:** Truman, Churchill, and Stalin meet at Potsdam in Germany to plan for peace in Europe

**Aug. 1945:** Atomic bombs dropped on Japanese cities of Hiroshima and Nagasaki

**Aug. 1945:** Japan surrenders; VJ Day, August 15

# More Books to Read

*Here are some books that tell about life during the period discussed in this book. Some were written for grown-ups—but they are not too hard to read, they tell wonderful stories, and they are the kind of books you will always remember. Besides these books, there is something else you should search out if you don't know about it:* Cobblestone, *which is a history magazine for young people. Each issue focuses on a subject in history, and back issues can be found in most libraries or ordered from Cobblestone Publishing, 30 Grove Street, Peterborough, NH 03458.*

**F. Scott Fitzgerald,** *The Great Gatsby* (First published in 1925.) Simon & Schuster, 2004. The best American novel of the 1920s. This story of crazy pleasure seekers and unrequited love is not very long, and it will make you laugh and cry at the same time. Then try some of Fitzgerald's short stories, which are quite easy to read.

**Anne Frank,** *The Diary of a Young Girl* (1958). Random House, 1996. In Dutch, the language Anne Frank wrote in, her diary is called *The House Behind,* because she and her family, who were Jews, hid from the Nazis in a few secret rooms inside a Dutch family's Amsterdam home. This book may make you cry, but you will love Anne and be amazed at what a marvelous writer she was at the age of 14.

**Ernest Hemingway,** *A Farewell to Arms* (1929). Scribner, 2003. An enthralling novel that draws on the author's own experience as a soldier in the Great War.

**John Hersey,** *Hiroshima* (1946). Vintage, 1989. This little book—it was originally an article in *The New Yorker* magazine—is a clear, sympathetic telling of the dropping of the first atomic bomb and its devastating effect on Hiroshima and its people. You should also try another very good book by John Hersey about the war called *A Bell for Adano* (1944; Vintage 1988).

**Gloria Houston,** *Littlejim* (1990). Harper-Collins, 1993. Littlejim Houston lives in the Appalachian mountains in North Carolina during the Great War. He's the best student at his school and works hard on the farm—but Littlejim's father wants his son to be a logger and hunter like him, and he thinks being good at studying is sissy. Then Littlejim enters a big essay contest on "What it means to be an American"; what will his father think if he wins?

**Jeanne Wakatsuki Houston and James D. Houston,** *Farewell to Manzanar* (1973). Houghton Mifflin, 2002. In 1942, when the author was seven years old, she and all her family, along with thousands of other Japanese-Americans, were sent suddenly to Manzanar internment camp in the desert of California's Owens Valley. Her father was sent even farther away; it was nine months before he was allowed to rejoin them. This book describes vividly the Wakatsukis' humiliations and hardships.

**Zora Neale Hurston,** *Their Eyes Were Watching God* (1937). HarperCollins, 2000. A terrific and very influential story about growing up poor and black in the South early in the twentieth century.

**Jerome Lawrence and Robert E. Lee,** *Inherit the Wind* (1969). Ballantine, 2003. This is a thrilling play (also made into a good movie that you might be able to find on video) which is a fictionalized dramatization of the Scopes trial of 1925.

**Lois Lenski,** *Strawberry Girl* (1945). Harper-Collins, 1995. Birdie Boyer is 10 when her family moves to the Florida backwoods to grow sugarcane, oranges, and strawberries. She finds out that it's hard dealing with drought and frost, but it's much harder to cope with unfriendly neighbors: the Slaters. This excellent story is all about how the Boyers farm, play, go to school—and deal with the Slaters.

**Sonia Levitin,** *Journey to America; Silver Days* (1970, 1989). Simon & Schuster, 1992, 1993. In 1938 Lisa Platt's father left Berlin for America in the middle of the night. Lisa, her sisters, and her mother have to wait until he has made enough money to send for them. But life for Jews in

Hitler's Germany becomes more and more scary; finally the Platts escape to Switzerland—where they wait and wait, with no money and not enough to eat, for a letter to arrive from America. It wasn't easy even when they got here. In *Silver Days,* the sequel, the author tells about the difficulties of being poor Jewish refugees in wartime California.

**Cornelius Ryan,** *The Longest Day* (1959). Simon & Schuster, 1994. A really exciting retelling of the story of D-Day and the invasion of Normandy.

**John Steinbeck,** *The Grapes of Wrath* (1939). Penguin, 2002. The Joad family are sharecropper victims of the Dust Bowl in the 1930s. Piling everything they own onto their decrepit car, they set off to look for work picking fruit and vegetables in California. This famous book helped bring home the plight of the "Okies" to the rest of the country. It is a great read.

**Mildred D. Taylor,** *Let the Circle Be Unbroken; Mississippi Bridge; The Road to Memphis; Roll of Thunder, Hear My Cry,* all published by Dial. Cassie Logan and her family live in rural Mississippi in Jim Crow times, when black people who got "uppity" could be risking their lives. Mildred Taylor's four books are about the racism of the Deep South in the 1920s and '30s and how it affects the Logans at different times during Cassie's childhood and youth. They are very well written and sometimes hard to take.

**Jade Snow Wong,** *Fifth Chinese Daughter,* (1945). University of Washington Press, 2003. Jade Snow Wong's parents owned a small overalls factory in San Francisco in the 1920s, when she was born. Until she was about 10, Jade Snow led a very sheltered Chinese life—looking after little sister, learning to cook rice perfectly, and discovering that grown-ups thought boys were more important than girls. Jade Snow decides to work hard in school; eventually she must convince her parents to allow her to be the first girl in her family to go to college. This is a splendid true story of the growing up of not just one Chinese daughter, but a whole family.

*Construction Worker on the Empire State Building* (c. 1930), by photographer Lewis Hines, a picture popularly known as "Sky Boy"

# Picture Credits

**AP / WW: Associated Press / Wide World Photos**
**CB: Corbis-Bettmann**
**FDR: Franklin D. Roosevelt Library**

**LOC: Library of Congress**
**NA: National Archives**
**UPI: United Press International**

5: Joy Hakim; 6: Freelance Photographers Guild; 7: Granger Collection, New York; 8: NA; 9 (top): detail from Nathaniel Currier, *The Way They Go to California*, 1849, Oakland Museum, Museum Founders Fund; 9 (left): NA; 9 (top right, middle right): Bowdoin College Museum of Art, Brunswick, Maine; 9 (bottom right): Museum of Fine Arts, Boston / National Portrait Gallery; 10 (top): U. S. Senate Collection; 10 (bottom): LOC; 11: NA; 12: Monticello / Thomas Jefferson Memorial Foundation; 13–14: NA; 15 (left): AP / WW; 15 (right): *The New York Times*; 16: Culver Pictures; 18: NA; 19 (top): Sir William Orpen, *The Signing of Peace in the Hall of Mirrors, Versailles, 28th June, 1919*, Imperial War Museum, London; 19 (bottom left): Harding, *Brooklyn Eagle*, 1919; 19 (bottom right): *Chicago News*, 1919; 20 (top): Harris & Ewing; 20 (below left): Holmes Papers, Harvard Law School Library; 20 (bottom right): LOC; 21 (top): National Library of Medicine, Bethesda; 21 (bottom), 22 (top): Sy Seidman; 22 (bottom): CB; 23: LOC; 24: Marcel Duchamp, *Nude Descending a Staircase, No. 2*, 1912, Philadelphia Museum of Art, Louise and Walter Arensberg Collection; 25 (bottom): Ben Shahn, *Women's Christian Temperance Union Parade*, c.1934, Museum of the City of New York; 26: Corbis; 27: Ben Shahn, *Bootleggers*, c.1934, Museum of the City of New York; 28: Ben Shahn, *Speakeasy Scene, Interior*, 1934, Museum of the City of New York; 29 (top): Brown Brothers; 29 (bottom), 30–31: LOC; 32 (lower left): Brown Brothers; 32 (bottom): LOC, French Collection; 33 (top): Douglass County Museum; 33 (bottom): League of Women Voters of the City of New York; 34: Culver Pictures; 35 (top left): Brown Brothers; 35 (top right): AP / WW; 35 (bottom right): Ben Shahn, *Bartolomeo Vanzetti and Nicola Sacco*, Museum of Modern Art, New York, gift of Abby Aldrich Rockefeller (photo © 1998, Museum of Modern Art); 36 (top and bottom): UPI / CB; 36 (right): *Philadelphia Inquirer*, March 13, 1919, New York Public Library; 37–38: LOC; 39 (top): Underwood & Underwood; 39 (bottom): Brown Brothers; 40 (top): Ellison Hoover, *Life*, March 6, 1924; 40 (bottom): Jacob Lawrence, *Migration Series, (No. 1)*, Phillips Collection, Washington, DC; 41: Culver Pictures; 42 (top): Brown Brothers; 42 (top right): UPI / CB; 42 (bottom): LOC; 43: Culver Pictures; 45: CB; 46 (bottom left): Metropolitan Museum of Art, Gift of David A. Shulte, 1928 (28.127.1); 46 (bottom right): Brown Brothers; 47 (left): LOC; 47 (right): Paul McFarlane—Mary Broderick; 48 (top): Culver Pictures; 49 (left): Bronx County Historical Society; 49 (left): Brown Brothers; 50 (bottom): John Springer / CB; 51 (left): National Baseball League; 51 (top middle): collection of Phil Dixon; 51 (top right): James Bell; 51 (bottom): Mike Anderson; 52 (top): National Baseball Hall of Fame; 52 (middle): National Baseball Hall of Fame; 52 (bottom): *Kansas City Call*; 53 (top): Don Rogosin; 53 (middle): National Baseball Hall of Fame; 53 (bottom): Mark Rucker; 54 (top): UPI / CB; 54 (bottom): *New York Daily News*; 55: Hogan Jazz Archive, Howard-Tilton Memorial Library, Tulane University; 56: collection of Leonard V. Huber; 57: Archibald Motley, Jr. *Blues*, 1929, collection of Archie Motley and Valerie Gerrard Browne, photo courtesy of the Chicago Historical Society; 58 (above left): LOC; 58 (bottom), 59: Hogan Jazz Archive, Howard-Tilton Memorial Library, Tulane University; 60–61: CB; 62 (top): *The Razor's Edge* (20th Century Fox, 1946); 62 (bottom): *The Little Colonel* (Fox Film Corp, 1935): 63–64: Time Pix, NASA Goddard Space Flight Center, Corbis; 67: Minnesota Historical Society; 68: NA; 68 (inset), 71: Corbis; 72 (top right): Culver Pictures; 72 (top left): LOC; 72 (bottom left): Granger Collection; 73 (bottom left): CB; 73 (top right): NA; 73 (bottom right): *The New York Times*; 74: Granger Collection; 75: Underwood & Underwood / CB; 76 (top): CB; 76 (bottom), 77: Corbis; 78: LOC; 79: Milton Brooks, *Detroit News*, July 1930; 80 (top): William Gropper, *Migration*, Arizona State University Art Museum, Tempe; 80 (bottom): LOC; 81: Dorthea Lange / LOC; 82: Alexandre Hogue, *Drought Stricken Area*, Dallas Museum of Fine Arts (1945.6); 83 (top): LOC; 83 (bottom): Special Collections Division, University of Washington Libraries; 84: Herbert Hoover Library; 85 (top): CB; 85 (bottom): NA; 86 (top): Granger Collection; 86 (bottom): Herbert Hoover Library; 87 (top): *Literary Digest*, November 21, 1931, New York Public Library; 87 (bottom), 88–93: FDR; 94 (top): CB; 94 (bottom left and right): FDR; 95 (top left): CB; 95 (top right): FDR; 95 (bottom): AP / WW; 96 (left): Special Collections, Van Pelt-Dietrich Library Center, University of Pennsylvania; 96 (top): UPI / CB; 96 (bottom), 97 (left): FDR; 97 (right): UPI / CB; 98–99: FDR; 100: CB; 101 (top): FDR; 101 (bottom left): John Tinney McCutcheon, *Chicago Tribune*; 101 (bottom right): LOC; 102 (top): UPI / CB; 102 (bottom): FDR; 103 (top): UPI / CB; 103 (bottom): Miguel Covarrubias, *The Inauguration of FDR*, 1933, *Vanity Fair*, National Portrait Gallery, Smithsonian Institution; 104 (top left and right, bottom): FDR; 104 (below right): LOC; 105: UPI / CB; 106 (top): Peter Arno, *The New Yorker*, 1936; 106 (bottom): LOC; 107 (top): Granger Collection; 107 (bottom): AP / WW; 108 (right): UPI / CB; 109 (left): collection of Kenneth W. Randell; 109 (top): Corbis; 109 (bottom): Otto Rösner / NA; 110 (bottom left): UPI / CB; 110 (bottom right): AP / WW; 111 (right): John Erikson; 111 (top right): Otto Hagel; 111 (bottom left): AP / WW; 111 (lower right): FDR; 112 (top): L. M. Muller; 112 (bottom): Hulton Picture Service; 113: Leo Baeck Institute, New York; 114: NA; 115 (top left): Yivo Institute for Jewish Research; 115 (top right): Peter Hunter, Riijksinstituut voor Oorlogsdocumentatie, Amsterdam; 115 (bottom): Lenni Sonnenfeld, University of the State of New York; 116: Wiener Library, London; 117 (top left and right, bottom): NA; 117 (middle right): Henry Beville; 118 (top): UPI / CB; 118 (bottom): Granger Collection; 119: courtesy of Liane Rief-Lehrer; 120 (top): General Electric; 120 (bottom): U. S. Immigration and Naturalization Service; 121 (top left): Los Alamos Historical Museum Photos Archives; 121 (top middle, top right, bottom): Los Alamos National Laboratory and National Atomic Museum; 122 (top): NA; 122 (bottom): *Washington Star*; 123: Stock Montage; 124: California Institute of Technology; 125 (left): NA; 125 (top right): Tita Binz, Mannheim, courtesy AIP Emilio Segrè Visual Archives; 125 (bottom): California Institute of Technology; 126: Charles Cundall, *The Withdrawal from Dunkirk, June, 1940*, Imperial War Museum, London; 126 (bottom), 127: NA; 117 (top left and right): Fox Photo; 130 (bottom): *Detroit News*; 131 (top): LOC; 131 (bottom): Roger-Violette, Paris; 132 (top): Bildarchiv Preussischer Kulturbesitz, Berlin; 132 (bottom), 133 (bottom left): Gillon Photo Agency; 134 (top): Bundesarchiv, Koblenz; 134 (middle, bottom): Sovfoto; 135–137: NA; 138: Corbis; 139 (top): NA; 139 (bottom left): UPI / CB; 139 (bottom right): Naval Historical Foundation; 140 (top): NA; 140 (bottom): Time Pix; 141 (top right): German Bundesarchiv; 141 (right second and third from top, bottom right): : 141 (bottom left) Corbis: NA; 141 (top left): UPI / CB; 142–143: NA; 144–145: Dorthea Lange / NA; 147: from Miné Okubo, *Citizen 13660*, Columbia University Press, 1946; 147: Northeastern Photo; 148 (top): NA; 148 (bottom): Toyo Miyatake; 149: U. S. Navy; 149–150, 151 (top): NA; 151 (bottom): Dwight Shepler, *Fighter Scramble—Guadalcanal*, Naval Historical Foundation; 152: Joy Hakim; 153: NA; 154 (top left): Frank B. Elam Photo; 154 (top right): NA; 154 (bottom right): Planeta Publishers, Moscow; 155, 156 (top left and right): NA; 156 (bottom): Ullstein-Birnback; 157 (top): UPI / CB; 157 (bottom): Bildarchiv Preussischer Kulturbesitz, Berlin; 158–159: NA; 160 (top): Dwight D. Eisenhower Library; 161 (top right): Robert Capa Archive, International Center for Photography; 163–164, 165 (top left and center right): NA; 165 (top right): *Arizona Republic*, 1943; 165 (bottom left): Dmitri Baltermants, Moscow; 166: NA; 167 (bottom): Ullstein-Bilderdienst, Berlin; 168–169: FDR; 170, 171 (top left and bottom): Harry S. Truman Library; 171 (top right): Stan Cohen; 172 (top): UPI / CB; 172 (bottom): FDR; 173–174: NA; 175: UPI / CB; 176, 177 (top left): AP / WW; 177 (top right): Keystone, Hamburg; 177 (middle left): Hulton Deutsch Collection, London; 177 (bottom left): NA; 177 (bottom right): Sovfoto; 178 (top right): UPI / CB; 178 (center left): Frederico Patellani, Milan; 178 (bottom right): NA; 179: Harry S. Truman Library; 180: NA; 182 (top left): UPI / CB; 182 (top right, bottom), 183 (top): NA; 183 (middle): Eiichi Matsumoto; 183 (bottom): Naval Historical Foundation; 184–185: NA; 186: George Wesley Bellows, *Cliff Dwellers*, 1913, Los Angeles County Museum of Art; 187: Edward Hopper, *Nighthawks*, 1942, Art Institute of Chicago, Friends of American Art Collection (photo © 1998, Art Institute of Chicago); 188 (top): Alfred Stieglitz, *Flatiron Building*, 1903, Metropolitan Museum of Art, New York, Alfred Stieglitz Collection (photo © 1998, Metropolitan Museum of Art); 188 (bottom): Alfred Stieglitz, *Georgia O'Keefe: A Portrait—Head*, 1922, National Gallery of Art, Washington, DC, Alfred Stieglitz Collection (photo © 1998, Board of Trustees, National Gallery of Art); 189 (top): Imogen Cunningham, *Magnolia Blossom*, 1925, courtesy of Christie's Images, New York; 189 (bottom): Georgia O'Keefe, *Cow's Skull: Red, White, and Blue*, 1931, Metropolitan Museum of Art, New York, Alfred Stieglitz Collection (photo © 1994, Metropolitan Museum of Art); 190 (top): Arthur Dove, *Fog Horns*, 1929, Colorado Springs Fine Arts Center, anonymous gift; 190 (bottom): Elie Nadelman, *Women at the Piano*, c. 1917, Museum of Modern Art, New York, Philip L. Goodwin Collection (photo © 1998, Museum of Modern Art); 191: Stuart Davis, *Landscape with Garage Lights*, 1932, Memorial Art Gallery, University of Rochester, New York; 192: Joseph Stella, *Battle of Lights, Coney Island, Mardi Gras*, 1913–1914, Yale University Gallery of Fine Arts, bequest of Dorothea Dreier to the Collection Société Anonyme; 193 (top): Charles Sheeler, *American Landscape*, 1930, Museum of Modern Art, New York, gift of Abby Aldrich Rockefeller (photo © 1998, Museum of Modern Art); 193 (bottom): Charles Henry Demuth, *The Figure 5 in Gold*, Metropolitan Museum of Art, New York, Alfred Stieglitz Collection (photo © 1996, Metropolitan Museum of Art); 194: Grant Wood, *American Gothic*, 1930, Art Institute of Chicago, Friends of American Art Collection, all rights reserved by the Art Institute of Chicago and VAGA, New York (photo © 1998, Art Institute of Chicago); 195 (top): John Steuart Curry, *Tornado Over Kansas*, Muskegon Museum of Art, Muskegon, Michigan, Hackley Picture Fund; 195 (bottom): Thomas Hart Benton, *Cradling Wheat*, 1938, The Saint Louis Art Museum, purchase; 196: Dorthea Lange / NA; 197 (top): William H. Johnson, *Li'l Sis*, 1944, National Museum of American Art, Washington, DC / Art Resource, NY; 197 (bottom): Aaron Douglas, *Aspects of Negro Life: From Slavery Through Reconstruction*, Art and Artifacts Division, Schomburg Center for Research in Black Culture, New York Public Library, Astor, Lenox and Tilden Foundations; 201: Lewis Hines, *Construction Worker on the Empire State Building*, c.1930, Avery Architectural and Fine Arts Library, Columbia University

# Index

# A Note from the Author

*It was the best of times, it was the worst of times, it was the age of wisdom, it was the age of foolishness....*

Charles Dickens was thinking about the 18th century when he began a famous novel with those words. But he might have been describing the first half of the 20th century.

The best of times? The worst of times?

Which was it? It was both.

Take that bomb, for instance. It was horrible to think of its hellish, destructive force. But there was another side to atomic energy. Wisely used, it held great hope for the future.

Wisdom and foolishness in modern times? You bet. And sometimes it was hard to tell them apart. Should the bomb have been dropped? The answer was obvious: of course not.

It was outrageous, and barbaric to bomb children and other civilians with any kind of bomb. The bombs dropped on Hiroshima and Nagasaki were the terrible outcome of a misguided idea—strategic bombing (which meant bombing of any targets, including civilian, that might aid the war). Strategic bombing was first tried in Spain in 1939 by Fascist forces. Hitler took the idea further when he bombed Britain. The Allies went still further.

But there was another question that had to be asked. What would you have done if you were Harry Truman? If you had a weapon that would end the war quickly (and save lives on both sides), would you have used it? Of course you would. In 1945, hardly anyone even thought of hesitating.

There was a lesson in all this. It isn't easy to be a citizen in a democracy. It takes work: reading, listening, and questioning. And yet, after the war, some people were still crying out for simple solutions. They were looking for leaders with slogans, not thinking explanations. They weren't willing to take time to become responsible citizens. A good citizen needs to be well informed, to get involved, and to know history.

Why history? Because it helps us make judgments. And history shows us that ideas set in motion sometimes head in unforeseen directions. They may lead to places we wish they wouldn't go.

The people in Germany who followed Hitler didn't expect his ideas to take them into the sewers of evil and destruction. But they didn't examine those ideas carefully. They didn't protest while they still had a chance. They didn't consider other people's feelings. They listened to simplistic messages, and they let others think for them.

The people in the United States who were racists and bigots didn't usually mean to hurt others. But they didn't do much thinking. History tells us that disgusting, ugly ideas are sometimes accepted by ordinary (but unthinking) people.

Did we learn anything from the history of the first half of the 20th century?

Yes. We learned of the horror and stupidity of totalitarian rule. (In totalitarian governments, a powerful leader is usually in league with the military, the police, and sometimes with business interests. Once they seize power, the ordinary citizen doesn't stand a chance.)

We learned of the waste of war. What if all those 20th-century children who died of violence had lived? What might they have accomplished?

And what of the waste of resources? Destroying a million dollars' worth of city buildings and streets usually costs the other side a million dollars in planes, bombs, and equipment. (Imagine if that money were spent to make life better for people.)

We learned something else: in a time of crisis, the best in people often appears. There was much real heroism during those years of war and depression. People worked together, and sacrificed, and felt good about that, and about each other. Is there some way to bring that sense of shared emergency to today's problems? How can we work together to make our cities safe? To improve our schools? To help all our citizens pursue happiness?

# ATLAS
# Map of My Country

This is part of a poem by John Holmes (1904-1962), poet, essayist who taught at Tufts University in Medford, Massachusetts.

A map of my native country is all edges,
The shore touching sea, the easy impartial rivers
Splitting the local boundary lines, round hills in two
    townships,
Blue ponds interrupting the careful country shapes.
The Mississippi runs down the middle. Cape Cod.
    The Gulf.
Nebraska is on latitude forty. Kansas is west of
    Missouri.

When I was a child, I drew it, from memory,
A game in the schoolroom, naming the big cities
    right.

Cloud shadows were not shown, nor where winter
    whitens,
Nor the wide road the day's wind takes.
None of the tall letters told my grandfather's name.
Nothing said, Here they see in clear air a hundred
    miles.
Here they go to bed early. They fear snow here.
Oak trees and maple boughs I had seen on the long
    hillsides
Changing color, and laurel, and bayberry, were
    never mapped.
Geography told only capitals and state lines.

I have come a long way using other men's maps for
    the turnings.
I have a long way to go.
It is time I drew the map again,
Spread with the broad colors of life, and words of
    my own
Saying, Here the people worked hard, and died for
    the wrong reasons.
Here wild strawberries tell the time of year.
I could not sleep, here, while bell-buoys beyond the
    surf rang.

Here trains passed in the night, crying of distance,
Calling to cities far away, listening for an answer.

On my own map of my own country
I shall show where there were never wars,
And plot the changed way I hear men speak in the
    west,
Words in the south slower, and food different.
Not the court-houses seen floodlighted at night
    from trains,
But the local stone built into housewalls,
And barns telling the traveler where he is
By the slant of the roof, the color of the paint.

Not monuments. Not the battlefields famous in
    school.
But Thoreau's pond, and Huckleberry Finn's island.
I shall name an unhistorical hill three boys climbed
    one moring.
Lines indicate my few journeys,
And the long way letters come from absent friends.

Forest is where green fern cooled me under the big
    trees.
Ocean is where I ran in the white drag of waves on
    white sand.
Music is what I heard in a country house while
    hearts broke,
Not knowing they were breaking, and Brahms wrote
    it.

All that I remember happened to me here.
This is the known world.
I shall make a star here for a man who died too
    young.
Here, and here, in gold, I shall mark two towns
Famous for nothing, except that I have been happy
    in them.

Seattle
Olympia ★  Tacoma
Spokane
WASHINGTON
Portland  Columbia River
Great Falls
Helena ★  MONTANA
NORTH DAKOTA
Bismarck ★
★ Salem
Eugene
OREGON
Billings
Yellowstone River
SOUTH DAKOTA
Medford
IDAHO
Boise ★
Snake River
WYOMING
Casper
Rapid City  Pierre ★
Missouri River
40°N
NEVADA
Reno
Sacramento ★
Carson City
San ★ Oakland
Francisco
San Jose
Salinas
Fresno
CALIFORNIA
Ogden
Salt Lake City ★
Provo
UTAH
Colorado River
Cheyenne ★
Fort Collins
Denver ★
COLORADO
Colorado Springs
Pueblo
NEBRASKA
Platte
KANSAS
Arkansas
Las Vegas
St. George
Bakersfield
Santa Barbara
Oxnard
Los Angeles
San Bernardino
Riverside
Flagstaff
ARIZONA
Phoenix ★
San Diego
Yuma
Tucson
Santa Fe ★
Albuquerque
NEW MEXICO
Roswell
Las Cruces
El Paso
OKLAHOMA
Oklaho
Amarillo
Lawton
Lubbock
Abilene
Odessa
PACIFIC OCEAN
30°N
TEXA
Aus
San Antonio
MEXICO
Laredo
Rio Grande
Brow

Barrow  ARCTIC OCEAN
70°N
Arctic Circle
ALASKA
Nome
Yukon River
Fairbanks
CANADA
Anchorage
60°N
Scale
0    200 Miles
0    200 Kilometers
Juneau
130°W
Ketchikan
PACIFIC OCEAN
170°W  160°W  150°W  140°W

PACIFIC OCEAN
N
W   E
S
Honolulu
HAWAII
Hilo
20°N
Scale
0    100 Miles
0    100 Kilometers
160°W  155°W

50°N
120°W  110°W  100°W

110°W

212

ARCTIC OCEAN

180
120W
60W
80N

Greenland
(Denmark)

Arctic Circle
Alaska
(U.S.)

60N

Iceland

Canada

**NORTH
AMERICA**

see
inset
below

40N

United States

ATLANTIC
OCEAN

Azores Is.
(Port.)

Midway Islands (U.S.)

Tropic of Cancer

Canary Is. (Sp.)

20N

Hawaii (U.S.)

Mexico

Cuba
Haiti

Western
Sahara
(Mor.)

Jamaica
Belize
Honduras
Puerto
Rico (U.S.)

Dominican
Republic

Maurita

Cape Verde

**PACIFIC   OCEAN**

Guatemala
El Salvador
Nicaragua

Gambia
Senegal

Costa Rica

Guniea-Bissau
Guinea

Panama

Venezuela

Guyana
Suriname

Sierra Leone

Colombia

French Guiana
(France)

Liberia

0
Equator

Galápagos
Islands
(Ecuador)

Ecuador

**SOUTH
AMERICA**

ATLAN
OCE.

Samoa
American
Samoa
(U.S.)

Peru

Brazil

Tonga

Bolivia

20S

Tropic of Capricorn

Chile

Uruguay

N

Argentina

W        E

40S

S

Falkland
Islands
(U.K.)

South
Georgia
(U.K.)

60S

Antarctic Circle

80S

120W
60W

### Europe inset

20W
70N
0
N
20E
40E
W        E
S

Iceland
Arctic Circle

Norwegian Sea

**Scale**
0        250        500 Miles
0     250    500 Kilometers

Sweden
Finland

Norway

60N

United
Kingdom

North
Sea

Estonia

Russia

Baltic

Latvia
Lithuania
Russia

Denmark
Netherlands

Belarus

Ireland

Germany
Poland

50N

Belgium

Ukraine

Luxembourg
Czech
Republic
Slovakia

Liechtenstein
Moldova

Switzerland
Austria
Hungary

**ATLANTIC
OCEAN**

France

Slovenia
Croatia
Serbia &
Mont.
Romania

Black
Sea

Monaco
San
Marino

Bosnia &
Herz.

Andorra
Corsica
(Fr.)
Italy

Bulgaria

Macedonia

Portugal

Sardinia
(It.)
Vatican
City

Albania

Turkey

Spain
Balearic Is.
(Sp.) Mediterranean
Sea

Greece

Gibraltar
(U.K.)
10E
Sicily
(It.)
Malta
20E

ARCTIC OCEAN

80N

Svalbard
(Norway)

60E                    120E              180

Arctic Circle

60N

Russia

EUROPE                                          ASIA

Kazakhstan

40N

Mongolia

Turkey                Uzbekistan        Kyrgyzstan          North Korea    Japan
                Turkmenistan                              South Korea
Tunisia    Lebanon  Syria    Tajikistan
        Israel    Iraq   Afghanistan          China                    PACIFIC   OCEAN
        Jordan            Iran

Libya    Egypt    Kuwait  Bahrain                    Nepal   Bhutan                    Taiwan          Tropic of Cancer    20N
                Qatar                                                                    Wake Island (U.S.)
ger    Chad    Sudan    Saudi   United            India   Myanmar                                    Northern
                        Arabia   Arab                    (Burma)  Laos                              Mariana Is.
AFRICA          Eritrea   Yemen   Emirates                Bangladesh   Thailand              Philippines    (U.S.)          Marshall Islands
                        Djibouti                                    Vietnam                        Guam (U.S.)
eria    Central                                                    Cambodia                              Federated States
        African    Ethiopia            Somalia            Sri            Brunei                        Palau      of Micronesia
        Republic   Rwanda  Uganda                        Lanka          Malaysia                                        Kiribati
Gabon    Rep. Congo         Kenya                                            Singapore                                Equator            0
al  Democratic         Burundi                        Maldives                              Indonesia                        Nauru
    Republic         Tanzania                                                                            Papua        Solomon
    of the Congo                                                                                        New          Islands
Angola    Zambia   Malawi        Seychelles          INDIAN                              Timor-Leste  Guinea              Tuvalu
                        Comoros                    OCEAN                                                    Vanuatu        Fiji
        Zimbabwe                Madagascar                                                                            20S
Namibia            Mozambique      Réunion (Fr.)                                                              New
        Botswana                    Mauritius                                    AUSTRALIA                      Caledonia
                                                                                                    (France)
    South            Swaziland        Scale
    Africa   Lesotho                0        1,000        2,000 Miles                                            40S
                                                                                                    New
                                    0    1,000   2,000 Kilometers                              Zealand
                                    Scale accurate at Equator

60S

Antarctic Circle

NTARCTICA                                    80S    180

60E                    120E

**Legend**

| | | | |
|---|---|---|---|
| Africa | | Europe | |
| North America | | South America | |
| Asia | | Australia & Oceania | |

**215**

**PACIFIC OCEAN**

CANADA

MEXICO

**Seattle** • WASHINGTON

Columbia River

OREGON

IDAHO

MONTANA

NORTH DAKOTA

SOUTH DAKOTA

WYOMING

Yellowstone River

Snake River

NEVADA

**San Francisco** •

CALIFORNIA

UTAH

Colorado River

COLORADO

**Denver** ★

NEBRASKA

Platte River

KANSAS

**Los Angeles** •

ARIZONA

NEW MEXICO

OKLAHOMA

TEXAS

Rio Grande

120W  50N  110W  100W

40N

30N

120W  110W  100W

## Legend

| | | | | |
|---|---|---|---|---|
| Automobiles and related industries | Au | Gold | Ag | Silver |
| Cattle | | Iron and steel production centers | | Textiles |
| Corn | | Meatpacking | | Wheat |
| Cu | Copper | | Oil and gas | Main railroads |
| Cotton | | Oranges | | Iron ore fields |
| | | | | Main coal deposits |

216

# UNITED STATES INDUSTRY AND RESOURCES, 1945

MAINE

MINNESOTA

Cu

MICHIGAN

Lake Superior

WISCONSIN

Lake Huron

VERMONT

NEW HAMPSHIRE

NEW YORK

Boston

Minneapolis

MASSACHUSETTS

Rochester

Buffalo

RHODE ISLAND

MICHIGAN

Milwaukee

CONNECTICUT

Detroit

Lake Michigan

Lake Erie

IOWA

New York City

Chicago

Cleveland

PENNSYLVANIA

NEW JERSEY

Pittsburgh

Philadelphia

INDIANA

OHIO

Baltimore

DELAWARE

Indianapolis

Washington, D.C.

MARYLAND

ILLINOIS

Cincinnati

WEST VIRGINIA

VIRGINIA

St. Louis

Ohio River

Kansas City

KENTUCKY

MISSOURI

Cu

NORTH CAROLINA

Au

Arkansas River

ARKANSAS

TENNESSEE

Au

SOUTH CAROLINA

ATLANTIC OCEAN

Birmingham

Mississippi River

GEORGIA

ALABAMA

MISSISSIPPI

LOUISIANA

New Orleans

Houston

FLORIDA

Gulf of Mexico

BAHAMAS

ale

150         300 Miles

150         300 Kilometers

Treaty with Britain, 1818

Treaty with Britain, 1818

CASCADE RANGE

WASHINGTON 1889

Columbia River

COLUMBIA PLATEAU

BITTERROOT RANGE

OREGON COUNTRY 1846

R O C K Y

Missouri River

MONTANA 1889

G R E A T

NORTH DAKOTA 1889

OREGON 1859

IDAHO 1890

Snake River

WYOMING 1890

SOUTH DAKOTA 1889

LOUISIANA PURCHASE 1803

NEBRASKA 1867

40°N

SIERRA NEVADA

Lake Tahoe

NEVADA 1864

Great Salt Lake

WASATCH RANGE

M O U N T A I N S

COLORADO 1876

Platte

Miss

P L A I N S

MEXICAN CESSION 1848

UTAH 1896

COLORADO PLATEAU

Colorado River

KANS. 1861

PACIFIC OCEAN

CALIFORNIA 1850

Salton Sea

ARIZONA 1912

NEW MEXICO 1912

OKLAHO 1907

GADSDEN PURCHASE 1853

TEXAS ANNEXATION 1845

RUSSIA

180° 70°N 160°W 140°W

ALASKA 1959 BROOKS RANGE

Arctic Circle

30°N

110°W

Yukon River

60°N

ALASKA PURCHASE 1867

CANADA

160°W

HAWAII ANNEXATION 1898

PACIFIC OCEAN

TEXAS 1845

Scale
0    200    400 Miles
0    200    400 Kilometers

PACIFIC OCEAN

PACIFIC OCEAN

HAWAII 1959

20°N

Scale
0    100 Miles
0    100 Kilometers

155°W

Rio Grande

100°W

# GROWTH OF A NATION

Treaty with Britain, 1842

Lake of the Woods

Lake Superior

CANADA

MAINE 1820

VERMONT 1791

Lake Champlain

NEW HAMPSHIRE 1788

MASSACHUSETTS 1788

RHODE ISLAND 1790

CONNECTICUT 1788

MINNESOTA 1858

WISCONSIN 1848

Lake Michigan

Lake Huron

MICHIGAN 1837

Lake St. Clair

Lake Ontario

NEW YORK 1788

MOUNTAINS

Lake Erie

IOWA 1846

OHIO 1803

PENNSYLVANIA 1787

NEW JERSEY 1787

ILLINOIS 1818

INDIANA 1816

WEST VIRGINIA 1863

DELAWARE 1787

MARYLAND 1788

Mississippi River

Ohio River

MISSOURI 1821

UNITED STATES 1783

VIRGINIA 1788

70°W

KENTUCKY 1792

OZARK PLATEAU

Arkansas River

TENNESSEE 1796

Tennessee River

APPALACHIAN

NORTH CAROLINA 1789

ATLANTIC OCEAN

ARKANSAS 1836

SOUTH CAROLINA 1788

MISSISSIPPI 1817

GEORGIA 1788

ALABAMA 1819

LOUISIANA 1812

From Spain 1810

FLORIDA 1819

80°W

From Spain 1813

Lake Pontchartrain

From Spain 1812

FLORIDA 1845

Gulf of Mexico

Lake Okeechobee

N
W E
S

## Scale

0        200        400 Miles

0     200     400 Kilometers

90°W

## Legend

United States, 1783

Acquired from Spain

Acquired from Mexico

Acquired from France

Acquired from Russia

Acquired from Britain

Acquired by annexation

**OREGON COUNTRY 1846**   Region and date of incorporation into the United States

OREGON 1859   State and date of admission into the Union

# NORTH AMERICAN CLIMATE

Greenland
(Denmark)

Alaska
(U.S.)

Yukon River

Mackenzie River

PACIFIC
OCEAN

Peace River

CANADA

Columbia River

Snake River

Sacramento R.

Missouri River

Mississippi River

St. Lawrence River

Hudson R.

Platte River

Ohio River

Potomac R.

Delaware River

40°N

UNITED
STATES

Colorado River

Red River

ATLANTIC
OCEAN

60°N

Rio Grande

MEXICO

Gulf of Mexico

BAHAMAS

Puerto
Rico
(U.S.)

CUBA

HAITI

Balsas River

20°N

JAMAICA

DOMINICAN
REPUBLIC

BELIZE

HONDURAS

GUATEMALA

NICARAGUA

EL SALVADOR

COSTA RICA

PANAMA

Chattahoochee R.

160°W

140°W

100°W

80°W

## Legend

- Tropical wet
- Tropical wet and dry
- Arid
- Semiarid
- Mediterranean
- Humid subtropical
- Marine
- Humid continental
- Subarctic
- Tundra
- Highland
- Ice cap

**Scale**

0        500       1,000 Miles

0        500    1,000 Kilometers

# EUROPE AFTER WORLD WAR I

SWEDEN

FINLAND
INDEPENDENT
1917

NORWAY

ALAND IS.
NEUTRALISED
1921

ESTONIA

LATVIA

LITHUANIA

NORTHERN
IRELAND

ULSTER

IRISH
FREE
STATE

GREAT
BRITAIN

*North Sea*

DENMARK

*Baltic Sea*

EAST
PRUSSIA

POLAND

NETH.

GERMANY

BELGIUM
LUX.

UPPER
SILESIA
BOHEMIA

CZECHOSLOVAKIA
MORAVIA

BU
VIN

*Atlantic
Ocean*

FRANCE

SWITZ.

AUSTRIA

TYROL

HUNGARY

TRANSYLVANIA

ROMAN

SLOVENIA

ITALY

CROATIA

SERBIA

YUGOSLAVIA
BOSNIA-
HERZEGOVINA

DALMATIA

BULG.

BASQUE
REPUBLIC
AUTONOMOUS
1936-37

CATALONIA
AUTONOMOUS
1932-38

PORTUGAL

SPAIN

MONTENEGRO

ALBANIA

MACEDONIA

GREECE

*Mediterranean Sea*

DISPUTED
TERRITORY

FRONTIER OF
GERMAN EMPIRE 1914

FRONTIER of AUSTRO-
HUNGARIAN EMPIRE 1914

FRONTIER OF
RUSSIAN EMPIRE 1914

NEW STATES

AREAS TEMPORARILY
AUTONOMOUS OR
INDEPENDENT

AREAS UNDER
ARMED OCCUPATION

AREAS UNDER
LEAGUE OF NATIONS
HIGH COMMISSIONERS

USSR

...SIA
...ENDENT
...9-21

UKRAINE
INDEPENDENT
1917-20

USSR

Caspian
Sea

...ARABIA

...OBRUJ

Black Sea

GEORGIA
INDEPENDENT
1918-21

AZERBAIJAN
INDEPENDENT
1918-20

ARMENIA
INDEPENDENT
1918-21

TURKEY

...NESE IS. TO ITALY
...012

GENERAL DWIGHT EISENHOWER

# EUROPE
# WORLD WAR II
# 1942~1945

NORW.

North Sea

DEN

IRELAND

UNITED
KINGDOM

LONDON

NETH.

BELG.

CALAIS

1944

1944

english Channel

LUX.

GER.

NORMANDY

PARIS

1944

Atlantic
Ocean

FRANCE

VICHY

SWITZ.

PORTUGAL

SPAIN

FROM U.K.

FROM U.S.
1942

1942

ALGIERS

1942

TUNIS

SP. MOROCCO

CASABLANCA

1942

GENERAL GEORGE PATTON

MOROCCO

ALGERIA